D1122043

CONTROVERSY CREATES CASH

ERIC BISCHOFF

WITH JEREMY ROBERTS

CONTROVERSY CREATES CASH

World Wrestling Entertainment BOOKS   POCKET BOOKS   NEW YORK   LONDON   TORONTO   SYDNEY

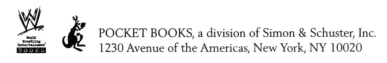

POCKET BOOKS, a division of Simon & Schuster, Inc.
1230 Avenue of the Americas, New York, NY 10020

ISBN-13: 978-1-4165-2729-9
ISBN-10:   1-4165-2729-X

This Pocket Books hardcover edition October 2006

Designed by Jan Pisciotta

10   9   8   7   6   5   4   3   2

POCKET and colophon are registered trademarks of Simon & Schuster, Inc.

Visit us on the World Wide Web
http://www.simonsays.com
http://www.wwe.com

Manufactured in the United States of America

For information regarding special discounts for bulk purchases, please contact Simon & Schuster Special Sales at 1-800-456-6798 or business@simonandschuster.com

DEDICATION

Writing this book was an interesting challenge. I rejected the idea of writing a book about my experiences in professional wrestling for a long time for a variety of reasons, including the fact that I just didn't think my story was all that interesting. But as time has passed, and as I've watched the evolution of the sports entertainment industry, I have begun to appreciate just how much the business has changed as a result of many of the things I was so closely associated with.

One of the biggest challenges for me was going back and remembering the key moments—the pivot points as I like to refer to them—that shaped the thoughts, strategies, and decisions that led to the explosive growth of WCW from the time I took over the company until the time I left in 1999. So many things happened in such a relatively short period of time that, for a guy who tends not to dwell on the past, it was like visiting an old friend I hadn't seen in years and reliving experiences I had long since forgotten about.

People warned me that writing this book would be difficult. The truth is that it wasn't. That's in large part because of Jeremy Roberts. Jeremy is the writer that spent untold hours with me, helping me to remember, organize, and structure my story in a way that would have otherwise been a vertigo-inducing literary train wreck.

Writing the book was relatively easy. The hard part was writing this dedication.

It is hard because there is more than one person to whom I want to dedicate this book. There is my wife, Loree, who has believed in, supported, motivated, and tolerated more of me than I ever thought possible. There are others, some of whom I credit in the following pages that gave me the opportunities to achieve what most people thought was impossible.

In the end though, the person I want to dedicate this book to is my mother. As I write this, she is in the third day of her second battle with cancer. The first go-round was about two years ago. My mother accepted the fight—took everything the bastard had to give—and walked out of the hospital a champion. In the process of watching her win this fight, I realized just how tough a woman could be. I learned what a positive attitude and a strong will truly is.

Three days ago she called and told us the news. She is in for a rematch. Characteristically, she has accepted the fight with dignity, strength, and a will to win.

So Mom, this book is dedicated to you.

Kick the bastard's ass.

CONTENTS

CONTROVERSY CREATES CASH

PROLOGUE
"Give Me a Big Hug"

ast Rutherford, N.J., July 15, 2002: I'm sitting in the back of a stretch limo in the parking lot of Continental Airlines Arena, waiting to make my appearance on a televised wrestling show. I've been on television hundreds of times before, on hundreds of wrestling shows, but tonight is going to be different—very different.

Tonight I'm appearing on the show I almost put out of business. And the person pulling open the car door to welcome me is the guy I almost forced into bankruptcy: Vince McMahon.

Could anyone have predicted this day would come? *Never!* But that's the thing about wrestling. There's a saying in our business: Never say never.

"How are you feeling?" Vince asks.

"Great."

"Nervous?"

"Not at all. Excited."

Vince looks at me for a second, like he's not quite sure he believes me. We go over what we're going to do onstage.

This is only the second time in my life that I've met Vince McMahon face to face. The first was more than a decade before, when he said hello to me after a job interview in Stamford. I didn't get the job. I didn't deserve it.

The history of pro wrestling might have been very different if I had.

The funny thing is, I feel as if I really know Vince well. We're like two soldiers back from a war; we've been through the same battles, albeit on different sides.

"Here's what I'd like you to do," Vince tells me. "When you hear me announce the new general manager of *Raw*, and you hear your music start to play—come out, acknowledge the crowd, shake my hand, and give me a big bear hug! And milk it for all it's worth. . . ."

He gets out of the car. Inside the arena, the crowd is hopping. They've been told *Raw* is getting a new general manager, one guaranteed to shake things up.

There's an understatement for you.

If you're a wrestling fan, you probably know that *Raw* is World Wrestling Entertainment's flagship Monday-night television show. You probably also know that Vince McMahon is the chairman of World Wrestling Entertainment, better known as WWE.

What you may not know is that almost everything that makes *Raw* distinctive—its two-hour live format, its backstage interview segments, above all its reality-based storylines—was introduced first on *Monday Night Nitro*, the prime-time show I created for the TNT Network. For nearly three years, my company World Championship Wrestling, kicked Vince McMahon's ass. *Nitro*, WCW's flagship show, revolutionized wrestling. The media called our conflict the Monday Night Wars, but it was more like a rout. *Nitro* beat *Raw* in the ratings eighty-something weeks running.

Then Vince caught on to what we were doing, and the real battle began.

Unfortunately for me, and the wrestling business in general, the fight wasn't really between WCW and WWE, which was called World Wrestling Federation at the time. In fact, the real battle was

between WCW and the corporate suits who took over Turner
Broadcasting with the merger of Time Warner and then AOL. That
was a fight I was never capable of winning, though, being stubborn
by nature, I didn't realize it until it was nearly over.

Stephanie McMahon pops her head into the limo. Stephanie, Vince's
daughter and one of the company's vice presidents, has come to
take me in to the show.

Ready? she asks.

I'm ready.

Nervous?

Excited.

She stares at me a second, probably convinced I'm lying. I'm
sure she thinks I'm a train wreck. The auditorium is packed with
people who hate my guts, or I should say hate my character's guts.

Not too many people bother to distinguish between the character I play
on television and who I really am. Worse, a lot of people think they
know who I am because of what they've read on the Internet or in the
"dirt sheets," the newsletters that cover the wrestling business for fans.

Wrestling fan sites are generally populated by people with too
much time on their hands, who have very little real insight into
what's going on in the wrestling business. A lot of them create their
own stories and realities just to watch other people react to them.
As a result of that, there's a lot of misinformation floating around
out there about a lot of people, not just me.

Which is one of the reasons I decided to write this book.

The truth is, I hate most wrestling books. I read a sentence, a
paragraph, sometimes a page, then quit. They don't take a serious
look at the enterprise. Most are bitter, self-serving revisionist history
at best—and monuments to bullshit at their worst. A lot of the guys
who write them seem desperate to have the last word on every-

thing. Rather than telling people what we're really all about, they refight old battles that everyone but them has forgotten. They come off like whiners, complaining about everything.

That's not me.

I've had some bumps and bad breaks. Everyone does in life. But pro wrestling for me has been full of good things. I started out as a salesman and then, by necessity rather than ability, became an on-camera talent. I went from that to being chosen, improbably, to head the second largest wrestling promotion in the country. We were a distant second to Vince McMahon's company, bleeding money every year. With hard work and against heavy odds, we became number one. What had been a company generating 10 million in losses on 24 million worth of revenue, became a company with 350 million in sales pumping out over 40 million in profit. Then things went to hell. After a wild roller-coaster ride I ended up back where I had started—as an on-air talent, ironically, with the guy I had been at war with for years.

And ultimately we became friends.

Let's go, says Stephanie. *You're on in a few minutes.*

We get out of the car and begin walking through the backstage area. My appearance has been a well-kept secret until now, and the looks of shock on the wrestlers' faces as I pass confirms it.

I can hear the crowd in the arena as I reach the holding area backstage. WWE writers have given me a two-page script to memorize, and the words are bouncing in my head. The funny thing is, I've rarely had to memorize a script before—all these years on camera, I've improvised my lines. But not tonight. The writers for WWE have spent a fair amount of time on this script; my job tonight is to deliver what they want.

But even before I look at the words, I know what I have to do tonight. I have to find my inner heel. Once I'm out there, the adrenaline will take over, and I'll be fine.

There's a hush outside. Vince McMahon has come onstage and is about to introduce me.

Wrestling began in the United States as a sideshow carnival attraction. It thrived and grew because it blended showmanship, unique characters, and illusion. It still does, in some respects. But it's also a business, and a very sophisticated one at that. The business structure and revenue model are extremely complex. No other form of entertainment, quite frankly, combines the different revenue streams and opportunities that WCW had, or that WWE has now. I hope to give you some idea of that complexity in this book.

What happened to WCW while I was there is as much about business as it is about wrestling. A lot of wrestling fans think WCW unraveled because of things like guaranteed contracts for wrestlers and the decision to give Hulk Hogan creative control over his matches.

The fact that we may have overpaid some wrestlers *was* one reason WCW ended up in a position that was difficult to recover from. But it had nothing to do with why WCW failed. If our talent budget was half of what it was, in the end, it would have made no difference. The company failed because of what happened inside Turner after it was bought by Time Warner. Turner's merger with Time Warner, and Time Warner's ultimate merger with AOL, was the single largest disaster in modern business history. WCW was just one of many casualties. There was a lot of collateral damage. Even Ted Turner suffered in the fallout.

Did I make mistakes? Sure. I'll list a few of the bigger ones here. But I'm tired of hearing things like, Eric Bischoff killed WCW because he overpaid wrestlers and was a Hollywood guy and so on. That's all bull. Take Eric Bischoff out of the equation, and WCW still goes down in flames, maybe even faster.

What happened to WCW is a cautionary tale. My story isn't just about wrestling and sports entertainment, but about what happens

to creative enterprises and individuals when they get caught in the maul of a modern conglomerate and the short-term "meet Wall Street expectations" thinking that's so prevalent today.

I know I'm not going to convince every reader who picks this book up that what I say is the absolute truth. It's possible that I've remembered some things subjectively or have a very one-sided view of them. Plenty has been written about WCW and my time there. But none of the stories of its demise have come from someone who was there. It's been written by people who were either just making shit up or hearing rumors. I was there, on the front lines. They weren't.

I'm on. I walk out toward the man who was my most bitter enemy for four or five years. We embrace.

That rumbling beneath your feet, I tell Vince, *is a whole lot of people turning over in their graves.*

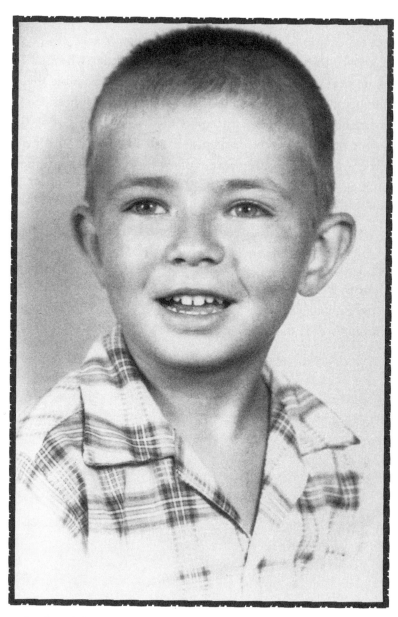

I'm about six here.

Throwing Rocks

Early Days

Motor City Boy

A lot of what people think they know about me is wrong. So let's start from the beginning.

I was born on May 27, 1955, in Detroit, Michigan. I lived there until I was twelve. I hated it.

We lived near the city line in a lower-middle-income area. It wasn't a great place. I did have a great mom and dad, though. My father—Kenneth—was a hardworking guy who had a pretty tough life. He was born prematurely in 1930. His spinal cord hadn't developed properly. There was a hole at the top of his spine, and as he grew older, it filled up with fluid. That gave him terrible, debilitating headaches. Even so, he was very active. He spent a lot of spare time hunting and fishing, and loved the outdoors.

My mom Carol was a typical 1950s housewife, very devoted to her family. She stayed home caring for me, my younger brother Mark, and my sister Lori while my father worked as a draftsman at

American Standard. My mother was also an extremely hard worker. She taught me in her own way to dream big.

Dreadful Surgery

About the time I was five or six, my father's headaches got so bad that he decided to try brain surgery to relieve the pain. I remember sitting on the couch, waiting, while my mom took him to the hospital, looking out the window, worried because my mom was worried, not understanding really what was going on.

When my father came out of that brain surgery, his headaches were gone. But he no longer had the use of his hands and had limited use of his arms. He couldn't even brush his teeth. For an active guy with a lot of pride who loved the outdoors and hunting, it was as if his manhood had been taken away.

It had a profound effect on him. He couldn't work as a draftsman anymore, so he became a purchasing agent. He became a workaholic in a good sense—he had a strong work ethic and just kept at it. But he became bitter.

My mom now had to take care of him as well as us kids. She was tough, one of the toughest women I know. Still is. When you've got a family of five living in a small house in a hard neighborhood, and all the kids turn out okay, then you know you've done something special.

My dad's mom, my grandmother Agnes, used to stay with us for a few months at a time while I was growing up. She was a tough old German farm broad, as ornery as any wrestler. More so. She could have made Stone Cold Steve Austin cry like a baby with a glance.

She also smoked like a chimney. To this day I can't stand cigarette smoke—or walk into a room filled with smoke—without thinking of her.

I went to Dort Elementary School, the same school rap star Eminem went to, quite a number of years later. It was a tough school in a tough neighborhood. There was really nothing good about it. I hated most of my classes, with the exception of geography and history. I loved to think about faraway places like China, India, Japan, and Europe, and often daydreamed about going to those places we were supposed to be learning about—generally during class, when the teacher wanted me to pay attention to something else.

Rocks

Even the games we played were rough. One game we would play was "army." Back in the sixties, a lot of TV shows, like *Combat* and *Twelve O'Clock High*, romanticized characters and events that took place during World War II. We copied them when we played. All of the kids from the neighborhood would choose teams, much like the way kids choose baseball teams. One team would be the Germans, and one would be the Americans. We didn't play with toy guns. Instead, we would literally have rock fights. We would chase each other through the neighborhood, throwing rocks and clumps of dirt at each other. The nurses in the emergency room at Saratoga Hospital on Gratiot Avenue knew me on a first-name basis.

Big-Time Wrestling

I was about eight years old when I discovered professional wrestling.

My father used to work Saturday mornings. We only had one car, so my mother would drive my father to work, drop my grandmother off at my aunt and uncle's for the day, and go grocery shopping. I'd stay at home with my younger brother while they were gone. We had the house to ourselves! We'd start the morning with some cartoons, raid the freezer, and make a gallon or so of chocolate malt. Then we'd catch *Dick Clark's American Bandstand*, and finally top things off with wrestling—*Big Time Wrestling* on CKLW, Channel 9, to be exact. I remember seeing the Sheik, Killer Kowalski, and Bobo Brazil, among others.

My brother Mark and one of his friends outside our house in Detroit.

My brother and I would practice the moves we saw on the living room floor. We got so we would script our fight scenes out and go through them in slow motion.

In those days, pro wrestling was divided into territories around the country. Every region had a different set of wrestlers, with their own "world champion." There were several large regional promotions with their own stars. Each had its own "world champion." But because this was the early sixties, before cable television, most viewers didn't realize that. Nor did they know anything about what happened behind the scenes. Even though matches were now being televised, wrestling was still very close to its original roots as a carnival sideshow. Kayfabe, the private language used by those in the business, ruled the industry.

The Working Life

I got my first job when I was six or seven, or maybe eight. An Italian couple owned a little grocery store named Lucy's down the block from my house. I used to hang around there a lot, and one day the owners asked me to pick up the litter in the parking lot and around the store. When I was done, I got to reach into the cash register; whatever coins I could get in my hands in one try was what I was paid. Soon I graduated to sorting and stacking their returned bottles. I've been working ever since.

School got tougher and tougher. From fifth grade or so, I was in at least one fight a day. I'd get into a fistfight on my way to school, and more often than not one on the way home. I rarely came out on top. I was kind of a scrawny kid and not very good with my fists, but that didn't matter much. The older kids were always picking on the younger kids, bigger kids always beating on smaller. Violence was a way to entertain yourself in Detroit, and it escalated as I got older. Kids brought weapons like lead pipes and knives to school. It was a small-time arms race.

Showdown for $7

The very last day I spent in Detroit, I purposely brought seven dollars to school. This was a time when thirty-five cents bought lunch, and having even that in your pocket was like walking with a sign around your neck volunteering for an ass-kicking.

But I said to myself, I'm going to have some fun today. I let everybody know I had seven dollars. By the time shop class came around toward the end of the day, there was a buzz going around: *Bischoff's carrying money.*

The thing about shop class was that the teacher always left early. Always. We'd sit in the class listening to the end-of-the-day announcements, and he'd be gone.

As soon as the teacher left, a kid came in to confront me. He hung with a tougher crowd, but he wasn't much himself. I pulled a metal handle from one of the vises sitting in the shop area and creased the top of his head with it. Then the bell rang, and it was time to go home.

For about twelve hours, I was a legend in the school. Of course, if I'd had to go back the next day, his friends would have beaten the hell out of me. But I didn't. We were off to Pittsburgh.

Moving Up

Pittsburgh

In 1968, when I was in eighth grade, my dad got a job opportunity in Pittsburgh. We packed up and moved to suburban Penn Hills, Pennsylvania. We thought we'd died and gone to heaven.

The development we lived in was more middle class, a definite step up from Detroit. Our house was twice as big as our old one. It had a finished basement where Mark, Lori and I could play. There were woods in the backyard where we could build tree forts and camp out at night, and a creek where we could catch crawfish. It was just amazing to see hills and mountains all around instead of city streets.

Saturday-morning wrestling was replaced with Saturday-night wrestling, but my brother Mark and I were still big fans. This was the first time I realized there were different "world champions" in every part of the country. Bruno Sammartino was the champion in Pittsburgh.

Sammartino began wrestling in 1959. During the 1960s, he was wrestling for what was then WWWF (now WWE), and already known as a wrestling legend. He was the shit at the time.

Besides his ability as a wrestler, Sammartino was a real and believable character. He was the workingman. Pittsburgh was a blue-collar town, with the steel mills and other industries. Sammartino

Pittsburgh. "Born to be wild."

really represented that, which was one of the reasons I think he was so popular.

He was also a local guy, and as it happened, he lived not too far away from our home. My friends and I used to cruise by his house on our bikes, hoping to maybe catch a glimpse of him. We never did, but we felt privileged just to live close by.

Wrestling

School in Penn Hills was very different than what I'd been used to in Detroit, and the only real fighting I did was as a wrestler. I believe I started out in the 126-pound weight class in junior high. I was an average wrestler, real average—not horrible, just real average. But I enjoyed it. I'd grown up fighting, and this was an organized way to do it.

I also continued to work. My neighbor, a guy named Bob Racioppi, hired me to do odd jobs and light construction around his home. He became kind of a big brother to me, doing things with me that my dad could no longer do, like hunting. He introduced me to martial arts, showing me some moves and whetting my appetite for karate. Then he got me my first job with a roofing company when I was fourteen.

I don't know if you're born with confidence, or if it's generated by the way you're brought up. Part of it for me, a big part, was the work ethic my father instilled in me. It lent itself to success. I've always felt a lot of confidence, and succeeded in what I set out to do by hard work. I give my father credit for that, and my mother credit for developing a desire to grow and not to settle for less.

Minneapolis & Wrestling

In 1970, when I was in tenth grade, my father got a new job in Minneapolis. I didn't really want to leave Pittsburgh. I had great friends there and really felt at home. But it wasn't up for a vote. It happened that the son of the real estate agent who sold us our home was the captain of the high school wrestling team and about my age. He introduced me to the coach and some of his teammates, and helped me fit in.

Wrestling quickly became one of the few things I really liked about school. I lettered when I was a junior, though I was never really a standout when it came to tournaments. I enjoyed it, and it was really where I made most of my friends. Besides wrestling on the school team, I joined a club that competed with others throughout the region.

Drugs

This was the late sixties and early seventies, when legend has it that everyone did drugs. But the facts are different. I was never into drugs myself, and neither were most of my friends.

One time I was tempted to try speed, the nickname for a particular kind of amphetamine. There was a girl I knew, a pretty popular girl, who experimented with Black Beauties in school. I saw her in the morning, and she could hardly stand still. Later on I saw her in the hallway, and blood was coming out of her mouth. She was so "speedy," she had literally chewed the inside of her mouth bloody. That convinced me to pass on the whole damn idea.

As I got older, I experimented with pot like a lot of other people did. I never really enjoyed that much either. Sitting around staring at a television and laughing about stupid shit you couldn't remember the next day just didn't appeal to me.

What I did like was riding motorcycles. I started riding a mini-bike when I was about ten and graduated to motorcycles when I turned sixteen. My first bike was a Honda 160. I soon traded that in for a Honda Super Hawk. The Super Hawk was a milestone motorcycle of the early 1960s, with overhead cams and a 305cc engine that redlined at 9,200 rpms. I went through maybe a half dozen bikes, each one getting bigger and faster, until I got a Kawasaki 900. At just over five hundred pounds, the bike could produce 82 horsepower. It was a rocket.

About the craziest thing I ever tried to do on a bike was jump the Kawasaki. Jumping dirt bikes is one thing; launching a heavy street bike like that is something else. On about the fourth or fifth attempt I crashed midair into the side of a garage next to my friend's house. I tore the bike up pretty good. That was the end of my motorcycle jumping career.

Verne Gagne & the AWA

Verne Gagne's *All-Star Wrestling Show* was big in the Minnesota area at the time, a must-watch for me every Saturday night at six.

A former marine and amateur college wrestler, Gagne had started wrestling professionally in 1948. He founded the American Wrestling Association in 1960, and within a few years built it into one of the country's strongest promotions. Besides Minnesota, the

AWA promoted wrestling in territories in the Midwest, Las Vegas, San Francisco, and a few other smaller cities and towns. Verne and his son Greg Gagne were among the featured wrestlers, with guys like Nick Bockwinkel and Chief Wahoo McDaniel, Larry "the Axe" Hennig, who had a head as big as a Corvair, Baron Von Raschke, and Ray "the Crippler" Stevens, among other stars.

I still remember enjoying a few of the big shows the AWA held in Minnesota. The promotion had an annual Thanksgiving show. Watching wrestling was just the thing to do after sitting around the house stuffing your face all day.

Meeting the Man

I met Verne Gagne once or twice over the course of my high school wrestling career. Verne lived in a little town called Mound, Minnesota, which was just three miles down the road from where I lived. Much like we did with Bruno Sammartino, we'd drive by Verne Gagne's neighborhood and hope that we might see him by his house.

When I was a senior, my AAU freestyle wrestling team was selected to compete against a team from Sweden that was touring the United States. We needed to sell tickets and get the word out, but we had no money for advertising.

Verne supported amateur wrestling in a lot of ways, often using his show to help different amateur teams get publicity So I came up with the idea of calling him and maybe getting a plug on one of his wrestling shows. I called the AWA offices and talked to Wally Karbo. Karbo was the "face" of AWA, the guy who viewers at home saw promoting the event.

"Hey, I'm Eric Bischoff," I told Karbo when the receptionist turned the call over to him. The words jetted out of my mouth. "I'm with the Minnetonka wrestling team, we're taking on Sweden, we need some support. Is there any way I can come on the air and do an interview and let people know when we're wrestling, where we're wrestling, and try and sell some tickets?"

"Sure, kid," he said to my breathless surprise. "Come on down to the studio, and we'll get you on the air."

I was ecstatic. I couldn't believe it.

My buddies and I drove over to Channel 11 on Saturday morning. We were sitting outside the building, waiting for the appointed time to arrive, when we saw Greg Gagne and Jim Brunzell come walking in. They wrestled as the High Flyers, the World Tag Team Champions at AWA. Then we saw Wahoo McDaniel, then Ray Stevens, Larry Hennig—we saw all these stars in person.

It was amazing. And we knew we were going to be on the same show *they* were going to be on. For real.

We went inside, and they gave us a place to wait right in the studio itself, near the television cameras. Sure enough, out came Wally Karbo and an announcer by the name of Marty O'Neill. Marty had an old-time cigarette-and-Scotch-whisky voice, a rasp that told anyone listening that something exciting was going to happen *right now*. He was about five feet nothing, sixty or seventy years old, and looked like an old-school carnival barker. Marty was the AWA's "stick man," the guy who conducted all of the interviews.

The camera went on a few feet away, and Marty starts interviewing Wally Carbo. And Wally says, *"Yeah, Marty, we got a guy in here we want to bring in, and he has something he wants to talk about. His name's Eric Bischoff. Eric, come on in here."*

So I went. I kind of looked into the camera and spilled out all this information. I was scared to death—but I was excited at the same time.

I don't recall how we did in the match, but I'm sure we got our butts kicked. Europeans were much better at freestyle than we were. But that was my first appearance on television.

Working for a Living

I worked all through high school, in just about any job you can think of. I ran a Bobcat bulldozer, drove a dump truck, flipped pancakes, and even worked in an animal hospital cleaning up after the dogs, cats, monkeys—you name it, I cleaned up after it. I'd take whatever I could to make money part-time during school and full-time during the summer.

I really wasn't that concerned with my studies. If it wasn't for wrestling, I probably wouldn't have stayed in high school at all. Money interested me a lot more than academics. I wasn't necessarily thinking clearly at the time, but school just wasn't my thing.

In the spring of 1973, when I was a senior, I blew out my knee wrestling a kid by the name of Joe Boyer. Joe was real strong—farm strong. He had great upper-body strength and a low center of gravity which combined to make him hard to take down.

He and I locked up at the start of the match. I tried to do a lateral drop. He overpowered me, reversed the lateral drop, and muscled me over so hard that my upper body went in one direction and my right knee the other.

There was a loud pop and a snap. It wasn't so much painful as eerie. My leg felt as if didn't belong to me anymore.

My knee swelled up to the size of a small cantaloupe. To this day I don't know exactly what I did, though over the years I've reinjured it probably two or three dozen times. I've never had it operated on or even looked at. Knee surgery in the seventies wasn't as advanced as it is today. Many of my friends at the time who had knee injuries and had surgery came out worse off than they were when they went in. I just said I'll deal with it.

While I wrestled later that summer, my knee bothered me so much that I couldn't work out regularly. That was pretty much the end of my amateur wrestling career.

Party School

In my senior year of high school, I suddenly realized all my friends were going off to college. I had never really planned on going to college, but when you're seventeen or eighteen years old, and your whole life has been your friends, and suddenly you realize they're all going away, it dawns on you that you might want to go away with them.

One of my best friends from high school had decided he was going to St. Cloud State in St. Cloud, roughly an hour northwest of Minneapolis. I applied there, and for some reason—I have no idea why—they accepted me.

My friend and I shared a dorm room. I was only there for the parties and wasn't really concerned about my studies. I did the bare minimum I had to do. Most of the time when I wasn't partying, I worked for a freight company unloading freight cars full of lumber. Not a fun job, but it kept me in beer and pizza.

I had a great time my freshman year, but I had to leave because I couldn't afford it. I transferred to the University of Minnesota so I could live at home and regroup my finances.

Passions

My Own Boss

For a couple of years during high school, I worked for a landscape construction company. I ended up as a foreman of my own crew during the summer before college and was pretty good at building retaining walls and overseeing some of the larger commercial projects I was assigned to. By the time I was a sophomore in college, I decided to start my own landscaping firm. In the winter I plowed snow; during the summer I maintained lawns and did construction work. It wasn't long before I was putting in a lot more time and effort into my business than into school. I went into a partnership with a friend of mine, and we ended up building a company that by 1975 or 1976 was one of the larger commercial landscape firms in the area. During our peak season we'd probably have thirty or forty employees, with eight trucks on the road. We got a contract with the city of St. Paul to replace thousands and thousands of elm trees after Dutch elm disease hit the city, and that helped the company grow. Not long after, we were doing in excess of a million dollars a year in sales. Not bad for a couple of college kids.

More and more, college was just getting in the way. I was making more money than any three of my professors combined, and after a while it just didn't make any sense to be going to college when I was building a business, so I officially dropped out.

By the way, that's contrary to my "résumé" posted on a lot of Web sites. They claim I have a business degree, and studied radio and television in school. I never did any of that. I don't even know where it came from. Someone says something in a chat room, and the next thing you know, it ends up on a Web page. It's crazy.

I bought my first house at age twenty one, a block off the beach near Lake Minnetonka, a high-end suburb of Minneapolis. I bought a new car, had plenty of money, was living life. But as the business got bigger, I enjoyed it less and less. The pressure grew. My partner and I stopped getting along. I've always believed that if you're not having fun doing what you're doing, you shouldn't do it. So I sold out my half of the company and took some time off.

I'd already found a new passion—martial arts.

Martial Arts

Somewhere around 1976, I enrolled in a martial arts class in tae kwan do, a Korean style of karate. My instructor was Gordon Franks, at the time the Professional Karate Association superlight champion of the world. He taught an American version of the traditional Korean fighting style that placed more emphasis on practical fighting.

I immediately fell in love with the sport. It was competitive, and something my knee would allow me to do. I really loved the contact. The school was known for being very aggressive and very physical. They prided themselves on the fact that their black belts were as tough as they could be.

I pretty much dove into it and started competing in tournaments when I was still a gold belt, which is a beginner's level. The only drawback with competing as a gold belt was that they didn't let you kick or punch your opponent's head. I liked kicking people in the head, so I didn't get real enthusiastic about the tournament format until green belt.

As I progressed, I worked out five or six hours a day and competed in tournaments all over the country, especially in the Midwest. A group of us from the karate school traveled together. The fighting was good, and the partying was better.

Karate stars have groupies just like rock stars have groupies, and there was no shortage of hot girls at the tournaments—or the parties afterward. It was just a great time. You'd fight all day and party all night. But there was no prize money, and after a while competition became pretty expensive. In 1978 I took a job as an instructor at the school, but karate teachers and their assistants don't make much money. I was probably earning about $600 a month and spending $400 on tournaments. Economically not the smartest thing I've ever done.

With Friends Like Me . . .

My matches have long since faded to a blur, except for the one I fought with a friend of mine named Randy Reid. Randy was one of the higher-rated black belts at the time. We became friends on the circuit, partying together. Once I made black belt, I knew it was inevitable that we'd meet. And we did, at a tournament down in Cedar Rapids, Iowa.

Randy was a lot faster than I was, but I hit a lot harder. Because of my knee injury, I'd had to reverse my fighting stance, putting my right leg forward and pivoting on my left. As a result of that, I became an unnatural southpaw. A lot of people were uncomfortable fighting me, for the same reason many right-handed boxers have trouble with a lefty.

When the match started, Randy blew across the line right at me. I caught him with a straight left that splattered his nose. I knew immediately that I had broken it.

Blood was everywhere.

They stopped the fight. He decided he wanted to continue. Once they restarted the fight, the first thing I did was sweep his legs out from underneath him. He hit the floor on his back.

Randy went down, and he was right on the edge of the ring, almost out of bounds. I kind of looked at him over my shoulder and did a little "fade-away" that made him think I was going to let him get up. As he put his hands down to prop himself up, I spun and stomped on his broken nose.

Which *really* splattered it. I think I have a picture somewhere around the house of three or four judges with towels mopping blood up off the gymnasium floor. That was the end of the match. I lost due to "excessive contact" (which was better than winning a trophy, as far as I was concerned). Randy and I had beers and chased girls that night. He would have done the same to me.

I gave up martial arts around 1981, after competing as a black belt for a little more than a year. There was no money in it, and being a karate instructor was not something I aspired to do. It had been an important time of my life, but it was time to move on.

A Knack for Sales

I went to work as a salesman for a company named Blue Ribbon Foods. Blue Ribbon made and delivered bulk frozen food to individual homes. They would generate leads and turn them over to salesmen to close the deals.

Most of the work was in the early evening, leaving the bulk of my day free. I tried it initially because I didn't want to work nine to five but still wanted to make a lot of money. Typically people who make a lot of money and don't want to work a nine-to-five job are either really good salesmen or drug dealers. Drug dealing wasn't a choice.

The guy I worked for at Blue Ribbon was named Irv Mann. Irv was an old-school direct salesman. He was Jewish, and in fact I was probably one of the only non-Jews Irv hired up to that time. Not only that, but I was under the age of fifty. Most of the other guys were all over fifty, Jewish, and old-school direct sales guys. Why Irv took a chance on me, I don't know.

Direct sales as a whole tends to use the hard-core, one-time sales closer. If you've ever watched the movie *Tin Men*, you'll see what I mean. The movie really caught what direct sales was like back then: pretty aggressive, don't take no for an answer.

Irv showed me how to structure a pitch and read a potential sale, how to overcome objections, when to close and when not to close. He really taught me a lot.

I worked at Blue Ribbon until 1982. I made quite a bit of money doing it. I probably closed 30 to 40 percent of my calls, which made me one of the better salespeople in the company.

Why was I good at sales? I don't know, really. Perhaps I had the ability to communicate, or convey a certain amount of trust to the person I was "pitching." I give a lot of credit to Irv Mann. He trained me well. Whatever the secret was, I've had decent success as a salesman my whole life.

While I was working for Blue Ribbon, I was approached by someone who suggested I might make a good male model.

A model?

It wasn't exactly a career choice I had ever considered. I didn't think much about the idea—until I found out that it was good money, and I'd only have to work during the day, leaving the evenings for my sales calls. I went down to a modeling agency, did a couple of different test shots, and within a few weeks started getting jobs for places like Target, which was based in Minneapolis. Modeling was a way to make extra money, and it paid pretty well.

It's also how I met my wife, Loree.

Romance

It wasn't any of that love-at-first-sight stuff. In fact, I wasn't really interested in a relationship at the time. But I *did* notice her instantly. She was hot—really hot. And this was in a room full of very attractive people. Little did I know this girl was going to become the love of my life and the mother of my children.

We hit it off right away. There was one stumbling block: Loree was not only a model, but part owner of an agency I was working with. And they had a "no fraternization" policy.

Yeah—right! I got her number, and we went out for drinks a week or two later. The relationship picked up pretty good steam from that point on, and pretty soon we were an item.

Loree had been modeling since she was four or five, and wanted to make a career of it. We knew if there was any future for either of us as models, it would be in Chicago or New York. We had some friends who'd moved to Chicago and really enjoyed it. We didn't have anything holding us back, so we both decided to give it a whirl. We were both up for a change. We wanted an adventure. So we packed everything we owned into a 1970 pickup truck and moved to Chicago. It was in the winter, and it was cold and miserable and overcast, but we enjoyed every minute of it.

We found a studio apartment downtown. Loree got a job as a cocktail waitress at night so she could run around town and attempt to launch her modeling career during the day, and I got a job as a bartender and doorman down on Rush and Division Street in downtown Chicago so I could do the same thing. Doormen were bouncers, but they didn't like to call them that on Rush Street.

Chicago was a cool town. We had a ball living there, but modeling is a very competitive business. After a year or so, we realized it wasn't there for us.

Money got tight. Things got to the point just after Christmas that the power company shut off all the power to our apartment.

I was twenty-six, maybe closer to twenty-seven. I realized it was time to quit playing around and start thinking about the things I needed to do to build a life for myself.

The Middle of Nowhere, Minnesota

My father had an acquaintance who ran a company called Dahlman Manufacturing. I think largely as a favor to my dad, he offered me a sales job.

Dahlman made agriculture equipment, particularly potato harvesters, in a small town about an hour and a half north of Minneapolis called Braham. To go from living in downtown Chicago and working in the modeling and nightclub industry to a 1,500-person town selling potato harvesters; that may define culture shock.

For the first few months, I lived alone. Loree was back in Chicago, finishing up some modeling gigs. It was cold, stark, uncomfortable reality. A wood stove supplied the only heat in the small house I rented.

I didn't like the job. It was okay, and it was in sales, which I was good at, so that portion of it I didn't mind. And the people I worked with were good people. But they were so different than me that it was hard to fit in.

Most of the people in Braham had probably only left town a handful of times over the course of a year. To them, driving an hour and a half south to the big city of Minneapolis was a major excursion. I didn't relate to any of them, other than the fact that I liked to hunt and fish, which was about the only thing to do up there other than drink.

But the job provided a weekly check and was a step in the right direction. It was necessary to transition into a more traditional job so I could move on to something better.

In the summer of 1983, I went to pick up Loree back in Chicago. We had a great celebration our last night, and then headed back to Braham. She was even more shocked than I was when she got there. But she tried real hard to adapt and make the most of it. That's the way she is.

Baby on the Way

Not too long after Loree settled in, we found out she was pregnant, probably thanks to our little soiree that last night in Chicago.

Until that point, I had no intention of being married. I knew that Loree was the woman I wanted to be committed to, but marriage just wasn't something I really gave a lot of serious thought to. Neither of us had any intention of having a child. When she found out she was pregnant, that was a defining moment of our relationship. She wasn't sure what I was going to do or suggest what she should do. It wasn't anything we had discussed.

I remember the day vividly. We were at my parents' house, and Loree got up and took a pregnancy test. I was outside target-shooting with my bow. Loree came out and told me the test was positive. Time stood still.

We went to a Perkins restaurant not far from my parents' home, and sat together at the counter. She looked at me and said, "What do you want to do?"

"You first."

We'd both decided, without knowing how the other one really felt, that we wanted to have the baby.

That changed everything quickly. For me, that crystallized where I was at in my life. I couldn't keep fucking around. I had to get serious.

Wrestling Is Serious Business

The Purest Form of Entertainment

We didn't have a lot of money. We were living in a two-bedroom house in the middle of nowhere with a wood stove for a furnace. It was very *Little House on the Prairie.*

We did little things to treat ourselves. On Sunday mornings, we would go to the supermarket, get some fake crab legs, a bottle of cheap champagne, some eggs, and have ourselves the nicest little brunch we could have for under twenty bucks. And typically we would watch Verne Gagne's AWA wrestling on Channel 9 out of Minneapolis.

My wife tolerated a lot of things regarding me and my personality and the things I liked to do. (She still does.) But I remember her looking at me one day and saying, "Why do you watch this?"

"Honey," I tried to explain, "in my mind, wrestling is the purest form of entertainment, and therefore the purest form of marketing that there is."

Wrestling as Marketing

Maybe it was because of my sales background, but where my wife saw big guys in their underwear hitting other guys over the head with chairs, I saw a marketing opportunity. Intuitively, I knew that professional wrestling worked on a lot of different levels for a lot of different reasons. I saw story, I saw psychology, and I saw a unique way to connect with an audience.

I studied wrestling. I'd ask myself what people liked about a particular character. I pondered the ways it was *different than* everything else people watched. It was obviously successful and popular, and I thought often about why. I tried to understand why it worked so well.

The early 1980s were a time of big change in the wrestling business, even though I wasn't aware of it. Vince McMahon was revolutionizing the business, using cable to deliver a national program. Cable was still very new, but Vince used it in what was then a radical way for wrestling. Until then, regional promoters like Verne Gagne and Vince's father (called Vince Sr., though their middle names are different) made local television deals and, for the most part, stayed out of each other territories. They didn't compete directly.

Vince changed all that by syndicating his show across the country and distributing the his wrestling show on nationwide cable. Instead of being confined to markets in the Northeast, it reached all over the United States, which among other things allowed advertisers to buy spots on his show and reach the whole country as well. He made a lot of other changes, but that was the big one. No one else would ever catch up—though maybe only Vince realized that at the time.

Back to Minneapolis

We spent about a year or a year and a half in Braham. Most of that time, people looked at us as if we were space aliens. We were that young couple who moved *into* Braham. No one ever moved *to* Braham. They might move out, but not in.

Soon after our son Garett was born, April 20, 1984, we decided it was time to move down to Minneapolis. We found a house to rent near my wife's parents in an older section of north Minneapolis. I went back to Blue Ribbon Foods as sales manager, managing a sales force of fifteen people. It was another step in the right direction, résumé-wise.

My daughter Montanna was born in November 1985. By that time, Loree and I had married. While Montanna's arrival was also unplanned, we both looked forward to having another child.

Irv Mann, my boss at Blue Ribbon, became—I don't want to say a father figure, because that would be going too far—but certainly he was a mentor. We developed a very close relationship. He and his wife would spend weekends with us out at the lake during the summer.

We were enjoying ourselves and our young children, and life couldn't have been better in many ways. Then one day a close friend of mine named Sonny Onoo came to me with an idea for a kids' game. I had no idea, but my life was about to take a very unexpected turn.

Ninja-Star Wars

Sonny and I had first met back in my martial arts days. Born in Tokyo, Japan, he ultimately ended up in, of all places, Mason City, Iowa. He owned a couple of karate schools, was a top amateur martial arts competitor, and turned pro in kickboxing in the late 1970s.

One night he and I were sitting at a bar and drinking way more beer than we should have. We started talking about the games we'd played when we were kids. Sonny told me about a tag game they called ninja. He and his friends would take milk bottle caps or whatever they found in the street and fling them at each other like five-pointed martial arts stars.

From that conversation, he proceeded to invent a game based on the game he'd played as a kid. We called it Ninja-Star Wars.

Players wore a ninja uniform: a black felt vest and a headband. Each player had five ninja stars, which were made out of Velcro and weighted down with a two-penny washer in the middle. The stars stuck to felt on the vest. Kids would put the ninja uniform on and chase each other around until someone got all five ninja stars on his opponent.

We thought it was the greatest idea in the world and were sure we'd make millions of dollars selling it. We were so convinced that we each put every penny we had (and some that we didn't have) into manufacturing the game. We found a manufacturer in Korea who would make these games for us, put them in boxes, the whole nine yards. But the economy of scale required meant our initial order was something like ten thousand games. We had a lot of friggin' games manufactured.

We didn't have a warehouse to keep them in. They were literally stuffed in every room of my house.

Sonny and I spent a couple of months trying to take them around to retailers, trying to get them on the shelves. That's when we learned how the toy business really works. Stores allocate square footage to toys based on the distributor's success in the marketplace. If you're Mattel, you're might get 60 percent of the shelf space. If you're Hasbro, you might get 30 percent. If you're Joe Blow's toys, you get whatever's left. And anyone else—Eric Bischoff and Sonny Onoo, for example—doesn't get squat.

We decided to try and create a buzz. Every Saturday my wife and I stood in front of independent toy stores, throwing these ninja stars at each other. People would come up and ask what we were doing, and we'd tell them about the game. The stores wouldn't inventory the game, but they would sell them that day while we were there.

It would have been years before we moved all that inventory. Fortunately, I came up with a better idea.

Wrestling to the Rescue

One afternoon while I was between appointments at Blue Ribbon, I stopped in at home. I happened to catch an AWA wrestling show on ESPN. Verne Gagne had recently begun airing his show on the sports channel, which was still relatively new.

While I was watching Verne's show, I saw some PI spots— Christmas albums and that kind of stuff. PI stands for "per inquiry" and is direct-response sales. As an ad or an infomercial for a product airs, a number flashes on the screen. You call the number, you get the advertised item.

I said to myself, Wait a second. Here's a guy who's got a wrestling show that I know a lot of kids watch. It's airing right in the middle of the afternoon. It's the perfect way to sell Ninja-Star Wars.

The AWA is obviously in the PI business. Why don't I go to Verne and cut a deal?

I knew that if I dropped the amateur wrestling card on the table, I'd get an appointment with Verne. And that was all I was hoping for, an opportunity to pitch him. From there I could rely on my sales skills to close the deal.

I picked up the phone, called directory assistance, got the number, and told whoever answered the phone at AWA that I was an amateur wrestler and wanted to talk to Verne Gagne.

Sure enough, she put me through.

"Mr. Gagne, my name is Eric Bischoff. You may not remember me, but I graduated from Minnetonka senior high school, I wrestled at 138 pounds my senior year tournament, I met you," yada yada yada. "I've got this idea I really want to run by you."

"Sure, kid Come on over. Let's see what you got."

Whether he was just the kindest person I ever met or what I had to say was interesting to him, I'll never know. But I went over the next day.

The Man Himself

The whole idea of being in the office of the AWA, even at thirty-two, was really cool.

Verne had this table that was probably twenty-five feet long, and could fit maybe fifteen people around it. He sat at the far end. Greg Gagne, Wahoo McDaniel, Ray Stevens, a couple of secretaries, the accountant—everyone who worked in the office—gathered around the table to hear my presentation.

I put on one of the vests and headbands, gave another set to the receptionist, and started throwing stars around.

Verne got a big kick out of it.

"How does this work?" he asked.

"I cover the cost of the commercial out of my own pocket. You run the commercial on your show. I handle all of the fulfillment. The games cost me $8.45 each. We'll sell them for twenty bucks each. You and I will split the profit, fifty-fifty."

"Jeez, now that sounds like a great idea."

I shot a commercial that was horrible, got an 800 number, and within a month we were selling games on ESPN.

It was relatively successful, but the economics weren't as good as we wanted. No one was losing money, but no one made enough to make it really work. Ultimately Sonny and I decided to pull the plug.

But by then, I'd become somewhat familiar with Verne and Greg, and in particular with a guy by the name of Mike Shields. Mike had come up with Jerry Jarrett and had done everything from running cameras to helping with booking. He handled advertising and syndication for Verne, heading up the production department. The AWA production department wasn't much—it was like three people and one camera. But they did a lot with what they had.

Mike and I developed a pretty good working relationship. He got a sense of what I was all about, and appreciated my energy and sales ability and just the way I operated.

For my part, I was extremely interested in what he did. I would ask a lot of questions, and he would explain for hours how something like syndication worked. I found it all very fascinating. One thing led to another, and a few months after I'd come to Verne with the Ninja-Star Wars idea, Mike offered me a sales job.

I snatched the opportunity in a heartbeat.

A Tough Place to Work

My first day was August 15, 1987. I didn't start selling right away, though. First, I needed an office.

Verne's operation was located in a one-story building that had once been a church. There were offices on one side of the building; the other was a large, open studio. The offices were all taken, so there was no place to put me. The only thing to do was to build a little office on the television side.

That was my first job. I took some two-by-fours and Sheetrock, and built a little freestanding cubicle not too far from the front door.

A few days after I was finished, all the wrestlers came to the studio to shoot promos. There were twenty, thirty guys in the studio, making a bunch of noise, cutting up, acting like wrestlers, all that happy horseshit. I was in my office, staying out of everybody's way.

All of a sudden I heard Sheik Adan El Kaissey and Kevin "Nails" Wacholtz yelling and swearing at each other.

Kevin, by the way, was the first guy to ever beat up Vince McMahon over a payday dispute. He was jacked up at the time and not the sharpest knife in the drawer to begin with. He didn't just play a hot-head on TV; he was one in real life.

The wrestlers began shouting, "Whoaaaaa! Whoaaaa!"

I looked up just as Sheik's head crashed through the Sheetrock beneath one of the photos on my wall.

I said to myself, Wow. This is pretty impressive.

And then: *What have I gotten myself into?*

Ken Doll

Smartening People Up

Lies and Bullshit

'd like to take a minute to address some of the more blatant lies, inconsistencies, and bullshit that have been spread about me and my time at the AWA.

For example, if you look at a lot of the Web site information about me, my background—none of which was ever supplied by me—you'll read that I took a job mowing Verne Gagne's lawn. That, I assure you, never happened.

More seriously, people have said that I was the architect behind the Team Challenge Series, which was a cute little idea that was horribly executed and was a dismal failure. I had nothing to do with that. It was not my idea, and I was not involved in executing it, but for whatever reason, that disaster has been attributed to me. People have called me AWA's booker, claimed I clashed with Verne over wrestling styles, even suggested I was the general manager.

None of it is true.

Behind the Curtain

During the time I was working with Verne, I had zero input—and I cannot emphasize *zero* enough—on anything that anyone had to do with anything on the screen.

I had *no* creative input. I was not asked for any creative input, and it didn't even occur to me to offer any, because my role was primarily that of a sales and marketing guy. The only time I even saw most of the wrestlers was when they came into town maybe once or twice a month to shoot promos. And then I kept my distance.

Quite honestly, Verne was one of those old-school promoters who didn't want to "smarten" anybody up, or explain the inner workings of the wrestling business to outsiders. He very much believed that the only people who needed to see what went on behind the curtain were the people who were behind the curtain. If you weren't a wrestler or a referee or one of the bookers, you had no business knowing what was going on inside the ring. You couldn't ask questions like, "Hey who's going to beat the Crusher?" You ask that, you'd be shown the door.

Verne was very strict about kayfabe, or the secrets of the business, as the term is used today. If I happened to walk out of my office near the studio, and Verne was talking to a wrestler, he'd whisper in their ear so I couldn't hear what they were saying.

I didn't try to ease my way in behind the curtain. I knew my role and knew what I could do and should do.

For a year and a half, all I did was syndication and sales—and I was *ecstatic* to do that. It was probably the first time in my life that I was doing something that I wanted to do for an indefinite period of time.

The pay was about thirty thousand a year, less than I'd been making at Blue Ribbon, but it was regular. And it was doing something I loved, as opposed to something I was good at.

How the Business Side Worked

Verne's operation at AWA had two main components—the live events or promotions in different locations, and television shows.

Primarily, Verne's live event business was driven by local television markets. The more television stations or local markets that carried his show, the better the live event side of his business did. The TV shows gave you an opportunity to promote the events. That was the best way of advertising the shows. Posters and radio time, the other options, were pretty ineffective for wrestling. Fans have to know your characters and storylines. That's the difference between wrestling and other live event businesses like the circus or music. That happens on the air.

When I came to AWA, Verne distributed a program on ESPN, Monday through Friday, and had a syndicated show that would play on various stations around the United States. My job was to increase the number of stations syndicating the show. I'd solicit interest in different markets over the phone, then go and visit them, hoping to convince them to air Verne's program. That in turn gave Verne a chance to expand his live event territory.

It also helped us increase advertising revenue. Advertisers like M&M Mars paid us based on our penetration into the marketplace. If we had 60 percent national penetration, say, we would get X; if we had 70, we would get X plus Y.

Within six months or so, I took us from thirty-two stations to sixty-five or seventy. That remained my primary focus for the first year and a half.

Pitching

I remember a lot of those pitches. This was a time when television was still very traditional, and the program directors tended to be older, in their fifties for the most part. They'd been around when wrestling was in its heyday in the 1960s. I liked talking to them, because they'd tell me great wrestling stories.

When I was a kid, I remember when this guy wrestled that guy, and my grandma took me to the wrestling matches and she got so upset she reached into her bag and pulled out a hairpin and tried to stab this guy.

That kind of stuff.

You'd hear all of those stories, because everybody has one, especially in the Midwest. Out there, you didn't get a lot of rock 'n' roll; you didn't get the circus coming to town on a regular basis. Cedar Rapids and Fort Dodge, places in Nebraska that outsiders have never heard of and I've forgotten—out there people didn't have a lot of entertainment coming to town. So when wrestling came to town, it was a big damn deal, especially back in the 1960s.

When I went to markets like Milwaukee or Chicago or some of the other big cities, I'd run into younger programming people at certain stations who were trying to be hip and cool. But invariably they'd reveal, yes indeed, they were wrestling fans. It was always fun getting that out of them.

Behind the Curtain

The Cockpit of a 727

About a year after I started, Mike Shields came to me and said, *"Why don't you come to Las Vegas and sit in on one of the shows and watch what we do?"*

Besides everything else Mike did, he directed the ESPN show that Verne shot in Vegas at a small off-strip casino called the Showboat once or twice a month. Mike made me technical director on the show. It was a pretty low-level job, but it was the first time I stepped foot inside the television production universe.

It was like walking into the cockpit of a 727. It was amazing.

I'm a product of the 1950s and '60s. Television was still relatively new to our culture when I grew up. We didn't even have a color TV when I was a kid. Very few people had more than one set in the house. But the television they did have was the center of every family's life. Everyone knew what television was—they just didn't know how it worked. I was fascinated to find out.

Mike gave me an opportunity to step inside a television truck and see how it all came together. It absolutely intoxicated me.

Equipment crammed the production truck. Eight or ten people worked elbow to elbow. You saw lights and buttons and levers and screens. Mike watched eight screens on the wall, all at the same time, each feeding a different shot. It was controlled, high-energy chaos. I was fascinated that he could pick the shot he wanted to take at any given moment. It's like watching someone juggle hand grenades.

"Ready, Camera Two, take two. Camera Four—take four. Camera one—graphics up—hit the music!"

By today's standards, it was pretty fundamental and basic, and, dare I say, crude, without any disrespect to Mike. But to someone who'd never seen it before, it was an amazing thing.

I think Mike invited me out to Vegas as a "It's time you learned another phase of the business" thing. He was a mentor that way. Whether he saw my enthusiasm for it, or because I asked so many questions, he invited me to learn more.

I was an eager learner, and he was a great teacher.

One More Step

At some point around late 1988 or early 1989—I wish I could recall when, but I can't—I went from being the sales and marketing guy to being an on-camera talent.

Which I had *no* intention of doing.

My goal, my aspiration, was *never* to be in front of the camera. I was thrilled to be in sales and marketing. I never assumed I could be a "talent," never hoped to be asked. But it just fell in my lap.

Edit Market Promos

The way Verne set up his business, the wrestlers came in every two weeks and cut edit market promos. Edit market promos would be edited into the syndicated show to advertise upcoming events. They were made in such a way to make it seem as if the syndicated show was actually a local production. That was the "magic" of the old territory system.

Here's how it all worked:

Verne used to shoot his syndicated show inside the soundstage at the local television station in Minneapolis. It was a small soundstage; probably seventy-five to a hundred people would come in and watch the show. A number of matches would be filmed at one time, then prepared for the syndicated TV shows.

At a later date, the wrestlers would cut the interviews, which were generally a minute and thirty seconds long. These would be edited and inserted into the show for each market.

Let's say I'm Greg Gagne, and Mean Gene is interviewing me. I have a match coming up in Milwaukee. Gene would say something like, "Okay, great. You're coming to Milwaukee and you're going to be wrestling at the Mecca Center on Saturday, January 19, at 8 P.M. tickets are available at all Joe Blow ticket outlets right here in Milwaukee. And who are you going to take on?"

And Gagne would say, "Well, right here in Milwaukee I'm going to be wrestling the Crusher and I'm going to show these people here in Milwaukee . . ."

The interview would make the viewer feel like the show was being produced specifically for Milwaukee. The wrestler and interviewer referred specifically to things in the Milwaukee area. They might mention the Green Bay Packers, or people that everybody in Milwaukee knew.

They would do that for every single market the show was in. The same basic show would air in Milwaukee and Green Bay and Minneapolis and Fargo and Mason City and Lacrosse and Cedar

Rapids, with dozens and dozens of these interviews edited into the proper segments.

If you were a wrestler, you would stand there for an hour and do the same promo, the same interview about the same guy you're going to wrestle, maybe fifty or a hundred times. Each time you'd change just enough to refer to the local market. The announcer would do the interview over and over with different wrestlers, feeding them their lines all day without, hopefully, getting hoarse or mind-numb.

The Worst Announcer Ever

By this point, Verne's longtime announcer "Mean" Gene Okerlund had left AWA and gone over to work for Vince. Verne hired a guy by the name of Larry Nelson, who had a deep, burly voice that Verne liked. He was an old-school radio guy, and he was also a pretty heavy drinker. In fact, I think the Scotch had a lot to do with his radio voice.

One day all of the wrestlers had arrived in the building. It was about ten o'clock in the morning, and they were getting ready to shoot. But Larry wasn't there. An hour went by and, no Larry Nelson. An hour and a half went by—they couldn't find Larry. No one could find Larry.

That's because Larry was in jail. Larry had gotten pulled over by the police and, for whatever reason, he never showed up to work. There were a lot of wrestlers, and a lot of work to be done, but there was no announcer.

I was sitting in my office, minding my own business, working the phone. I had a sales call that I had to make later that day, so I'd worn a shirt and a tie and a sport coat to work, which turned out to be my undoing.

At some point—I'm not sure who it was, it may have been Greg Gagne, it may have been Verne, it may have been Mike Shields— someone said, "Hey, why don't we get Eric to do it? He wore a tie today, let him do it."

"Do what?"

They brought me in, put a microphone in my hand, and told me what to say

I tried. But I sucked really bad.

Really bad.

I might add that even today, the announcing job is one of the toughest jobs there is on camera. You can't really compare it to being a wrestler, because there's no physicality involved, but getting the information out and getting it out in an entertaining way, without a teleprompter—the AWA didn't have one—is tough. You have to remember where the event is, what time it is, where you can get tickets. You have to introduce the wrestler, feed him a line so he can feed the camera his line: "When I'm in Rochester this Saturday night, I'm going to kick Baron Von Raschke's ass because of what he did to me last week. . . ." Then take it back and button it up, reminding people where and when to buy, and get it all done in exactly one minute, thirty seconds. All the while there's a guy behind the camera going, "Ten, nine, eight . . . ," counting the spot down because if it's a minute and thirty-five, you had to do it over again.

It's a real skill. And I didn't have it.

Cracking Up the Audience

My first interview was with Larry Zbyszko, who by the way happened to be married to Verne Gagne's daughter. All the wrestlers were kind of standing around watching, waiting for their interview with the new guy. Anything that would give them a laugh was a good thing, and they were all at the edge of their seats waiting for this new little "Ken Doll"—as they referred to me—to break into the business.

I don't know what I said or how I screwed it up, but as I opened up the interview and turned to feed the microphone to Larry, he looked at me for probably four or five seconds (which seemed like an eternity) and then just busted out laughing. Loud, eye-watering, cramp-inducing, belly-laugh laughing. At which point everyone else in the room busted out laughing with him.

For a very long time.

I got through the day. How, I don't know. I'm sure it was painful to watch, and painful to produce, because it was painful for me to do. But we got through it.

Verne immediately went out looking for someone who could really do the job. I was more than happy to go back to my office and not embarrass myself.

Getting Better

They hired someone else right away.

Quite honestly and incredibly, he was worse than me.

They gave him about two weeks. He got worse instead of better, and then he was gone.

They came back to me. *We're going to look for someone else, but in the meantime, you fill in.*

I did a little better this time, thanks to some coaching from some of the guys who worked with me at night after everyone went home—Brad Rheingans, Sgt. Slaughter, and Sheik Adan El Kaissey are the ones I remember. I was still painful to watch, but may be not excruciating.

We got through the day, and everybody thanked me—not profusely, but at least they weren't laughing. I went back to my office and selling. Verne continued looking for another announcer.

They found another guy who washed out after a few weeks, and I filled in again. This time I did a little better. They kept looking. I kept filling in.

Eventually, maybe because they just got used to the pain, they stopped looking for somebody else. And I became the AWA's announcer.

The Old School's Last Holdout

Burning Cash

My new role as on-air talent may have had as much to do with the economics of the AWA as improvement in my announcing skills.

At the time Verne was burning cash trying to stay in the business. He was losing money every week trying to hold on to his dream and compete with Vince McMahon.

I only know one side of the story—Verne's. I heard that Vince came in and tried to buy Verne out, but Verne would have nothing to do with him. I can believe that. The AWA was Verne's baby. Selling it would have felt like stomping on his legacy. And Verne was a stubborn guy.

When Verne Gagne was in his heyday in the sixties and seventies, there was an unwritten code that regional promoters stayed out of each other's territories, nobody tried to steal anybody's wrestlers, and that kind of stuff. They were all happy making their money in their respective territories. Then Vince Jr. came along and bought out the company from his father. He said, "You know what, I'm not going to operate the old way. I'm going to take it all. I'm going to take over the entire country and aggregate the best talent from different regions. I'm going to take this thing nationwide."

Up until that point, no one had ever thought of becoming a national product. The television business didn't allow it. With the advent of cable television, and with the cable networks reaching the entire United States, you could. When Vince did that, the old territorial model began to crumble.

Verne held on to the belief that what Vince was doing would fail. And when it failed, Verne would be in a position to take advantage of it.

Or, if it worked, he could compete, thanks to his ESPN connection and syndicated show.

The problem was, Verne didn't really have an understanding of what it would take to compete. He was an older guy at the time, in his mid-sixties. Verne had a certain understanding or philosophy of how the business should be operated, and I don't think he could adapt to the changing television landscape. He didn't have the vision. He was still thinking about territories and wrestling as small-town entertainment.

He wasn't able to go to another cable network and say, "Look what Vince McMahon is doing over here; why don't we do the same thing with your network." The ESPN deal wasn't enough of a platform to compete on a national level. His show felt small, with production values that were severely lacking compared to Vince's.

He also couldn't hold on to the top talent. Vince was making a lot of extraordinary deals with wrestlers, effectively luring them away from the regional promotions.

Ironically, years later Vince would accuse me and Ted Turner of stealing his talent, when in fact that's exactly what Vince did to these regional promoters in the 1980s. A lot of the big names who had been at AWA had moved on to work for Vince. Even the wrestlers who were there when I arrived, like AWA World Champion Curt Henning and Kevin Kelly, had their eyes on a World Wrestling Federation career.

Most of the guys who were left were, quite honestly, guys Vince wasn't interested in. There's not a kinder way to say that. I wish there was, but it's true. Baron Von Raschke had been a big name, but he was in the twilight of his career; Sheik Adan El Kaissey, the same thing. Jerry Blackwell, kind of along the same lines.

The rest of Verne's talent tended to be young guys who hadn't gotten a lot of attention. For most, it was a great opportunity to break into the business—it certainly worked out for me—but it made the AWA feel less than World Wrestling Federation.

What McMahon Did Right

Vince McMahon didn't get to be the king of professional wrestling simply by skimming the best talent from the other promotions. He did a lot of things right. He brought a lot more production value to his television product—a lot more. Even the earliest *WrestleMania*, Pay-Per-Views, and weekly television shows were clearly better in terms of production and entertainment value than anything Verne or the other regional promoters produced. Vince's shows looked bigger, used more cameras, and had more elaborate costumes. Its characters were more colorful and attractive. Everything was bigger, louder, sexier, more entertaining than what we as fans had recognized wrestling to be.

But to Verne, Vince's product wasn't what wrestling should be. He thought it was too cartoonish, with too much emphasis on characters and costumes, too much emphasis on entertainment. Verne was a lot more wrestler than showman. Vince McMahon was all showman. Like a lot of old-school wrestlers, Verne was stuck in the mud. Audiences preferred Vince's product, but Verne didn't realize it, or if he did, he refused to accept it.

By the time I joined the company in 1987, the nose on Verne's airplane was already in a steep dive, and it just kept accelerating, quite honestly, into a death spiral. Verne burned truckloads of his own savings trying to keep it in the air.

I really didn't have a good understanding at the time just how bad off the AWA was financially. I was insulated from that. But it was probably one of the reasons Verne kept me on board as the announcer. I was cheap. Using me didn't cost him any extra money.

Night Shift

The AWA may not have been doing well financially, but I was having a ball. Besides my announcing and my sales job, I became fascinated by television production. I'd literally spend my nights and weekends from eight P.M. to eight in the morning "dubbing" or duplicating tapes. I liked being in the control room running those one-inch machines and having a real hands-on experience. As silly and insignificant as it may sound in retrospect, just learning how to thread a one-inch tape machine and operate the duplicating equipment was a big deal to me. I wanted to be part of the process.

The technology in the late 1980s was nothing like today's. Verne had one switcher, two one-inch machines, and two three-quarter-inch machines that we used to dub tapes. It could take the better part of a weekend to get what takes a couple of hours to get today.

I also started promoting some live events. Shawn Michaels and Marty Jannetty—I believe they were called the Midnight Rockers at that point—were on the very first card I ever promoted in Mason City, Iowa.

Promoting, even on the small scale I got involved in, was a lot of work. You had to find a venue, and find local radio stations to help you promote the event. Oftentimes you'd tie into a local fundraising event to help move tickets. It was Promotion 101. Working at the AWA for me was really like getting a master's degree in professional wrestling while getting paid to do it.

Again, if the AWA had been successful, I would never have been able to get these opportunities. There would have been other people much more qualified than I was. But because Verne was on his last legs financially and couldn't afford to pay anyone who was more experienced or talented than I was, I had the unique opportunity to be involved in every aspect of the wrestling business that I was interested in.

Lessons Learned

The Energy of the Live Show

Besides the technical aspects of producing a wrestling show and running events, I learned a great deal about wrestling itself from

Verne Gagne and the people around him. Wrestling isn't just a sport and a business. In many ways, it's an art form.

When you watch wrestling, what you see looks fairly simple. It looks like a staged, choreographed fight between two people who supposedly have an issue, something that they're fighting over. What you don't see is the psychology that goes into creating that story. What you *really* don't see is the skill and the art that's required to engage the third person in that ring.

The third person in the ring is the audience.

The audience has always been the most important ingredient in a wrestling show, but it's really critical in a television show. If the wrestlers are not connecting with the audience, no matter what they do, the match doesn't translate to the viewer at home.

Try this experiment. Pick the two best wrestlers you know of— take Ric Flair and Ricky Steamboat, just as examples. Put them in a Broadway—a sixty-minute match that ends in a draw—that's the best match of their careers. Put that match in front of fifteen thousand people who know Ric Flair and Ricky Steamboat, real fans who have followed their careers, are caught up in their storyline, and know their moves.

Close your eyes and imagine what that match is going to look like. Imagine what that crowd is like.

Now open your eyes.

Take the fans out of the building. Close your eyes and have that same match in front of empty seats.

What's the viewer at home going to do ten minutes into the match?

Change the channel.

The crowd validates what the viewer at home feels. If the crowd isn't there, most viewers aren't going to feel the same way about what they are seeing. The audience is one of the most important ingredients in wrestling, much more so than in most other forms of entertainment.

Where the Art Comes In

Truly accomplished wrestlers read the audience. They learn to "feel" the audience and work to get the reactions they want. They have a whole arsenal of tools to utilize to tell their story. Therein lies the art.

An accomplished wrestler is a little like a Broadway actor who appears in the same play over and over again during a two-year run. The Broadway actor is going to get the same reaction at a Wednesday matinee that he or she gets on a Friday night. He may have to go about it in a different way, but he'll get it.

The same is true in wrestling. The really good wrestlers—whether it's Ric Flair, Triple H, Hulk Hogan—they know how to get the reaction they want. They can read and manipulate the audience.

People criticize Hulk Hogan because he doesn't have a lot of physical tools, but I don't know anybody who can read an audience better than Hulk Hogan. He knows when to give that special look to just the right person at ringside, so that everyone else in the arena thinks Hogan's looking right at him. Hulk Hogan can get more of a reaction with a single look than many more athletic performers can get during an entire match. Sometimes the changes are subtle—sometimes they are over the top. But he knows how to get the reaction he wants to get. That's an art form. That's a skill.

Good Guys and Bad

In wrestling, you need a good guy and you need a bad guy. The problem these days is, no one wants to be a bad guy.

We all want to be liked. It's human nature. We all have egos. I have an ego—a fairly large one, at that. There are things that Vince McMahon has asked me to do that, as a person, as Eric Bischoff the real person, I didn't want to do because I didn't want to be perceived a certain way. That's ego. But as a *character*, it was the right thing to do. I've matured enough, and am comfortable enough, that I can separate the real person and the character. You'd be surprised how many performers have a hard time separating their self-image from the character they are asked to play.

A lot of wrestlers who are supposed to be bad guys don't have that ability. Sometimes I see it in guys who are really experienced—they don't want to be the bad guy. They don't want to be booed. But for a story to be successful, there *has* to be a villain. You have to have the characteristics that people truly hate. You have to be a liar, a cheat, a sneak, a coward—and the fans need to believe it.

Most performers are uncomfortable with that.

And sometimes it's not just ego. In today's environment, much of your income is determined by your ability to sell merchandise. This is a vulnerability in the WWE formula. If the crowd doesn't like you—in other words, if you're an effective villain or heel, to use the wrestling expression—fans generally don't buy your T-shirts and other merchandise. That translates into less money in your pocket.

But if no one *really* wants to be the villain, no one *really* gets to be the good guy. People start to feel ambivalent about the storylines and characters. They may come to enjoy the action and the communal experience of being in an arena with 15,000 other people. They will react the way they know they are supposed to, but will they really care about the outcome of the match?

In my opinion, probably not. At least not as much as they should. That's the difference between what I refer to as "Pavlovian heat"—an automatic reaction that's not deeply felt—and real heat—loathing that comes from the heart.

I have a hard time today pointing to one person who is really a babyface or a good guy. I can't even point to one guy that the audience believes is a villain.

Look at a guy like Triple H, and how people react to him when he comes out. He goes into that Incredible Hulk–like stance. He scowls and spits water straight up into the air like he owns the arena. They dim the lights, and he has a spotlight on him like Elvis Presley as he makes his way to the ring, growling for the camera.

What guy doesn't want to be him?

I don't want to pick on Triple H, but unfortunately his character is an example of what I'm talking about. He's one of the best modern heels out there, but his entrance is a hero's entrance. If you give someone a hero's entrance week in and week out, and he gets a hero's response, the audience doesn't hate that guy. They can't—they wish they were him.

Guess what? Once that happens, you're not a heel. You cannot achieve heel status with the audience when, consciously or subconsciously, they wish they were you. It's absolutely impossible.

Its like: *Yeah, I'll play the role of a bad guy, but I want people to think I'm cool. I want people to buy my merchandise.*

You have to establish a heel character the second you walk through the curtain. You have to want people to hate you. They should be throwing shit at you. Then when you step in the ring and the good guy across from you hits you and knocks you on your ass, the roof blows off. And that good guy, that babyface, is *truly* a good guy And they buy *his* merchandise. The audience is living vicariously through him.

Verne Gagne told me it doesn't matter if people love you or hate you, as long as they feel strongly one way or the other. The worst place you can be is in the middle.

The Road Gets Rockier and Rockier

Superclash

Maybe because we were a struggling company, there were never any really standout moments—times when you stand back and say, Holy shit, *this* is an event, *this* is big time. But one that came close was a Pay-Per-View in 1989 dubbed *Superclash III*.

The show was held in Chicago. Verne joined forces with some of the other regional promoters still around at the time. Jerry Jarrett, down in Memphis, was one; Don Owen and Bob Geigel in Kansas City were among the others. I think the show was Eddie Guererro's professional television professional debut; he managed his brothers Chavo and Mando at the time. It's interesting how a lot of us crossed paths early in our careers.

Seeing all this different talent from around the country that we had never worked with before was really quite interesting. I said earlier that I wasn't going to talk about some of the crazy shit guys did backstage, and I'm not going to start now, but working with Kerry Von Erich was interesting. He was a lunatic. Kerry was definitely "Kerry" in quotes.

Besides doing the interviews for *Superclash*, I built the interview set. I loaded it into a van, put a mattress on top, and then with my three-year-old son and wife left Minneapolis in a rented van and drove from Minneapolis to Nashville to Louisville to Memphis, doing shows that promoted the Pay-Per-View the whole way. Then we went on to Chicago. We had a great time. We thought we were living like kings and queens.

Diamond Dallas Page

During my time with AWA, I crossed paths with many guys who'd play an important role in my later career. One was Diamond Dallas Page—though things between us started out very rocky.

At the time, Page was managing the tag team of Paul Diamond & Pat Tanaka. We were all in Rochester, Minnesota, for an event, which I had put together as the AWA promoter. We were in this bar, and Page was there, along with a lot of other wrestlers. Page was a very loud and sometimes obnoxious individual—and actually still is. He wore white leather pants and snakeskin cowboy boots and looked real flashy with his "Diamond Dolls" (a couple of local strippers) hanging off him.

Page was being rude and loud, and, well, just being Diamond Dallas Page. He said something at one point that struck me wrong. I don't know what I said back, but it was probably pretty aggressive. Then either he called me out or I called him out. I put down my drink and followed him to the door, muttering to myself, "I'm going to kick this guy's ass."

I got outside, and the only thing I saw was Page going down the street, driving away.

On one level, I was proud of myself that I didn't get into a fight in the bar, because that would have been inappropriate. I was probably somewhat relieved that we didn't end up getting in a fight in the parking lot, because even if I had kicked his ass—and I sure thought I could—it would have caused a scene. And my ego was pretty happy that this loudmouth who thought he was a tough guy thought twice about it and left.

I went back inside and proceeded to pound a couple more beers. Then my wife and I went back to my hotel. We got in the elevator to go to our room. When the doors opened, Diamond Dallas Page stood right in front of me.

We had a few more words. I don't remember how intense it was, and I don't remember how or why we decided not to get into a fight there and then, but he went back to his room and I went back to my room.

I woke up in the morning, and I just felt like an idiot. I knew the way I'd handled myself was wrong. So I went to Page's room and knocked on the door. He came out looking like a hundred miles of bad road. I'm not sure what he was thinking—he's got his version of the story, naturally, and I have mine—but I said, *Hey, I just wanted to come by and apologize.* He kind of chuckled and shook my hand.

Breeding Ground for Greatness

Toward the end of 1989 and the beginning of 1990, I put together my first video from beginning to end. It was a tape for the home video market called *Best of the Eighties* and was a kind of greatest hits of AWA wrestling events. Verne had a tremendous wrestling library at the time—in fact, it's now part of WWE's 24/7 offerings. Working through that catalog really drove home how much Verne had done for professional wrestling.

When you look back at that library, and you look back at the history of AWA, you see that some of the great names of our business during the late 1980s and early 1990s had really come out of the Verne Gagne territory—Hulk Hogan, Jesse Ventura, Jim Brunzell, Gene Okerlund, Scott Hall, Shawn Michaels, and Curt Hennig were just some of the many wrestlers who worked for Verne.

Minneapolis itself produced a significant number of the real superstars. Among them were the Road Warriors, Animal, Hawk and "Ravishing" Rick Rude—who went to the same high school as my wife.

Curt Hennig also came from the area. I don't believe he wrestled in high school, but he had a brother named Randy who I wrestled my senior year. I think he was the captain of the Robbinsdale High School team. I was a little intimidated because he was a Hennig—his father, Larry "the Axe" Hennig, was a big pro wrestling star at the time.

I did fairly well, even though he beat me. He had a figure-four leglock on me, riding me around my midsection. It was just a grinding technique. I remember looking up and seeing Larry "the Ax" looking right at me. I remember thinking I didn't know which was worse—this kid crushing my ribs, or the big burly mean bastard who looked like he'd just as soon do it himself.

Anyway a lot of those guys who made it big later on came from the AWA and made it big in Minneapolis first.

Audition

Verne's business was sinking lower and lower. My own finances were being stretched, as paychecks began coming later and later, and finally stopped altogether. If I stayed at AWA and things continued the way they were, it would be just a matter of time before I went bankrupt.

In June or July of 1990, World Wrestling Federation advertised for an announcer. I put in a call, and within a day or two they sent me an airplane ticket and arranged for an audition.

Needless to say, I was extremely excited—and somewhat intimidated—at the opportunity.

The interview process was very informal. A couple of people in production put me in front of what they call a chroma key or blue screen. They gave me a script and said, "Sell us a match." I gave them my very best pitch.

Someone—I think it may have been Kevin Dunn, who's now the executive vice president for TV production—said, "Hey, Eric, sell me that broom over in the corner."

I wasn't sure if it was a rib—a joke—or if he was serious, but I figured what the hell. That's what they want me to do, I'll sell my ass off. I picked up the broom and interviewed it.

When I was done, Vince McMahon came over and shook my hand. He made a couple of jokes about Verne Gagne. They were gentle, along the lines of "Is he still as bald as he's ever been?" Vince and I talked for probably three minutes, and that was the end of it.

I didn't get the job. Looking back, I didn't deserve it. I wasn't ready for the big time.

Time Runs Out

While I was enjoying the opportunities at the AWA, Verne was going out of business one day at a time. It started getting so bad that he had a hard time paying talent. He cut costs any way he possibly could.

I'd gotten to know Verne at a different level at that point. I'd become friends with both Verne and his son Greg. We used to do a lot of things together socially. I took some fantastic hunting trips with them, and that sort of thing. I hated what was happening to them.

Besides having trouble competing with Vince, Verne was in the middle of a major lawsuit with the state of Minnesota. A lot of his money was wrapped up in an estate on Lake Minnetonka outside Minneapolis. Verne had built a beautiful home there, but the state of Minnesota decided they wanted his property to build a park. They enforced eminent domain to take it from Verne, in exchange for what they thought the property was worth. Unfortunately, what they thought it was worth was significantly less than what it was really worth.

That put Verne in a double bind. He no longer had the property to draw equity from to keep AWA afloat. And not only did he not have that property, he had to fund a lawsuit against the state.

I stayed on, even as the ship kept sinking. We ran less and less shows, had fewer events, lost talent left and right. The last six months I was there, I literally worked without a paycheck.

Still, we all still showed up for work every day. Between the loyalty I had toward the Gagnes, the passion I felt for the business, and the knowledge that if I left, I probably wouldn't get back into wrestling anywhere, I was reluctant to leave the business.

That decision took a significant financial toll on me and my family My car was repossessed out of my driveway, and I fell four or five months behind on my house payments. My kids ate rice and beans and hot dogs. My wife worked nights as a waitress in a restaurant, but the money wasn't enough to keep us going.

The reality of my situation came to me when we came home from visiting my parents one winter night, and the house was freezing cold. We were out of propane. And we weren't going to get any more, because we owed the propane company money. I had to heat our house with a couple of portable kerosene heaters.

I needed a miracle, or I needed to get out of pro wrestling. Or maybe both.

WCW: The Early Days

How Soon Can You Get Down Here?

Two Possibilities

People looking for a new position are often told that it's a lot easier to get one if you're already in a job. That's always been especially true in wrestling, where a lot of the hiring has traditionally been done by word of mouth. Someone knew someone who needed someone and could vouch for you, that sort of thing. Once you were outside of the network, it could be very difficult to get back in.

The problem for me was, there were only two other organizations in professional wrestling big enough that it seemed possible for me to get a job.

One was World Wrestling Federation, which seemed like a distant possibility. They were the juggernaut, and after I failed to get a job as an announcer following my audition, I couldn't imagine that I'd be able to carve out a place for myself without any relationships whatsoever.

The other was World Championship Wrestling, WCW. I knew some people who had gone down there. So I put together a demo tape and sent it off to Jim Herd, the company president.

Ted Turner & the History of WCW

WCW's prehistory is quite complicated, but it essentially rose from the ashes of the National Wrestling Association, or NWA. The NWA had started as a loose alliance of regional pro wrestling companies, including storied promotions such as Georgia Championship Wrestling. Jim Crockett Jr. consolidated many of the southern franchises in the NWA, promoting them all as "NWA World Championship Wrestling" in the 1980s. (Technically the NWA remained separate from Crockett's promotions, though most people did not distinguish between the two entities.)

There were a lot of very big names in the NWA at the time. Ric Flair had been the champion for quite a while. Dusty Rhodes was there. But like the AWA, the NWA wasn't big enough to compete with Vince on a national level, and as a regional business, it floundered. By 1988, it was on the verge of bankruptcy.

At that point, Ted Turner stepped in and bought Jim Crockett Promotions, ultimately renaming the company WCW.

Why He Did It

People unfamiliar with Ted Turner's history may wonder why a billionaire who first rose to national fame racing yachts bought a wrestling promotion. In fact, it made a great deal of sense.

When Ted launched the Turner Broadcasting System in the 1970s, he did it with very inexpensive programming, things that he could afford. None of it really got much of a rating—except for wrestling. For a variety of reasons, wrestling was one of the most popular things on the TBS network from its very beginning.

In 1987 Crockett Promotions remained relatively popular on TBS. As original programming went, wrestling was also cheap to produce. That's why Turner acquired the company.

I started watching WCW around 1991. While I'd heard of many of the wrestlers, I wasn't familiar with most of them. The presentation was better than the AWA; they had more money and better production values. But the shows were still a far cry from Vince's.

They had a national cable platform thanks to Turner, but WCW seemed very southern in its orientation. The announcers had heavy southern accents, which worked great in the South, but didn't play so well in the rest of the country. The rest of their presentation was very regional as well. The WCW didn't look like much of a competitor stacked against Vince, and the fact that it had only barely escaped bankruptcy a few years before didn't really inspire me.

Nonetheless, it was one of very few opportunities out there.

We Got Your Tape

About a month after I sent the tape to Jim Herd, I was sitting on the edge of my bed one morning when the phone rang.

It was Herd.

"Eric, we got your videotape. We want to get you down here. How soon can you come for an audition?"

I was very calm talking to him, very calm. From a point of pride and not wanting to embarrass myself, I didn't want anyone to know how bad the situation was. It was pretty fuckin' bleak, but I played the call very calmly.

"How soon do you want me?"

"We'll send you some tickets right away."

I hung up the phone, turned around and looked at my wife. Then I jumped about four feet in the air and yelled at the top of my lungs.

I knew at that moment I was going to end up getting that job.

Sunk . . .

Two weeks passed in a blur. I flew down to Atlanta and got to the Omni Hotel, which Ted Turner owned. I got checked into my room, went down to the bar, had a beer, and kind of collected my thoughts. Life was about to get a whole lot better.

The next morning, I got up early. I was excited and couldn't wait to get to the audition. I watched the clock in my room, and the second it hit 9:00, I called the number they'd given me to get the information for the audition. Keith Mitchell, the head of production, answered the phone.

Diamond Dallas Page.

"All right, Eric. Come on down around ten or eleven. You're going to be working with Diamond Dallas Page."

Diamond Dallas Page?

Aw fuck!

The guy I almost came to blows with in Rochester, Minnesota, a few years back?

This is the guy I have to work with? He hates my guts. I'm toast.

I didn't say any of this to Keith, of course. Even though I pretty much knew I was sunk.

You Look Like a Movie Star

I hung up the phone and proceeded to call Page, who already knew what was up. To my great surprise, he was very gracious. And not only gracious—Page went out of his way to tell me what he knew about what WCW was looking for in a play-by-play guy.

Page is a unique guy. He's loud, he can be obnoxious as hell, and he's the most relentless self-promoter you will ever meet. But he is also one of the most generous people you'll ever know. Page would give you his last dime and not even ask why you need it.

Page had been at WCW for about a year and a half, and knew a lot about what was going on. He really stepped up when he didn't have to. He could have just as easily allowed me to bury myself.

Or, if he was a typical wrestler, he could have told me the exact *opposite* of what they were looking for, so he could get a kick watching me go down in flames.

But he was honest and straightforward. He told me what they liked and what they didn't like, and how to impress them. Page and I worked really well together in that audition and ended up working on camera a lot afterward.

Following the audition and lunch, I had an appointment with Jim Herd. He told me he liked what he'd seen on the audition tape, and offered me a job.

I can't even describe how I felt. Relief, gratitude, enthusiasm—

they all overwhelmed me. I couldn't believe that the last year and a half was finally going to pay off.

Jim Herd was kind of a crusty, gruff character. He was a businessman, but he was direct and to the point. He looked at me, and he said something like, "Kid, you look like a movie star."

I think that was a compliment.

"Here's what I'm going to do. I'm going to hire you. I'm going to bring you in. I'm going to pay you seventy thousand dollars a year. Here's your job. Your job is to put pressure on Jim Ross and Tony Schiavone. Schiavone and Ross need to know there is someone else here who can take their jobs if they don't stay in line. That's why I'm bringing you in here."

I didn't know Jim Ross, and I didn't know Tony Schiavone. I couldn't have cared less. If my job description was to make the Marquis de Sade miserable, I would have done that.

At Work in the WCW

Like Winning the Lottery

Seventy thousand a year was twice what I'd been making when Verne was still managing to pay me. The idea of making that much money in 1991 was just unbelievable. I remember telling my wife, "Honey, this is how much money attorneys make. I'm making attorney money."

By that time, we'd already filed for bankruptcy. I had a massive IRS issue. Nonetheless, our family's situation changed literally overnight. Little things like making sure the house was heated properly and the phone bills were paid became possible again. The kids could get decent clothes. I could actually buy a dependable car.

We certainly didn't live large by any stretch of the imagination, but considering what we had been going through, we felt like we had just won the lottery.

Plus, I only had to work two days a week, which meant I could commute from Minneapolis and not uproot my family. I'd leave Sunday night or Monday morning, fly into Atlanta, work Monday and Tuesday, and then fly home.

The Backup to the Backup to the Backup

I was the backup to the backup to the backup announcers, but I still had a lot of work to do.

Each week WCW produced a Saturday-night show for TBS, a Sunday-night show for TBS, three or four syndicated U.S. shows, and a number of international shows. I did play-by-play on a couple of the syndicated shows, a voice-over on one or two of the international shows, and stand-up edit market interviews or promos.

There was a lot of on-camera work, but a lot of it was very low-profile—grunt work, if you will. It was the work that Jim Ross or Tony Schiavone didn't have time to do or didn't want to do because it was not as high-profile or seem as important as their main jobs.

Comparing the AWA production facilities to what the WCW had was like comparing a go-cart that you build from scraps in your garage to a Ferrari.

WCW had phenomenal facilities. They were cramped, but phenomenal. The production offices were in the lower level of the CNN Center, right in the same building as CNN and Turner Broadcasting. When you were there, you felt like you were in a real network environment.

Often when I'd get done, I'd take a walk around. I'd pass the gift shop and I'd think, Wait a minute, I work for the company that has this gift shop. I work for Turner Broadcasting.

CNN at that time was really exploding. They were the international leader in news. To me, this was all just amazing. I was working for one of the biggest entertainment and media conglomerates in the world.

There were plenty of celebrity moments, with standout personalities from every walk of life. Every so often we'd get a glimpse of Ted Turner or Jane Fonda going through the atrium at the CNN

Center. Once in a while you'd see a dignitary—or mostly their security people, guys with dark suits and sunglasses talking into their wristwatches. You knew something was going on, but you weren't quite sure what.

A Role Player

When I was announcing, I didn't look at myself as a character. I looked at myself as more of a utility player.

My role was all about getting information out in as entertaining a way as possible. It was never about driving a television show.

The truth of the matter is that, in wrestling, if the announcers become lead characters, there's something desperately wrong. Announcers don't wrestle. Announcers don't drive television ratings. No one pays money to come to an arena and watch an announcer perform. You're garnish on the plate.

What you should be doing is making the talent look better, making the stories more interesting. Sometimes the best way to do that is to keep your mouth shut and say as little as possible. That was the way I was trained with Verne Gagne, and I still believe it to this day.

Getting the wrestlers over doesn't happen by accident; you have to work at it. As an announcer, you're very familiar with all of the characters and their storylines, and you look for things to bring up that will enhance the perception of these characters. Whether it's their background or personal interests, or unique things about them physically, you look for that one thing that you can talk about that will make the character or the story more compelling.

When you're sitting down to do play-by-play, you have a whole laundry list of things that have to be done. You've got to talk about the Pay-Per-View that's coming up. You've got to sell each one of the stories that are involved in that Pay-Per-View. You need to sell magazines. You need to sell home videos, merchandise, and next week's show. You need to keep people interested in the main event coming up at the end of the show. You've got a number of items to check off during that forty-four minutes of a broadcast hour.

The best wrestling announcers are the ones people don't even remember. There are exceptions. A guy like Jim Ross, who has been out there as long as Jim was out there, becomes a household name. But one of the things I like about Joey Stiles right now is that Joey makes the show better without becoming a character himself. And I think that's a great quality in an announcer.

Herd Is Out

I came to work one day in early 1992 and found out that Jim Herd had been fired.

I didn't work with Jim a lot. Jim Ross was my immediate supervisor, the guy I answered to. But I felt really bad for Jim Herd. I saw him in the atrium as he was leaving the building. I told him I wanted to thank him for the opportunity he'd given me. "I don't know what's going on here," I said, "but I want you to know that I'm very appreciative of what you did for me and my family."

He acknowledged that, but I could tell he didn't really want to talk to me. He had tears in his eyes, and I'm sure now that he would have preferred it if I hadn't found him walking out the door. But I felt I owed him, and still do.

Jim was pretty smart in some ways, but he could also be pretty gruff and painfully straightforward. He didn't really have an instinct for the business. Toward the end of his tenure, things had gone bad enough long enough that the people around him knew he was coming to the end of his rope, and it was a pretty miserable time for him.

I don't think that there was any singular thing that led to Jim being fired, but the Ric Flair affair was probably part of it. The conflict not only involved a contract dispute but saw the WCW Championship belt show up on a World Wrestling Federation broadcast, followed shortly thereafter by the Nature Boy himself.

I came in a week or two before Flair left WCW, so I can't really address any of that. Ric is an interesting guy. People either absolutely love him or absolutely don't. Those who were big Ric Flair fans within WCW certainly thought that his going to Vince was a big nail in Herd's coffin. But there were others who for their own reasons didn't mind the fact that Flair was gone.

Probably more important than the conflict with Flair were the things that were *not* happening, in terms of generating revenue and improving the brand and the ratings. When Jim left, there was a sense of renewal. People hoped Turner would bring someone in who could run WCW and turn it into a more profitable business.

That proved to be a false hope.

Kip Frye

Often, Turner Broadcasting would find an executive who, for one reason or another, wasn't working out in the division or department he was in. Inevitably he would be earmarked to be the next WCW president.

Kip Frye was one of those guys. He was a young attorney in the entertainment division, probably in his mid-thirties. I guess because he was an attorney and had some background in entertainment, they probably felt like he'd be the best executive for WCW. Who knows what anybody was thinking? That was one of the problems at WCW. Turner Broadcasting really had no idea how to run it.

Taking someone with no experience as an executive and no experience in wrestling and making them head of WCW wasn't the worst thing. On the contrary—many of the people who were involved in WCW were wrestling people with many years in the business. And that was worse.

Inheriting Problems

I'm talking about former wrestlers turned bookers, people who worked for the Crocketts in the NWA and stayed on after the sale to Turner. Most couldn't adjust to the changing times. They didn't understand what Vince McMahon was doing with wrestling and cable television.

They also all had their own political and personal agendas. More often than not, depending on their political faction, these groups of people would conspire with each other to work against what should have been the best interests of the company. Most had histories of one sort or another with each other, some good, most bad. It was a very, very political environment.

Turner had acquired a lot of the very same problems that had forced the Crockett family to sell in the first place. When you buy a company and bring everyone over that was associated with it, the odds are you're bringing over a lot of the cancer. That happened to WCW. A lot of the deadweight, a lot of people with limited abilities and vision but plenty of baggage, came along with the purchase.

That was why people like Jim Herd had such a hard time. Not only was he working against the forces of a competitive environment, but he was working against internal political bullshit that undermined him.

And the same thing happened to Kip Frye.

The Sharks Circle

I think Kip came in with his eyes wide open. He was enthusiastic. He embraced WCW and genuinely wanted to turn the company around. But after about two or three weeks, when the vultures and the sharks around him smelled weakness, they pounced.

I don't want to characterize all of these people as sharks, but I think anyone who had any sort of political stroke within Turner Broadcasting at the time had a self-serving interest, whether it was Jim Ross, Tony Schiavone, Dusty Rhodes, or the Sharon Sidellos of the world. Sharon Sidello was a vice president of Pay-Per-View and marketing, and she certainly had her own agenda.

Then again, all of the department heads at WCW had their own agendas, and were politically aligned in different camps. They spent a lot of effort aligning themselves so they could take over another part of the company, instead of doing the kind of things that would turn the company around.

Kip was naive about the wrestling business, and easily swayed on decisions. He didn't have a real clear-cut vision for how to turn the company around. So the sharks tried to manipulate him to fulfill their own self-serving agendas.

Initially, I think Kip made a good impact. He increased management's communication with the talent on creative decisions, for example. But within sixty or ninety days, he was overwhelmed by forces he didn't understand and shown the door.

No Stroke, No Poke

I was somewhat immune to maneuvering, because I had no stroke. I also had no aspirations to be anything more than what I was, which was a second- or third-string announcer.

It's kind of funny. When people don't think you're paying attention, they'll all talk to you, because they know they don't have anything to fear. I was constantly hearing one individual badmouth another, criticizing someone else's effort or ideas. Then that person would come back and criticize the other person. I was exposed to enough political maneuverings and inner-office drama that I knew I didn't want to get caught up in it.

I'm not sure anyone at Turner Broadcasting really intended Kip to be executive for any length of time. I think he was always seen as a transitional executive. But whatever, they put together a search for an individual they felt had the right credentials. And they ended up picking Bill Watts.

The Bill Watts Error

A New Sheriff in Town

Frye's replacement was "Cowboy" Bill Watts.

I'd heard a bunch of stories about Bill Watts, what a monster he was and how tough he was to deal with. As a young wrestler, Watts won a variety of NWA titles in the 1960s and '70s. He'd headed the

Universal Wrestling Federation during the 1980s before selling it to Jim Crockett.

I knew that Verne Gagne knew Bill Watts, so I called Verne and asked what Bill was like.

"Bill's a tough guy. He's got his own way of doing things, he runs a real tight ship. A lot of people don't like working with him, but he's a good guy. He knows the wrestling business."

Didn't sound *too* bad. Verne gave me one word of warning, though: "Be really careful, because he can be a hothead at times."

I thought, Okay. I'll just see how the cards play out. I was still loving my job, had gotten a raise, and was making six figures. I was also under contract, so I didn't worry about losing my job.

Emotions about Watts coming in varied from complete ambivalence to—I don't know if "fear" is the right word, but strong concern doesn't cover it. I think Jim Ross may have been the only one really enthusiastic about Bill Watts. Jim had a long-standing relationship with Watts, going back to early in his career when he was with Mid-South, which later became Universal Wrestling.

Jim was a big advocate of Bill Watts. I never talked to Jim about this, so I don't know if he thought, "Better the devil you know than the one you don't," or if Jim felt that his bread was going to be buttered on the right side. Maybe he knew that from the political point of view he was going to have a lot more stroke or leverage with Bill Watts in a position of power as opposed to a Kip Frye or someone else from the outside, who might not appreciate Jim's long history in the business.

The Ball-peen Hammer Approach

Watts had had some success in the past. For a brief time in the 1980s, his Universal Wrestling Federation had national exposure and was considered a hot franchise. (To simplify the history a bit, the UWF was basically Mid-South Wrestling, rebranded for national exposure. Watts created Mid-South in the 1970s from Tri-State Wrestling, which he'd bought from Leroy McGuirk.) Among Mid-

South/UWF's most famous wrestlers were the tag teams Rock 'n' Roll Express, Road Warriors, and Dirty White Boys. The older Guerrero brothers also wrestled for Mid-South.

But that was all in the past. Watts hadn't changed with the times. He wanted to come and use Turner's resources to reinvent the business that he used to know. And it didn't work.

Clearly.

I think Bill Watts at WCW—that whole era—was the darkest, most miserable time in the company's history. The impact he had was devastating.

Bill first tried cutting as many contracts as he possibly could. In and of itself, that may not have been completely bad. There were a lot of people under contract who shouldn't have been. But the way he went about it was a disaster.

Guaranteed Contracts

Traditionally, wrestlers were paid according to formulas based on how much they worked. No work, no pay. Additionally, the paychecks could go up or down depending on things like how many people came to their events, how much merchandise with their names on it sold, how well the promotion was doing in general, and enough other factors to keep accountants sharpening pencils for a year. WCW's contracts, however, were much simpler, guaranteeing wrestlers a specific amount for each year, provided they met the specified terms.

Life and contracts are more complicated than that, but you get the general idea. WCW's contracts were "guaranteed"; Vince's were not.

I often get "credit"—in a negative way—for inventing guaranteed contracts for wrestlers. Nothing could be further from the truth. I was hired with a guaranteed contract. Jim Herd was giving out guaranteed contracts a long time before I knew what WCW was.

Anyway, Bill Watts came in, and because guaranteed contracts were not a part of the old formula, not the way they used to run wrestling businesses, the first thing he wanted to do was cut as many of those salaries as he could.

He couldn't take a wrestler's contract away, since it was already signed, but he let them know that when they came up for renewal, it was going to be a whole different day. In effect, he told his talent he didn't think they were worth what they were getting, and that he planned on knocking them down a few pegs at his earliest opportunity.

I don't disagree with the idea of reducing compensation for some, but you can do it with a velvet hammer. You don't have to do it with a ball-peen. And Bill Watts did it with a ball-peen hammer. Watts was a bully in everything that he did. If Bill Watts said good morning to you, you felt like he was doing it to intimidate you.

This was a guy who wore a gun to work in the CNN Center. The guy tried so hard to convince everyone what a badass he was. Pretty friggin' weird. It's not like he needed to be armed in the CNN Center, for cryin' out loud.

Watts loved to bully the talent. He was loud and he was vulgar, even by wrestling standards. Whenever possible, whether he was demonstrating a move or talking about something, he'd get physical with the talent and take cheap shots. He'd abuse his power, constantly trying to prove he was tougher than the wrestlers. It was obvious to me that he was a very insecure person.

Back to the Future

Watts didn't really have a clear vision on how to be competitive. His approach was to take the product back to the way it was presented in the 1970s, not unlike what Verne Gagne had tried.

One of the big discussions we had was about lights and audiences.

"Why do we have all these big lights?" Watts wanted to know. "Why do we need to see the people in the audience? Back in my day, the only lights were on the ring, and you couldn't even see past ringside!"

WCW had trouble drawing people to the events we used to produce television shows. When the lights were turned up for the show, you saw a lot of empty seats and a very unenthusiastic audience. Rather than addressing the fact that we weren't drawing people, Watts decided to turn down the lights so the home viewer didn't see what was going on. Or in WCW's case, what wasn't going on.

The end result was a television product that looked small, dim, and dull. It also happened to look *a lot* like the product Bill was used to from the 1970s.

But that only exacerbated the problem. Now, besides people not wanting to come to our events, they saw a product on television that literally paled in comparison to Vince's.

No More Mats, No Big Moves

One of the other big initiatives, if you want to call it an initiative, was taking the mats away from the area outside the ring. Watts apparently believed that if the audience knew that if these guys went outside the ring, and landed on their heads, they really got hurt, then it would make them believe more in the product.

I couldn't think of anything more ridiculous. All it did was take away a lot of the talent's working area. They were confined to the ring because of safety issues. Again, that made the product feel less exciting, less dynamic, very stale, and very old.

Wrestlers also weren't allowed to do moves off the top rope. That was another retro-wrestling idea, limiting the performers' ability to thrill the audience with their athleticism.

If you go back to watch wrestling from the 1960s and '70s, you'll see that compared to today, it was very basic. Wrestling has evolved a great deal since then.

In fairness, it's no different from the NFL. If you sit down and watch game film from the 1960s, you see very basic running and pass plays, nothing like we have today. The athletes got bigger, faster, smarter. The coaches got smarter and developed more complex offensive and defensive strategies designed to use their players better. The game evolved.

Well, wrestling evolved, too. But Bill Watts's approach to that evolution was to stop it—or more accurately, reverse it—primarily because he didn't understand how to do it any other way.

Looking for a Way Out

Small Towns

Another disastrous back-to-the-future idea was the decision to add house shows in small markets. Because WCW was a dying brand, we couldn't draw in bigger venues. So we were forced to run in smaller markets, cities with five or ten thousand people, who typically wouldn't get live wrestling. We couldn't be successful in Atlanta, Charlotte, or New Orleans, but we could be friggin' rock stars in Rome, Georgia.

No knock on Rome, Georgia.

The truth is, we didn't do well in the small towns either. We lost money every time we went out the door. Adding the shows increased our red ink, and upped everyone's workload, especially the wrestlers'.

Understanding a Carnival Act

The company sank into in a downward spiral. Audiences shrank, and revenue plummeted. It was miserable.

I was pretty miserable, too.

I gave it a fair shot for a few months, but it became clear to me that I had nothing in common with Bill Watts or what he was turning the WCW into. I don't think he disliked me personally. He didn't know me, and we didn't interface. But he probably looked at me the way a lot of wrestlers looked at me and people like me who didn't "lace up the boots." They thought that unless you had been in the ring, you could never understand the business.

A lot of the staff at my level and below were sick of that "you don't know anything about the wrestling business unless you're a wrestler" mentality. You get tired of hearing that after a while if you're someone who works in production or you're a cameraman or an editor or an announcer. If your opinions have no value, you're demoralized after a while.

No Space Shuttles Here

The truth is, there's nothing magical about pro wrestling. The business isn't hard to understand at all. It's not like flying a space shuttle. It's pretty basic. You give the audience what they want, they give you their money. Entertain them with plenty of action, suspend their disbelief, surprise them, keep them guessing about what happens next, and you'll be a success. The real complexities involve changing your model to adjust to changes in viewing habits, industry shifts, and revenue opportunities.

A lot of the attitude toward nonwrestlers in the business has to do with professional wrestling's history. If you look at professional wrestling and how it evolved before television, it was very much a carnival act run by con men. Those con men kept the secrets that made the business successful. They didn't share them with the outside world. The people who were inside all knew how things worked, but they worked very hard to keep the outsiders from understanding. Magicians never reveal their tricks, and these guys basically thought of themselves as magicians.

The culture of secrecy continued into in the 1950s and '60s. That's why Verne Gagne went to such lengths to hide story angles from me when I was a salesman. He was old-school. It was a tradition.

Of course, a lot of people who have never been in the wrestling business understand it a lot better than people who have been in the business. But that wasn't Watts's philosophy.

A Sinking Ship

My personal workload became really high after Bill Watts took over. I went from working two days a week to five, and most of them ten to twelve hours on camera. That's a lot of time on camera.

I moved my family down to Atlanta to accommodate my schedule in 1992. I didn't mind that, or the work, but what I didn't enjoy was the feeling that the ship was sinking. Most people didn't know what to do about it. The rest tried to convince themselves they were going to be the captain of a submarine.

My personal dislike and disrespect for Bill Watts grew more, the longer I stayed. He was not a professional and didn't understand the level of business he was being asked to play at.

Another Chance

A Game Show Shot

About that time, I had become friendly with an actor named Jason Hervey. Jason was one of the stars of a hit series on ABC called *The Wonder Years*, which ran for six seasons, from 1988 to 1993. He played Wayne Arnold, the older brother.

Jason's family has been part of Hollywood for two generations. Jason's uncle is a business manager for some of the biggest names in the industry. His mother is a talent agent, and his brother is an entertainment attorney. Jason has probably learned more about the entertainment business at family reunions than most midlevel network executives will ever know. Besides acting, he's worked behind the scenes as a writer and producer.

Anyway, around the time I met Jason, I was working on an idea for a television game show that had a wrestling theme. I had originally developed it with a guy out of Miami who had a background in game shows. I thought I'd present it to the WCW people and see if we could get it produced.

I'd come up with the idea after looking at what we lacked at WCW. Our audience tended to be very old because of our style of wrestling and the traditional feel of the shows. Younger viewers, the more desirable audience from the advertisers' point of view, had left our product in droves and gone over to Vince. So what I did was reverse-engineer a wrestling-themed game show that I thought would appeal to kids. While it would air separately from the WCW shows, it would carry the WCW wrestling brand. That would hopefully bring the youth audience to our network so our advertisers could enjoy a younger audience.

Given the mentality of Bill Watts and his back-to-the-future approach to the business, this would have been like selling ice cubes to Eskimos. Watts clearly would not have understood what I was trying to accomplish. It would have been alien to everything that he believed in, so I didn't pitch it.

I didn't give up, though. I made up my mind that I'd pitch the show out in Los Angeles, independent of WCW. Since Jason had Hollywood relationships and knew the business, I asked him what he thought.

He looked at the storyboards and concept. He liked it.

"Do you know anybody out there?" I asked.

"Sure. We can go out there and pitch it together."

I went out to Los Angeles and pitched it in a couple of places. We got a lot of traction at Universal and Fox Kids Network. Molly Miles, an executive at Universal Studios at the time, knew Jason. She ended up giving us an option to develop it. Universal Television would have been the producer, and Fox Kids Network the buyer, if you will. So we said, "Wow, this is great."

I walked out of that meeting, and I made up my mind I was leaving WCW. I was going out to Hollywood.

I could feel the energy on the street. The environment was positive and creative, a hundred and eighty degrees from the dark, prehistoric feel of Bill Watts's WCW.

I went home and told my wife, "The good news is, I think we've sold the show—it's going to be great, it's going to work. The bad news is, I can't stand going to back to Bill Watts and WCW. I'm going to resign."

She was cool with that. We started to make arrangements to move.

Out with the Old

It was just about that time a rather tasteless racial remark Bill Watts made spread around the offices at CNN. I wasn't there, but the published reports have said that during an interview Watts gave to Mark Madden at the *Pro Wrestling Torch*, he made a number of comments that appeared to put down blacks or question their rights. One concerned Lester Maddux, a restaurant owner involved in a civil rights fight over whether he has to serve blacks or not. Watts supported Maddux. Years later in his book, *The Cowboy and the Cross*, Watts said that while he wasn't a racist, he felt that a restaurant owner should be able to deny service to anyone he wanted. He also claimed that his comments were misinterpreted, and that Madden sent them to Hank Aaron only because he wanted him fired.

That's Bill Watts's side of the story.

Turner Broadcasting was a great environment to work in because Ted Turner was an entrepreneur; Ted Turner was a visionary. He rewarded people who were like him in that respect. He appreciated people who had put it all on the line and made things happen. Consequently, most of the people who worked under him had that same kind of temperament.

But the one thing that Ted Turner didn't tolerate was discrimination. Turner Broadcasting was one of the most progressive companies in terms of breaking down barriers for minorities. So when Bill Watts's comments filtered over to the north side of the CNN Center, where all the real executives were, Bill's days were numbered. They got rid of him rather unceremoniously and without a lot of delay.

Bill Shaw

Watts had been hired and fired by Bill Shaw, a very well respected, highly regarded, long-term executive with Turner Broadcasting. Besides being president of WCW, Bill was corporate vice president of administration for Turner Broadcasting. Ted Turner had added WCW to Shaw's portfolio roughly a year before with the directions "Sell it, shut it down, or run it." He was determined to take another go at turning it around.

Bill came over and had a meeting with everybody in a conference center at CNN. He was very forceful, extremely professional, but very clear about where Ted Turner wanted WCW to be. Bill let everyone in the room know what he would tolerate and what he wouldn't.

"First and foremost, this is a television company," he told us. "Turner Broadcasting is a television company, it is not a wrestling company. And this company is going to be run like a television company, not a wrestling company."

When Bill said that, it made me realize that there might be a chance for WCW to turn around. If he meant what he said, there'd be no more old-time wrestling guys trying to re-create what they had back in Oklahoma in the 1970s.

His speech made me second-guess whether I wanted to leave WCW.

One of the things Bill said they were going to do was hire an executive producer. He wanted someone who understood wrestling and had a vision for the product, but was *not* a wrestling person. They specifically did not want somebody who came from that old wrestling mentality.

I went home, and I told my wife I was going to throw my name in the hat for the job. It would be a tremendous opportunity for my career. "And you know what? The fact that they're going to hire someone to come in and make it look more like a television show than wrestling in the sixties means maybe we have a chance. I'm going to stick it out for a while, whether I get the job or not."

Running the Show

From Disadvantage to Edge

A Leap Off the Top Rope

pplying for the executive producer's spot was a big leap. I thought there was a very slim chance that I'd get the job. I had only one real advantage—I wasn't a wrestling guy.

Looking back now, I realize that because of my experience in the AWA, I also had a pretty good understanding of the business in general. There weren't many aspects of the wrestling business that I hadn't touched in one way or another. I came in to the AWA with a sales and marketing background. I had developed corporate sponsorships with some large and sophisticated companies. I had a lot of insight into the advertising side of things and understood where the revenue came from. I understood demographics and how syndication worked. I'd promoted events, and understood what it took to promote a live event. Hell, I'd even built my own interview sets!

And I was a talent. I had all of the important bases covered, without having the disadvantage of being a "wrestling guy."

But I didn't have that perspective then. Frankly, I thought they would see me simply as a second- or third-string announcer. I didn't think in their minds I'd be qualified.

I called Bill Shaw's office, and I said, I understand that you're going to be looking for an executive producer. I'd like to be considered. I'd like to come in and meet you and tell you what I think it will take to turn WCW around.

After I hung up, I was convinced he wouldn't even bother to interview me. But about a week or two later he called and said, "Okay, Eric, come on up."

The first thing I did was tell Bill about the kids' game show. I explained that I wasn't trying to sell him the show, but wanted to explain that it was the type of thing the brand needed to shore up the demo.

Whether the idea was good or bad, I think he was impressed that I was coming at WCW's problems from a different angle of attack. I wasn't thinking like a wrestling guy. I was thinking like a television guy who understood wrestling.

I impressed him enough that I was soon under consideration. There were three or four people inside and outside the company they were looking at. David Crockett, who was part of the Crockett family, and Keith Mitchell, the head of production, were among the WCW contenders I knew about. There was at least one other person from the outside up for the job as well, though I was never told any of the names.

I had three or four meetings with Bill Shaw as the interview process continued into the summer. One day Bill called me to his office to talk again. To be honest, I didn't really think I was going to get the job. But I was so excited to have gotten this far in the interview process that I made up my mind that no matter what, I was sticking with WCW. I respected Bill and wanted to work for him in any capacity.

"Congratulations, Eric," he said when I walked in. "You're the new executive producer."

I almost swallowed my tongue.

My Job Was TV

As executive producer, I was in charge of everything we saw on television, with the exception of the wrestlers. Bob Dhue came in as executive vice president, overseeing the creative and business sides of the WCW. Accounting, live events—all of those departments reported up to him, as did the wrestlers.

Bob was a very likable guy, with a charming personality. He also had the attention span of a fruit fly. He was far more interested in golf than he ever really was in trying to turn WCW around. He would go anywhere that had the slightest connection with wrestling—as long as there was a good golf course nearby.

Bob brought in a friend of his by the name of Don Sandefur to run the live events side of the business. Don had a pretty extensive background; I think he may even have been involved with the Harlem Globetrotters and the circus at one point. But I think the real reason Don worked there was so that Bob had someone to play golf and drink martinis with.

Ole Anderson was handling the booking at the time. Ole, who was born in Minnesota, started wrestling in 1966; his career in the ring included a stint as one of the Four Horsemen. He retired from the ring in the late 1980s.

Ole, Bob, and Don did their things, I did mine. I tapered off my announcing so I could focus on my day-to-day job.

We started making some changes. I put the ring mats back around the ring. I turned the lights back up. We developed some new graphics packages. In general, I tried to dress up the product to make it look like it belonged in the 1990s.

Mister Unpopular

Even though I'd been with the company for a while, I was viewed as an outsider by the dirtsheets and other media that covered wrestling.

I didn't come from the old NWA territory, and I certainly hadn't been around long enough to "pay my dues." I didn't lace up the boots—I wasn't a wrestler. I was a young upstart. Plus, I was part of a regime that replaced people who, whatever the realities inside the company, had long histories in the business.

All of that helped make me instantly unpopular with the dirtsheets and the Internet community, which was still in its infancy at the time. No matter what I did, no matter how positive the outcome, the reaction was negative.

As far as the wrestlers themselves went, I had different relationships with different guys. To a lot of the old-time guys, I was an outsider, not a wrestler, and they resented that. But I had good relationships with some veterans. One of them, at least at first, was Ric Flair.

Ric came back to WCW in 1993 while I was executive producer. I went over to Techwood, the original Turner office building in Atlanta, with the other WCW department heads for a kumbaya moment where everyone welcomed Ric back. I wasn't part of the decision to bring Ric back; no one asked me for my opinion or input. But that was the beginning of my relationship with Ric— shaking his hand and congratulating him.

Firing People

One of the big misconceptions that's been created is that Eric Bischoff went around firing a lot of people as soon as he got a management job. Nothing is further from the truth. The truth is, I should have fired a lot of people, but I didn't.

If you go back and look at the people who claim they were fired by Eric Bischoff, there are some holes there.

Jim Ross is a good example. I had no more influence in the decision to let Jim go than the receptionist did. The truth is, the company didn't fire him—Jim decided he wanted out after the change in management.

Jim Ross between Lawrence Taylor (L) and Paul Heyman.

Jim Ross

A lot of the changes that followed Bill Watts's departure came about because of an internal audit by the international consulting firm Booz Allen Hamilton, which had been reviewing WCW before Watts's infamous racial remark. Besides all of the management and internal human resources problems—and there were *a lot*—the audit looked at the programs WCW was putting on.

Besides being WCW's lead announcer, Jim was also vice president of wrestling operations. This meant Jim oversaw the production department, the announcers, and live event booking. He worked closely with Watts on talent issues and television booking. In short, Jim was tied so closely to Watts that he got thrown out with the bathwater.

I want to make it clear: I didn't like working for Jim Ross at the time. Jim Ross was—I won't say a tyrant, but he was a miserable human being. A lot of that had to do with the fact that he reported to Bill Watts and had to take a lot of Watts's shit. Jim had to support Bill Watts's decisions, whether he agreed with them or not. He had to be his hatchet man. Jim took responsibility for a lot of what Bill Watts chose to do. It was a miserable position to be in.

One of things I respect about Jim Ross is that he's an incredibly hardworking, loyal person. If the guy above him says, "This is what I want to do," he goes and does it with one hundred percent effort. With respect to Bill Watts, that put Jim in a very difficult position.

A Kick in the Balls

Bill Shaw moved Jim out of wrestling operations and put him into sales and syndication. Jim took that as a real kick in the balls. He looked at it as a demotion. Jim didn't have to take a cut in pay, and there were no changes to his contract, but it must have been hard on his pride.

A few days later, I was appointed the new executive producer of WCW programming.

Jim took that as an even *bigger* kick in the balls. Here's Eric Bischoff, a guy who's barely been in the business long enough to have a cup of coffee, a guy who worked for him, probably three levels below him, now that I think about it, coming in and giving him orders.

Jim Ross, because he was so miserable, contacted Vince. It became obvious to Jim that McMahon would hire him. So Jim called Bill Shaw and asked if Bill would let him out of his contract.

At that point, I did get involved. Bill Shaw came to me and asked, Eric, what should we do? Should we just hold on to him and keep him away from Vince? Force him to work out his contract in sales?

I said—and not as any big favor to Jim, just as the right thing to do—*"Why keep a guy here when we've been surrounded by negativity and bad morale and political infighting? Why would we want to keep a guy here when he's miserable? Let him move on with his life."*

I told Bill Shaw to let him out of his contract so he could go work where he wanted. That's the real truth. I didn't fire him at all. I helped Jim get what he wanted.

Getting Himself Over

But Jim got himself over by claiming that I fired him, and that WCW was being run by a bunch of unqualified idiots. Jim would run around and say in his good-ol'-boy drawl, "I got fired because of that damn Eric Bischoff."

I don't know how Jim reconciled what had been going on under Bill Watts—a group of Cub Scouts would have done a better job running WCW than Watts had done. But criticizing me endeared him to a lot of people. People looked at me as this young kid who had come out of nowhere and was wielding *all* this power and abusing *all* these people who'd been in the business for so long and had contributed *soooo* much and had a legacy in the wrestling business yada yada yada. I was totally disrespecting them.

Right.

A lot of people got themselves over that way, and Jim Ross was one of the first.

Part of it was probably that he was hurting. And maybe he thought in his mind that I was pulling all the strings behind the scene, but I wasn't.

Tangled Mess of Political BS

Before Bill Shaw there were no lines of communication between WCW and Turner execs. Things got filtered through various parties.

Take Jeff Carr. Jeff was, I think, the vice president of programming at TBS at the time. He was a real wrestling fan—almost too much of a wrestling fan. He thought more like a wrestling fan than a programming executive sometimes.

This cut both ways. Jeff was a big supporter of WCW many times when executives in CNN's North Tower—where all the top brass worked—had questions or even suggestions about WCW. Rather than walk across the atrium and come talk to us, they would talk to Jeff Carr because, *Well, Jeff Carr's a wrestling fan and he works at TBS, therefore he's the best person to talk to.*

Unfortunately this was problematic. Jeff might have been a wrestling fan, but he wasn't running WCW and wasn't familiar with what we needed or were trying to accomplish.

Another link—or maybe *supposed* link—to Ted Turner was a guy by the name of Jim Barnett. Jim was a longtime promoter who'd been part owner of Georgia Championship Wrestling and had a long history in Chicago dating to the early days of televised wrestling. He'd also had some experience working for Vince. He was recognized at Turner as a guy who knew the wrestling business. Legend had it that Ted Turner relied on him quite a bit when he decided to buy WCW. It was a legend that Barnett propagated.

Rest his soul, but Jim was one of the most political people I've met in my life. He was a great old guy, and it was hard to dislike him, but he was a lot more of a politician than he was an expert on modern wrestling.

No one at WCW really knew how much Ted Turner talked to Jim, or even if he had relied on his advice when Ted decided to buy WCW. But I can assure you that Jim let everyone know that he had Ted Turner's ear. And Jim Barnett played that for all it was worth.

Jim was essentially a consultant who was there to voice his opinion on anything that anyone needed an opinion on. He had an official title—I think when I was there, he was in charge of international—but he was really there just to say what he thought of things.

Mind you, the franchises Barnett had been associated with had been sold or put out of business years before, left behind in the wake of Vince McMahon's wrestling revolution. But to the executives at Turner, Jim was an invaluable resource.

It was laughable, but you have to put yourself in Turner Broadcasting's shoes. The company didn't have anyone they could rely on who was a seasoned wrestling executive, someone with a corporate memory, if you will. Jim Barnett had a lot of wrestling experience, he knew the players, and he knew the culture. That's why he was there—so the Turner people could get their basic questions answered.

Straightening Things Out

As likable and well-intentioned as the Jeff Carr and Jim Barnetts of the world were, these informal and circuitous lines of communications hindered the organization. And there were plenty of other people who were neither as likable nor as well-intentioned toward WCW. Their agendas, at best, were personal, aimed at making themselves look good, no matter what the cost.

Bill Shaw, though, really engaged. He was one of the first executives from the North Tower who spent time in the WCW offices and made an attempt to learn firsthand what was going on. He developed his own opinions instead of depending on consultants and people who were supposed to be knowledgeable.

Bill attended meetings, spent time on the sales calls, went to arena shows, attended television tapings—he really got in and tried to understand the business. Once that happened, it minimized a lot of the communications problems. People in the North Tower stopped making decisions that affected us based on things that had filtered through the tortuous lines of communication.

It soon became evident that anyone who needed to get to Ted would do so through Bill Shaw and no one else. This had a significant impact on the politics within WCW. All of a sudden, people at midlevel management no longer jockeyed for position. The politics and all the BS that went with it ended.

Righting the Ship

Hemorrhaging Money

In 1993, WCW was a $24 million company that was losing $10 million a year. There was a tremendous amount of pressure on all of us to turn that around.

The one thing we didn't contemplate was laying anyone off. The cumulative effect of the Watts era had taken its toll, and Turner wasn't anxious to go on a whole-scale firing spree. They wanted to figure out how to shore up the business instead of hacking and slashing staff.

We discussed what to do from all different perspectives. Although I wasn't in charge of the other departments, I was happy to speak my mind.

Coming from Minnesota and being an outsider, I wasn't really familiar with the history of WCW and the NWA. I didn't know much about the old promotions' legacies, which everyone else thought were so important. In my mind, if they *really* were important, the company wouldn't have had financial problems to begin with. Maybe in retrospect I should not have disregarded the history and traditions of the NWA/WCW quite as much as I did.

What I was most concerned with was giving our company a national rather than regional feel. We were competing for national ad-

vertisers, the M&M Mars Candies of the world, the toy manufactur-
ers and big retailers. Focusing on regional personalities and histories
didn't ring my bell. I didn't think that would help convince advertisers and audiences that WCW was a legitimate alternative to
World Wrestling Federation.

Heresy

Bob Dhue and I started butting heads early. Some of the things Bob
wanted to do made absolutely no sense. For example, his solution to
increase revenues in the live events side of the business was to produce more shows. So instead of doing, say, one hundred and fifty
shows a year, he wanted to do two hundred and fifty.

Well, the problem with that is, it doesn't scale properly. If you're
losing money every time you go out the door, why would you want
to step out the door another hundred times? Until the perception
of the product changed, increasing the live event schedule would
only increase our losses.

My position was, let's just cut live events all together. Let's go
out the door twenty-four times a year or whatever we need to make
television and Pay-Per-Views, and that's it. While we wouldn't be
making any money from live events, we'd be losing less. A *lot* less.

That was completely contrary to everything everyone "knew"
about the wrestling business. It was as about heretical as you could
get. Back in the old days of the territories, the associations kept the
guys on the road every week. That's how wrestling was supposed to
work. The focus was on live events.

I said, *Screw that and let's just produce television. Dump all of our
resources into TV, acquiring new talent, and dressing up our product.*
Then eventually, whether it was six months from now or a year
from now or five years from now, people would start parting with
their cash and come out to see us live.

People dropped over dead.

As much as no one wanted any more political infighting or power struggles, they started surfacing again. Meanwhile, the financial pressure increased. I kept speaking up and speaking up and becoming more adversarial. It gradually became me on one side and just about everyone else—especially Bob Dhue, Don Sandefur, Ole Anderson, and Sharon Sidello (who was rumored to be having a "secret" relationship with Ole at the time)—on the other.

Burned to the Ground

In the meantime, the product burned down to the ground. People didn't like what we were doing. On the live events side, we went from not being able to draw in big markets to not being able to draw in small ones. When we had to go out and produce our television tapings, we'd end up with an audience of 250 people. Bob Dhue and Don Sandefur would give away free tickets and paper half of the arena—sometimes even more. We'd have a Pay-Per-View in a ten-thousand-seat arena, and seven thousand people would be inside free.

It drove me crazy.

"When is this trend going to stop? As long as you're going to keep giving it away, why do you think they're ever going to pay for it?" I'd ask. People would stare at me, and I'd continue trying to explain.

"Bob, say you go to a bar and you sit down next to a pretty girl. You buy her a drink, and the next thing you know you're up in a hotel room with her. You come back the next night, and the same thing happens. And the next. And the next.

"Then on the fifth night she says, 'It'll cost you a hundred bucks to go up to my room.'

"What are you going to do? You've already been there for free. You're not paying for it."

I had to paint a picture that they could relate to. We'd been giving tickets away for so long people thought we had no value.

This wasn't just a problem for our live events business. We shot our syndicated programming on the road in arenas. We'd go out to produce a television show, and we'd have a miserable looking crowd, half of them winos with a bottle of cheap wine in paper bags on their laps, or no crowd at all. It affected the performance of the wrestlers because they were performing in front of people who were dead. And forget about what a shot of the audience told the viewers at home.

Even the best shows looked tired. They looked regional. They looked dull. That was what the world thought of WCW.

Finally I came up with an idea that pissed everyone off even more.

M-i-c-k-e-y

Wrestling with Disney

In late 1993, I took a trip down to Orlando, Florida, to check out the Disney-MGM Studios. I thought that, if it were possible to shoot our syndicated show on a soundstage at Disney World, we could turn perceptions around.

It was a much smaller venue than those we'd been using, but we had the ability with camera technique to make it look a lot bigger than it really was. It had better production and lighting facilities, so the shows would be colorful and bright. We could shoot three or four shows a day every day for six or seven days, saving a lot of money. *And* we'd have train cars full of fresh audiences who had all their teeth.

The people visiting Disney for the most part weren't wrestling fans, but we didn't have many of those anyway. All we had were winos and brown paper bags.

From a purely television point of view, an advertiser's point of view, and a syndication point of view, shooting at Disney would give us a product that looked a whole lot better than what we had been producing. It wasn't ideal by any stretch of the imagination, but it would be a vast, vast improvement.

More importantly, I knew that if our show could open up with an announcer saying, "Coming to you from the Disney-MGM Studios in Orlando, Florida," and combine that with a wide cover shot of the Disney towers, the perception of WCW as a tired, regional promotion

Our "set" at MGM-Disney.

would immediately change. As incongruous as this may seem today when you think about it in relation to a wrestling company, the fact that we co-branded with a powerhouse like Disney would help us in a big way with advertisers as well as audiences. It would make us look like a national operation. We could finally be seen as competition.

But shooting a wrestling show at Disney-MGM Studios?

Where Mickey Mouse is? And Pluto? And Donald Duck?

Are you crazy?

I went from being a heretic to being the Antichrist.

Just Do It

There were certainly negatives to the idea. A sound stage was a sound stage and didn't have an arena feel. This sound stage could hold only about eight hundred people. And the audience would be primarily vacationers who came for Disney, not us. For the most part, they wouldn't be following our storylines or get into our characters. But overall, the pluses far outweighed the negatives.

Bob Dhue, Don Sandefur, Ole Anderson, Sharon Sidello, and Gary Juster (he headed arena relations) all thought I should be hung by the neck until dead. And frankly, it wasn't just the Bob Dhues of the world who thought I'd lost my mind. Dusty Rhodes, who I get along with just about as well as anyone, was reluctant at first. Most wrestlers couldn't imagine producing the show in a sound stage. It was a real battle.

There were weeks and weeks of meetings and debate back and forth. Everybody had a point of view, and none of them agreed with mine. Finally, Bill Shaw got involved.

Bill thought it was out of the box, a little progressive—not necessarily in a good way—but he finally said, "Quit your bitchin' and bellyaching, we're going to go do this."

Wrestlers? In Disney World?

As wacky as the debate got inside the offices of WCW, it was nothing compared to the reaction of the seven or ten Disney executives when I met with them to discuss the idea.

My first meeting was with Bob Allen, the vice president of Disney-MGM Studios, who oversaw all of the production inside the sound stages there. I sat down and explained what we did, telling Bob that I'd like to produce all of our syndicated shows inside one of his sound stages.

Keep in mind, part of Disney-MGM's business was trying to attract outside television production. They wanted to keep those sound stages full. Tourists would go in and see actual television shows being produced, which made the studios a draw for the park. And, of course, the companies using the studios were charged a good sum for the facilities.

Bob loved the idea of wrestling at Disney. But he knew that he had to sell it up to his superiors, because it would be—

Controversial?

The word doesn't quite cover it. *Radical,* maybe. *Insane* was probably closer. "Professional wrestling" and "Mickey Mouse" had never been uttered in the same sentence before.

Two or three weeks later, myself and another WCW executive, David Crockett, went down for a follow-up meeting with some of the more senior Disney people. We were surrounded by a dozen very corporate, very Disneyesque execs. I could tell by looking at them that most of these guys had no desire to see 300-pound guys running around in wrestling tights in Disney World.

After all the introductions, I began the presentation. The more I talked, the more uncomfortable the Disney people got. When the meeting started, they were all looking at me, making eye contact, shoulders squared with me, receptive or at least not openly hostile.

Halfway through the meeting, most of the people in the room

were turned ninety degrees from me. It was small room, so they couldn't *quite* turn their backs on me, but they would've if they could've.

These executives had a very strict view of the Disney brand and what worked and didn't work. For me to convince them that professional wrestling worked—I felt like I was selling ice cubes to Eskimos.

To be fair, they did have some cause for concern. Wrestling, and WCW in particular, had been positioned as very violent and got a little bloody at times. That wasn't the Disney way. I had to convince them that things wouldn't be nearly as violent as they had seen on the TBS cable side of things. The syndicated show had always been more family friendly: we'd make sure it was even more so.

The meeting didn't go well, but Bob Allen was still pretty enthusiastic. He must have gone to work on his bosses, because after a third meeting we managed to convince them to give it a try.

Don't Feed the Wrestlers

But the Disney people did give us rules.

First, I had to promise that the wrestlers would be bused in. We were coming down there with sixty or eighty wrestlers at a time. They didn't want wrestlers parking in the lot and walking over to the sound stages.

It wasn't just a logistical issue. Basically, they didn't want us to be seen.

They asked if it would be possible not just to bus our guys in, but to cover the windows so people couldn't see them. I wasn't doing that. But we did agree to bus everybody in, because that part made sense. Everyone coming in their own cars would be too chaotic.

"Also," they said, "we don't want the wrestlers walking around the park. When they're here, they have to stay in the sound stage. We don't want the guests to see a bunch of scary-looking wrestlers walking around."

Okay.

I didn't tell the talent. I had enough people fighting the idea without telling everyone that we had to hide when we went there.

The Survey Says

I knew what we were up against with Disney. So I asked Turner's research department to come up with some "research" to overcome their negativity. We distributed questionnaires to everyone who came to the first shows and asked them questions designed to tell the Disney people that the WCW experience was a good one.

Ninety percent of the questionnaires came back positive. We asked questions we knew would allay the execs' fears: Did your children enjoy the show? Do you feel comfortable bringing your kids back to another WCW event? Do you have anything negative to say about the show?

People said things like, "It was the most fun we had at the park," "Great time," and so on. I gathered up all this research for my next meeting with the Disney executives. We walked through some of the logistical issues we'd had, catering, simple stuff. Then I said, "Oh, by the way, here's what your guests said about the experience."

When I came back to negotiate the second set of tapings, the Disney executives who had objected to having WCW earlier had changed their tune. Now they were excited about having us. They still wanted me to bus the wrestlers in, but they let us film in other parts of the park. Jesse "the Body" Ventura could interview people in Epcot and at other areas. They let us out of the box.

Well, they didn't let us into Magic Kingdom, where the rides were. Maybe they were afraid we'd break something expensive.

But otherwise we had the run of the place.

Telling Stories

Changing the Product

Disney had an immediate positive impact on the product, and on WCW. There was more buzz, better shows, and more interest from the national advertisers. The hard-core wrestling fans hated it, but there weren't enough of them to support the brand, and I wasn't going to cater to them.

We'd gone from filthy arenas with a few hundred people who, if they were sober enough to realize where they were, didn't care, to being in front of families with children who were excited to be in front of a WCW ring and seen on television. All of that translated to the viewer—not the hard-core wrestling fan, mind you, but the passive or peripheral viewer and the advertisers. They were my target.

Taping at the television studio changed the product in more subtle ways. Since we now produced ten to twelve weeks of shows at a time, our writers had to think long-term when they came up with their angles. None of them were used to doing that.

Most of the writers on the creative side of the business were born out of the monthly or in some cases weekly territories, where they only had to think two or three weeks in advance. There was very, very little long-term planning at the time.

That was something I knew had to change. According to people who claimed to have worked somewhat closely with Vince, they planned six months in advance, sometimes as far out as a year. Vince would always have a pretty good idea of where storylines were going. He'd know what he wanted to do at, say next year's *Wrestle-Mania*, and would work backward from that.

I thought that was absolutely necessary for our success. Having never been a wrestling booker or having worked on the creative side of the business, I was kind of amazed at how little planning went into it. To me, whether you're writing a sitcom or a dramatic series, there has to be an arc. It's fundamental to any storytelling. There has to be a plan.

Storylines

How do you tell a story in the ring, thirteen weeks in advance, without giving away so much information that people can figure out what's going to happen and ruin the surprise? Word of what happened at the Disney shows inevitably leaked, and was then spread by the dirtsheets, the Internet, or the 900 wrestling gossip lines that were so prevalent at the time. We wanted to preserve as much suspense as possible.

That was a difficult challenge. We experimented with different approaches. We'd even send someone out carrying a championship belt to do an interview, though we knew that guy was never going to have that belt or even be in the title picture.

Eventually, what we figured out was that we could film just the wrestling match without the storyline. Then we could cut the storyline in later on, adding interviews and color commentary from the studio. We'd also use the Saturday-night show, which was a weekly show, to advance the stories.

It was all very similar to the way edit market promos were cut, with interviews and commentators actually supplying the storyline. We were able to tell a story in commentary without revealing it to the people in the arena.

We were modifying, learning, experimenting as we went. We made a lot of mistakes, but eventually we got there. It was far from an ideal solution, but it beat the hell out of what we had been doing.

Success

We had to deal with some problems with the taping, but overall it went much better than most people thought it would. Those who said the idea would never work were grudgingly forced to admit, "Wow, it *was* a great idea."

Bill Shaw sent me a letter saying he was impressed and proud of me for standing up for what I believed in and sticking with it. Getting that kind of pat on the back from Bill meant a lot to me. I respected Bill a lot and wanted to deliver for him.

One thing I noticed: some of the people who'd fought the Disney strategy as hard as they could claimed afterward that they'd known all along it was a good idea. They said they voiced a negative opinion to get everyone else on board, as if they'd been playing devil's advocate.

That was bull, of course.

I would have had a lot more respect for them if they'd just said, "I'm glad it worked." They were so two-faced and transparent that it was ridiculous.

Running Things

Vice President

Bob Dhue was the kind of guy who tended to support whoever talked to him last. So when there were issues under debate, he exacerbated the political problems by the way he managed. He was such a nice guy that anybody felt like they could talk to him. And they would, pushing their point of view constantly, whether they understood an issue or not. A lot of times the decisions made had to do with whoever talked to Bob Dhue last.

The more I saw of that, the more frustrated I became. I pretty much call things the way I see them, and I'm not very subtle. I started calling Bob on a lot of things. Our relationship became steadily more adversarial.

Even though I was not a direct report to Bob—I answered to Bill Shaw—he still had a lot more capital within the company. In deference to his position on the food chain, I had to bite my tongue to a certain degree in management meetings. But when a conflict came up and we'd go before Bill Shaw alone, I'd be very candid. The more I pointed out what was going on, the more strained my relationship with Bob became.

The biggest example was with our live event operation, which was still a money-losing dog. But the creative side of the business was another mess.

Old-School Storytelling

Ole Anderson was the booker at the time. Ole, being first and foremost an old-school wrestler, was great at reading a crowd. In Bob Dhue's case, he read Bob like a picture book. He manipulated him, and had no problems getting what he wanted.

Ole's heyday had been back in the 1970s and '80s. He was a regional tough guy very much like Watts. He liked hard-core, old-school wrestling. I, on the other hand, wanted to take us into the 1990s. Wrestling with Mickey Mouse put Ole and me on opposite ends of the philosophical spectrum.

Truth is, I liked Ole. He was funny. He had integrity, and he spoke his mind. I might not like what Ole had to say, but I didn't have to spend much time reading between the lines, trying to figure it out. I respected that. But we were constantly bumping heads.

It was inevitable. As booker, Ole was in charge of the talent and the creative side of things, while I was in charge of everything that was happening on TV. There's only so much you can do to change the product if all you can do is move the lights and cameras around and change graphics. We would constantly disagree about how storylines should play out.

Those disagreements went before Bob Dhue. And inevitably Ole would win them, because he (and Sharon Sidello) spent a lot more time politicking with Bob. I wasn't going to "work" or manipulate anyone to achieve my goals.

Push Comes to Shove

It's been said that I wanted to push Bob Dhue out of the way so I could run WCW myself. But my goal was never to get Bob Dhue or take over. My goal was to make WCW better.

Increasingly I'd press the issues, and force our arguments to a head. We'd end up discussing them in front of Bill Shaw.

More and more, Bill sided with me. Ultimately those types of situations put so much strain on the company management—and Bob—that Bill decided in early 1994 that one of us had to go.

He kept me.

I took over as vice president of WCW. Bob Dhue was reassigned, and ended up leaving the company. Don Sandefur had his office packed as soon as he heard.

The truth is, I don't even remember the moment. It wasn't a seminal revelation, the heavens didn't open up—it just kind of occurred. I can't even put a date on it now.

I'd never envisioned a time when I would run the entire company. Whether I was executive producer or vice president or the dishwasher, I really didn't give a damn. What was important to me was that we got the job done and reached a goal. Titles didn't motivate me. Nor, for that matter, did power.

I *did* enjoy power for its ability to allow me to effect change without a lot of resistance. But power for the sake of power was never that attractive to me.

By the time I took over, I had spent a lot of time in WCW executive committee meetings. I was familiar with all of the department heads and the function of their departments. I felt like I understood their businesses well enough to oversee them.

That didn't mean I understood them better than the people who worked in them. I knew enough that I could speak the language—and more importantly, I could see through the bullshit.

The Creative Process

I didn't have a good feel for the creative side of the wrestling business, but I did know enough to know what was wrong—the old-school approach to booking. We had to focus more on entertainment and less on hard-core "wrasslin'." The show needed to be more of a spectacle.

I wanted to be involved in creative, but I never aspired to be "the guy." I never wanted to be the head writer. I was quite content to find the right person, the guy who could manage the process and be successful. I wanted to focus on the other parts of the business.

Quite frankly, I was intimidated by the creative process. Wrestling is a much more complicated storytelling form than people give it credit for. I knew back then that I didn't have a handle on it.

I knew what I liked and didn't like, just as I could look at cars and decide that I really liked Ferraris and not Lamborghinis. But I couldn't tell you how they were made. That's how I felt about the creative process. I knew what I liked, and I knew what I didn't like, but I wasn't able to tell anyone how to get me what I liked.

I needed people to listen to my vision, and then tell me how to get there.

Ole Anderson

I tried working with Ole Anderson first.

I got frustrated with him because he was stubborn and ornery and hardheaded. As much as I liked him, I just got to the point where I couldn't work with him anymore. So I sent him off to head the Power Plant, which was our training facility. I wasn't exiling him. Ole was a great teacher and well suited to the job. But he didn't see it that way.

Ole had saved his money and was really smart with it; he never really needed the paycheck when he was at WCW. But he wasn't anywhere near ready to retire, and he wanted to be involved in the business. And what he really liked to do, even as booker, was get down in the ring and roll around with the wrestlers, teaching them the craft.

When I listened to Ole talk about strategic activities and where the business should go, it was obvious he didn't understand wrestling's new direction. His ideas were dated and unsophisticated. He had zero understanding of the business side of wrestling. He understood the world the way he used to know it.

But when he would talk about the mechanics of a match, what you should do or shouldn't do in the ring, Ole glowed. Passion filled his voice. Ole's "feel" and understanding of the basics of the physical side of storytelling were very valuable. We desperately needed talent with good basic skills, wrestlers who understood psychology as well as the athletic side of our business. Ole could teach them all of that.

I think he did well at the Power Plant. But unfortunately, Ole had a hard time letting go. I'm sure he saw the move as a demotion and blamed it all on me. The resentment festered.

Ole's Undoing

One day, Ole was down at the Power Plant mouthing off about what a son of a bitch I was. We had a guy working for us by the name of Blackjack Mulligan. Blackjack was Barry Windham's father and a friend of Dusty Rhodes. He'd been around the industry for a long time. I gave him a job as an agent during a stretch when he desperately needed a job. Honestly, I gave him the position not as a favor, but because most of the wrestlers really respected him, which is one of the most important qualities you need in an agent. Blackjack had everybody's respect for all the right reasons. But at the time I hired him, he also really needed a job. He was grateful—and, unfortunately for Ole, loyal. God forbid anyone said anything bad about Eric Bischoff.

Life at the Power Plant.

Ole made the mistake one day of badmouthing me while Black-jack was around.

Now, if I'd have heard the things he said, they wouldn't have bothered me. I let that crap roll off my back. But Blackjack over-heard him, and knocked him out with one punch.

Ole was a tough guy. He had a head like a cinder block. But Blackjack could punch a hole through a refrigerator, and he just reached back and knocked Ole out cold.

That was pretty much the end of the road for Ole. The humilia-tion of being demoted from booker, and then being knocked out in front of everybody in the wrestling school—Ole had had enough embarrassment for a decade, and he moved out.

Dusty Rhodes

Dusty Rhodes followed Ole as booker. It was a much better situation, but we still couldn't get the right feel to our stories.

Dusty could be pretty progressive. But like most other wrestlers, he thought just one week or maybe one month at a time. Bookers generally weren't used to building story arcs and understanding character development ahead of time. This had become important because we were now shooting thirteen weeks of shows at a time; if you didn't think ahead, you were sunk.

So, I wondered, how do we fix this?

Okay, I thought, bring in people who have more of a traditional writing background, who understand episodic television, structure, story arcs—everything that works in TV.

I brought in two Hollywood writers I met down in Disney-MGM Studios and forced Dusty to work with them. I didn't want them to drive the storytelling. I wanted them to take Dusty's vision and help formulate a structure, or a "bible," that would give us a plan to work from. Dusty would say, *Okay, this is where these guys are going to end up, and here's the personal issue between them.* The writers would go back and add detail, put in dialogue, and create a long-term structure.

Dusty is one of the most imaginative, creative people I've ever met. But he was used to going from week to week. He had a tremendous understanding of all the little nuances of wrestling storylines; I just couldn't get him to wrap his head around what I really wanted and buy into it.

To Dusty's credit, he really tried hard, but it was so alien to his nature that it was ultimately a failed attempt. Dusty, like the business in general, wasn't quite ready for more sophisticated storytelling.

Nature Boy as Booker

Anybody who's ever met Ric Flair will tell you that he can be the most charming person you've ever met. Ric Flair can also be extremely persuasive. It's not that he's trying to deliberately manipulate or deceive you. Ric truly believes the things he says.

After Dusty didn't work out, I was convinced Ric Flair would be a good booker. He took the job. I have to say, though, it wasn't without some reluctance on his part. Ric knew that, as a booker, you're a target. Booking wrestling is the most thankless, no-win position anyone could ever be in. When things go well, it's because the talent makes it work. When they go badly, it's because the booker doesn't know what he's doing.

Ric Flair knew he was going to be in that position, but he took the job anyway. I forget now, but it's very likely he didn't even get any extra money for doing it.

The one negative thing about Ric is that he doesn't handle pressure very well. He's the type of person who wants everybody to love him. He doesn't like to be in a situation where there's dissension, or where he feels like he's being personally attacked or questioned. Ric's the life of everybody's party. He doesn't like being in a position of authority or responsibility—which pretty much comes with the territory when you're the booker.

I know this now, but I didn't realize it then. I knew only the positives. Ric supported where I wanted to go with the company. He had a huge amount of experience in wrestling, and of course he was well respected by people inside and outside the company. While some of my ideas were pretty far outside the box of wrestling tradition, Ric was a good counterweight. I think that's why I stuck with him for as long as I did.

That, and he's such a charming son of a bitch.

For the first few months, it seemed to me that it was working rather nicely. I was moving so quickly and in so many different directions, I probably didn't look at the situation as closely as I should have.

Aiming for Profitability

Four Wheels of Revenue

The wrestling business, in theory, has four streams of revenue—like the four wheels on a car, if you will. When the business is operating efficiently and well, 25 percent of your revenue comes from arena ticket sales or live events. Twenty-five percent is going to come from ad sales on television. Twenty-five percent should come from Pay-Per-View. And 25 percent from licensing and merchandising.

That's when you're hitting on all eight cylinders and driving down the highway at the speed limit.

In WCW's case, since we weren't a successful brand, we couldn't get out of first gear. We didn't even have four wheels on the car.

WCW hadn't developed a licensing platform. For people to want your license—the company logo and images, wrestlers' faces, etc.—you need a high-profile entertainment property. We had no profile, so we had no licensing or merchandising to speak of, and 25 percent of the revenue we needed was nonexistent.

Another of our four wheels, live events, was so badly off I can't think of a suitable metaphor. We not only had no arena revenue, we were bleeding money every time we went out the door.

New Goals

Once I took over as vice president, my first goal was to shore up Pay-Per-View and ad sales, and then work on live events and merchandising.

The truth is, I was learning on the job. I knew a little bit about advertising, but I had to learn a lot more. I had to learn about merchandising and licensing. In short, I learned how to run a wrestling business on the job.

I asked a lot of questions. I sat in on a lot of meetings. I read everything I could read. I talked to anyone who would talk to me, inside Turner and outside Turner. I sought out experienced people in advertising and marketing and television, and I learned as much as I could from them. Then I applied what I had learned, or thought I'd learned, to our particular situation at WCW.

Looking back, I was putting in something like seventy hours a week. I didn't really notice the hours then, though. Frankly, I worked hard because I didn't know what else to do other than work. I didn't have many hobbies, didn't socialize much, and was obsessed with turning WCW around.

The one surprising thing about the job was its intensity. Something was always happening. It wasn't unusual to get home at ten or eleven o'clock at night and have to deal with a contract or, a little later on, a scissor fight in a hotel room between Sid Vicious and Arn Anderson. It never stopped.

It was one of the most difficult but rewarding periods of my professional life. Even now I look back on it and wish I had stopped long enough to realize just how wonderful an experience it was.

A No-Lose Position

Quite honestly, I was in a no-lose position. Everyone who had tried to come and save WCW had failed miserably. I couldn't possibly fail any worse than Bill Watts did. I had nowhere to go but up.

People within Turner Broadcasting were convinced that no one could turn that company around. A lot of executives were politicking to pull the plug on WCW.

Scott Sassa, the president of Turner Entertainment, hated wrestling. It wasn't Hollywood, it wasn't glitzy. In his opinion, it didn't have any place in the Turner portfolio. With his stroke—he was generally considered the heir apparent to Ted Turner—combined with the amount of cash that WCW was bleeding, there was a lot of weight against WCW on the Turner Broadcasting executive committee.

Fortunately, Ted Turner loved wrestling. He believed in it. I'm not so sure he loved it as a fan, but he appreciated it and understood it in terms of its ability to draw an audience to the network. That was enough love for me.

Counting Pencils

Contrary to the bs about WCW having money to burn, my mandate was to save money. One of the first things I did was make people count the number of pencils they had in their drawers.

Literally, I told everyone to do a complete inventory as we looked for ways to cut back. I was trying to make a point. There was no expense too insignificant for us to consider. I remember saying at meetings that we would do whatever it took to turn a profit, even if it meant standing at the street corner and selling those pencils.

We cut a lot of costs. A lot of that was uncomfortable, but it was necessary.

One area we paid a lot of attention to was our travel budget. Triple H still tells a story about the time when he wanted to try out for WCW. He says that when he told me he lived in Massachusetts, my response was, "Sorry, you are a GUD—Geographically UnDesirable." According to him, I refused to allow him to try out because it would have cost too much to fly him around.

I'm not positive it's true—some of Triple H's stories should be taken with a grain of salt—but it does sound possible. One of the things I did to cut costs when I first took over was look at the talent expenses. Unless a talent was at least mid-card, they had to either move to Atlanta where we were working, or we would cut them.

In the end, Triple H flew himself in for the tryout and ended up doing so well he got the job, GUD or not. (Later, he went over to Vince's company, where he's a major star today.)

Legitimate expenses were one thing. We also had a lot of illegitimate ones draining the budget. Having been on the talent side, I knew firsthand some that could be fixed.

The Turner Gravy Train

When I came to WCW in 1991, Larry Zbyszko came up to me, the first day I walked in, pulled me aside, and said, "Kid, this is the greatest gravy train you'll ever be on. Once your name goes on the payroll list, it never comes off."

That was the perception that everyone had. And they weren't far wrong.

But things were worse than that. WCW was so unorganized, and so big, that if you were a dishonest person or a con artist, it wasn't hard to figure out ways to take advantage of the company. Before I got into management, a wrestling personality—he'll remain nameless for reasons that will soon be obvious—showed me a stack full of unused airline tickets: "Buddy, this is as good as cash."

He was right. And nothing was stopping him from using the travel system as his own personal ATM.

See, Turner Broadcasting had a travel department that managed travel arrangements for everyone in Turner—WCW, CNN, the Braves. If you were a talent and needed to go somewhere, you called up the travel department and said, "I need a ticket for such and such a date and place." They made the travel arrangements and sent you a ticket (this was in the days before e-tickets, when everything was done on paper).

But say you then changed your plans, so you were traveling on a different day or to a different place. You then got *another* ticket, without the first one being canceled or collected.

That first ticket could then be redeemed, either for personal use or money. I can only imagine the hundreds of thousands of dollars that Turner was conned out of. It was stealing, plain and simple.

If I'd come in as an executive, I doubt too many people would have come up to me and clued me in on all the ways to cheat the company out of money. But because I'd been a talent, I knew a lot of the problems. So I started putting an end to all of those things, instituting a new travel policy and the like.

We started saving money. In the meantime, morale began to improve. People felt better about working for WCW. Our momentum was starting to build, not just within WCW but in Turner Broadcasting as a whole. They no longer looked at us as a redheaded laughingstock of a stepchild.

The jury was out. We didn't belong yet—far from it—but there was the faintest glimmer of a possibility that we might.

Hulk Hogan

The Next Big Step

Midnight Phone Call

I was in bed when the phone rang. It was late, maybe midnight, but I reached over and picked it up.

"Hello, brother. I understand you'd like to talk to me."

The fatigue I'd felt just a moment before vanished. Hulk Hogan had a very distinctive voice, and I sure did want to talk to him.

An All-Time Great

I doubt anyone reading this book needs to be reminded who Hulk Hogan is, or how big a star he was when I picked up the phone in early 1994.

He'd been wrestling since 1978. While he'd once held the NWA Southeastern title, he'd been a World Wrestling Federation Champion since defeating the Iron Sheik in January 1984. His red-and-yellow wrestling gear and his signature "Don't forget to take your vitamins" line for kids were as well known as any celebrity's trademarks. He was one of pro wrestling's biggest draws ever.

But after a fallout with Vince McMahon and the lure of a career as a movie and television star, Hogan left the company and wrestling in 1993. No one was sure for how long. He'd told people that he was done with wrestling. He was not part of the company's plans at that time, and he wasn't under contract to them.

Coincidentally, the Disney tapings brought us into contact with Hulk Hogan. He was taping a television show at the Disney-MGM Studios called *Thunder in Paradise.*

I don't know how I got his phone number, and I don't recall whether I put a call in to him or someone else passed his or my number along. Legend has it that Ric Flair made the first contact, and I'd be inclined to believe it. Anyway, as soon I picked up the phone that night, I knew who it was. I explained to him that we were shooting our shows down at Disney-MGM and invited him to come on over. And I added that I would love to have him come over to WCW.

He didn't jump at the hint, but he didn't hang up on me either.

The Turner Draw

The fact that WCW was changing the way it produced wrestling and taking big chances may have made Hogan think that WCW was an interesting opportunity. But I think part of what made us attractive to Hulk had to do with Ted Turner. Ted was in the television and movie business, and that was interesting to Hogan at the time.

Sure that Hogan would come to WCW if the circumstances were right, I went to Bill Shaw to get his approval. I wasn't authorized to make a decision that big, because it involved *a lot* of money. I went to Bill and said, If we want Hulk Hogan, here's what it's going to cost us.

"We've taken the first step. We've come out of that dark, dingy, miserable arena look, we're starting to change the way people are looking at us as a brand. I want to take the next big step—I want to go get Hulk Hogan."

Bill took it to Ted, who was very enthusiastic. They gave me the green light.

This was right around the time that Vince McMahon was scheduled to go on trial for allegedly supplying steroids to wrestlers. Hogan had been called to testify at the trial. The steroid matter was probably one of the reasons Hogan had had problems with the company. Then, as now, it was a controversial matter.

We knew it was going on. We knew there was a chance that Hogan was going to end up getting some not so favorable press, but we were prepared for that. I spent a lot of time talking to Bill Shaw about it.

Wrestlers as Politicos & Backstabbers

Closing the Deal

I put on my salesman shoes and set out to persuade Hogan to come over. Ric Flair helped me and was instrumental in convincing Hogan to come to WCW. We had countless meetings and conversations as we slowly got Hogan to come back to wrestling.

Hogan and I remain good friends to this day: we speak every week. He might not say this because he wouldn't want to hurt my feelings, but it's true: he didn't have a tremendous amount of respect for me at the time. He certainly didn't look at me as a Vince McMahon. He just looked at me as a young guy who had a unique opportunity and was working for some of the most powerful people in entertainment. I'm sure he looked at me as raw meat.

Even so, Hogan was very cautious. He still is, to this day. He doesn't make moves that he doesn't think through very carefully. He knew there was a negative stigma attached to WCW. He also knew that if he came over, and WCW crashed and burned, he would have to wear that badge of dishonor. He would have looked like a failure if WCW failed, even if that failure had nothing to do with him.

Wrestling Politics

Wrestlers, particularly back then, could be very political, very manipulative. Hogan was concerned that he would be caught up in that. He knew there would be a number of people who would do anything they could to make sure that Hulk Hogan tanked.

Ric Flair really helped reassure him. He traveled with me over a dozen times to meet with Hogan. He talked about storylines, about wrestling politics, and assured Hogan that if he came over, he'd have a team of people in the locker room who would work together to make it successful. I can't give Flair enough credit. I couldn't have gotten Hogan on board if it weren't for him. Trust was a bigger issue for Hogan than money.

Hogan also knew he could have a good match with Ric Flair. Ric was one of those guys, especially in 1994, who could have a great match with just about anybody. Anyone who's ever worked with Ric loves to work with him because he has that ability.

At the same time, there was a great story there: Hulk Hogan versus "Nature Boy" Ric Flair, two wrestling legends with large followings butting heads. Hogan and Flair had been touched on briefly in World Wrestling Federation, back when Flair was there in 1991, but it never really happened for them on a large scale. This was the opportunity.

Old vs. New

A Hogan-Flair showdown would capitalize on the differences between the companies. Wrestling for Vince, at the time, was seen as more entertainment-based, more appealing to a mass audience.

WCW was more old-school wrestling. Hulk Hogan was, or had been, an icon. Ric Flair was a guy who, in the eyes of a lot of guys inside wrestling, was a much more credible *wrestling* champion, a guy who represented traditional professional wrestling. He was old-school to Hogan's new.

Bringing in Hogan and putting him against Flair would bring the two audiences together. In a way—and in retrospect, because I didn't think of it this way at the time—we were creating a war between the two brands.

We weren't looking for a confrontation with Vince, although some people thought we were. Admittedly, some of our statements made it look that way.

Around this time Bill Shaw and I gave an interview to the *Miami Herald,* where we both said we were hopeful that eventually we would overtake Titan, WWE's parent company at the time. "The biggest challenge we have ahead of us is making people realize we do have a better product," I told the columnist, Alex Marvez. "I think the consensus is we are better. But not enough people know that."

We were trying to rally our troops. We wanted people to know we were serious about building the WCW brand, and we wanted our people to feel good about the company A lot of what we said was hyperbole; we knew we were outgunned in 1994.

We had no idea that in a year and a half's time, we'd be the ones with the heavy artillery—a prime-time show, a ratings lead, and more momentum than a runaway M1A1 tank.

The Power of a Heel

Distrust

Given all of the things that had gone on with his departure from Vince's company and the controversy with the steroid trial, Hogan was worried that if he stepped over to WCW and crashed and burned, he'd be dead as a character. He was right. Knowing all that, he held out for creative control over his character.

Historically, wrestlers have always distrusted the people they wrestle for, and even other wrestlers. The business subtly encourages that. If you're a wrestler, you're only paid what a promoter thinks you're worth. And you can only look as good as your *opponent* makes you look.

Wrestling is a unique art form, in that, if you and I are in the ring together, and I like you, I can do everything in my power to make you look good. That ensures that you and I can make money together for a long period of time.

If, on the other hand, I'm threatened by you, for any reason—if I think too much attention is given to you, or I just personally don't like you—I can do any number of subtle or not so subtle things that will ultimately make you look bad.

Being a Heel

Bad guys—heels—are an important part of any wrestling match. More often than not, they control the tempo of the match. It's the bad guy's heat that makes the match.

The only way to be a "good" bad guy is to be a liar, cheat, or coward. You can be tough, yes, but primarily you're one of the other three. You have to rely on something from one of those categories to win because you're *just not good enough.*

There's a basic architecture to every wrestling match. The fight starts out strong, with the good guy in charge. The crowd is behind him. Then the bad guy finds some way to cheat. Let's keep this all very simple: the referee isn't looking, and the bad guy does something illegal to take advantage.

Now the bad guy is in charge. The tide of emotion rises. The bad guy gets his heat. He's beating the good guy to a pulp. The crowd hates it because it looks like the good guy is going to go down. They don't want that to happen. Their emotions build as the bad guy's victory looks more and more inevitable.

Then, at just the right moment, the good guy finds a way to start his comeback. He digs deep, breaks a hold, throws a right hand, and before you know it, is starting his finishing move.

So how is the bad guy in charge?

Say you're the good guy, and you hit me with a right hand when you're going into your comeback. If I look at you and smile—you're screwed. You have no credibility. Your comeback is toast. The audience goes flat, whether they know why or not.

Now granted, that example is extremely simplistic—extremely—but there are a million little variations and tricks of the trade. A heel can utilize all sorts of subtle tricks of the trade to make his opponent look good—or bad.

Creative Control

Hogan knew he was surrounded by a hornets' nest. He was surrounded by people whom he was completely dependent on in the ring to make him look good. But he knew that those people were intimidated and resentful because he was coming over. They were fearful that Hulk Hogan was going to take over the company.

That was why Ric Flair was so important when it came to convincing Hogan to sign with WCW. Ric couldn't guarantee anything, of course, but he made Hogan a lot more comfortable about the people he'd be dealing with.

Even so, Hogan worried that eventually the "us vs. them" mentality prevalent in the WCW would eventually sabotage him. And while he respected Ric to a large degree, he didn't feel Flair understood the best way to utilize the Hulk Hogan character. He was worried that a storyline that looked good on paper might turn out to be a trap, letting other wrestlers sabotage his character. That's why he wanted—and got—creative control. It assured him he wasn't going to be sabotaged.

Hogan was not subtle or shy at all about this.

"Look, brother, the money's great. The opportunity to work with Ted Turner is great. Eric, I like you. Yeah, there can be a lot of great opportunities here, but I have a real problem with some of the people in this company. They're going to look at Hulk Hogan as the guy who's going to come in and have too much control over their lives, and they're going to do everything they can to make that unsuccessful. The only way I'm making this move is with creative control. So if the situation is not comfortable for me, I won't have to do it."

A Sensible Move

It made sense to me then, and it makes sense to me now. It was the right thing to do. You can't take an asset like Hulk Hogan, an established brand, and throw him into a lion's den to be shredded up by a bunch of insecure people with their own agendas.

Maybe Hogan boasted about it, or maybe he just told people that he had creative control written into his contract. In any event, word of the clause quickly leaked, and I was roundly criticized.

Admittedly, it was the first time in WCW that anyone ever had creative control in an agreement. But for years, if you were on top, if you were Ric Flair at WCW, say, whether it was written into your contract or not, you had a lot of control. You had the title, and you were the champion. If a booker or promoter or an executive wanted you to do something you really didn't want to do, you had a lot of options.

Even though it doesn't exist in a WWE contract today, at least not that I'm aware of, anyone with real stroke has it. Look at Stone Cold Steve Austin. If anybody wants to pretend that, at the peak of his career, Stone Cold did not have creative control, they're kidding themselves. If Scott Hall, Kevin Nash, Shawn Michaels, didn't have creative control, then someone has to explain to me why Vince McMahon would jump on an airplane and fly to a house show in the middle of nowhere to sit down and talk to these guys about something they didn't want to do.

Creative control has been around in some way for a long, long time. It's just that in Hogan's case, it was the first time it had been put in a contract. In effect, it forced arbitration between whoever the booker was and Hulk Hogan. We had to sit down and talk through it.

Out of Whack

As it turned out, we talked a lot.

Hogan had a number of ways to let me know when he wasn't pleased with the way a particular storyline was going. He'd take days to get back to me on the phone, or maybe I'd get the word through Jimmy Hart, Hogan's assistant at the time. Jimmy would come in with his tail between his legs and give me the puppy-dog eyes.

"I don't think Hulk's very happy about this. I think you should just give Hulk a call. I know he'd like to talk to you."

So I'd get on the phone and convince him that no one was trying to screw him. Or at least, that I wasn't.

A lot of times I'd have to just drop what I was doing and go to see him. I remember one time going down to Tampa where Hogan lived because he wasn't happy about something. I found out that he was in a gym, working out. I drove over and waited for an hour and a half for him to finish before he'd talk about the subject at hand. I remember sitting in the corner of the gym thinking, *Wow, how out of whack is this? I'm running the company, not him.* But at the time, it was one of a lot of things we had to do as a company—that *I* had to do as the head of the company. The stakes were starting to get pretty high.

"Mean" Gene Okerlund and me taking in the crowd's reception of Hogan's arrival.

Momentum

Ticker-Tape Parade

After months of negotiation, we were set to announce that Hulk Hogan was coming to WCW in June 1994. By this time, our relationship with Disney had improved to the point where we had the run of the park. We wanted to film something really special, so we arranged a ticker-tape parade on the Main Street back lot at Disney-MGM. There were a lot of people in the park, and Hogan was a big deal. Fans surrounded him, and it looked great. It gave the whole announcement a big feel, exactly what we wanted.

Not Moving the Needle

But the truth is, Hulk Hogan didn't boost our viewership very much that year. Except for the first Pay-Per-View match between him and Ric Flair, where the buy rate was 1.3 percent, he did not have the impact on ratings we'd hoped. His shows didn't really move the needle.

There were a number of reasons. Hogan's character had gotten a little stale. And the whole red-and-yellow, say-your-prayers, eat-your-vitamins thing clashed with the steroids controversy. His credibility had been damaged.

Vince's audience didn't come to check out Hulk Hogan. They'd gotten a little tired of him, and turned off because of the steroid controversy and the issues between him and Vince. So we didn't drag that audience over to our product.

Hogan also didn't play that well with the audience WCW already had. Viewers who had watched WCW when it was NWA and Georgia Championship Wrestling, going way back, looked at Hogan kind of like an unwelcome guest. Hogan coming to WCW was like Roger Clemens coming to the New York Yankees. Yankee fans thought of him as a member of the hated Boston Red Sox, and didn't warm up to him right away. To bring in Hulk Hogan appeared to be a version of wrestling blasphemy. The hard-core fan just didn't understand why we would bring him in, and many peripheral mainstream viewers just didn't care.

Hogan wasn't a flop by any means. We brought Hulk Hogan in to get media attention, and convince the entertainment industry that we were no longer the retro-wrestling league. It was our attempt to reposition the WCW brand as a national franchise. This re-branding was the most important goal, and judging on that basis, we succeeded without question.

Of course, the only thing the dirtsheet "experts" talked about were television ratings. They didn't get it.

Working the Audience with *USA Today*

We invested a lot of money to make sure this rebranding was successful. Some of the things we did were unheard of in wrestling at the time. For example, I took out an ad for the Hogan-Flair Pay-Per-View in *USA Today*. I believe this was the first time anyone had ever advertised a wrestling Pay-Per-View *there*. I wasn't trying to attract viewers directly with the ads; I didn't think many wrestling fans were reading *USA Today* regularly. I did it because I knew that a lot of morning-drive shock jocks got their topics for the day out of *USA Today*. I figured that I would probably get some "free" buzz or radio time just by virtue of the fact that it was in there. And it worked.

I also knew that a lot of advertising executives read either *USA Today* or *Wall Street Journal* while traveling. So advertising there was another way of telling them we were a national platform where they could spend their clients' money.

Hogan helped us tremendously in New York, where most ad sales take place. Our salespeople could go out and talk about a big star that people outside of the wrestling business recognized. Hogan gave us credibility in the advertising world. He gave the people in the Pay-Per-View department something to be excited about as well. The amount of "lift" Hogan provided mitigated a lot of the potential for corporate backbiting. Everybody benefited, at least temporarily.

There were issues with the wrestlers, though. They all knew that Hogan was making a lot of money. The storylines were going to be built around Hulk Hogan, and everybody's job was to make Hulk Hogan look good. That's just the way it works. Still, there was quite a bit of apprehension. Everyone wanted to know what it would mean to *them*. A few felt directly threatened, and even the most secure person in the world would have been at least curious about his future.

After a few months went by and Hogan really didn't move the needle with the audience, I think there was a lot of relief. Some wrestlers were relieved that he didn't have the impact they thought he would have, because if he'd had that impact, he'd have had a lot more power. And believe me, he had plenty of capital to begin with.

Hulk Hogan Kool-Aid

Hogan helped WCW tremendously, but he could also be a handful. The politics between Hogan and Flair, and the politics between wrestlers in both men's camps, gave me waking nightmares. There was always plenty of maneuvering, backbiting, and politicking going on.

Truth be known, the same thing exists today in WWE. Anytime you've got performers—I don't care if they're musicians, actors, dancers, ice skaters, or jugglers—any time you have people who perform for a living, those people are fueled first and foremost by their self-image and their egos.

Combine that with the fact that the better positioned a performer is, the more money he or she can make, and you've got a highly political situation. Dealing with those politics was one of the most draining aspects of my job.

I was not drinking Hulk Hogan Kool-Aid by any stretch of the imagination. There were times when I would rather slam my own hand in a car door than hang out and have a burger with Hulk Hogan because of the shit he put me through.

At the same time, I have to say that, if push came to shove where Hogan was involved, and I wasn't sure in my own heart what to do, I would probably call it for Hogan. He'd earned that kind of consideration.

The same thing held true for Ric Flair. I didn't question his booking decisions. It was when they were working against each other that things got tense. And that didn't help Ric, frankly.

As 1994 went on, things started to fall apart with Ric. We'd have meetings where he'd get up in the middle and say, "Excuse me, guys, I gotta go call Beth." We'd be sitting around for an hour and a half, two hours, wondering where Ric went, only to find out he was on a plane heading home. Ric just couldn't handle the pressure. And there were some real pressure situations with Ric as a booker.

So if there was a jump ball, and the parties couldn't agree, I bet on Hogan. Hogan had a better track record, and fell in line with the look and feel our company needed. It wouldn't have made sense to bring him in and then do things the way we used to do things back in the NWA.

Some people took that personally They'd look at me and say, *He's in love with Hulk Hogan.* I wasn't. There were plenty of times he frustrated me so much I'd go bang my head on a curb.

Beyond Hogan

Missy Hyatt

Hogan wasn't the only thing we were doing to improve WCW, of course. We were starting to grow and gain momentum.

But it wasn't smooth path, either for the company or me personally. Missy Hyatt was one the nastier bumps I encountered that year.

We were taping a set of shows at Disney in mid-February 1994—I think it was the second set, but I could be wrong—when Missy Hyatt and I had our infamous "disagreement," which led to her filing a sex discrimination suit against Turner Broadcasting. Eventually, she accused me of saying she had to sleep with me to get ahead.

What a crock.

Take a Hike

Up until this point, Missy Hyatt was probably one of the top women in WCW, if there was such a thing then. There may have been only a handful of women there, but she was the one who got the most camera time. From time to time she was an announcer and a manager. Her role was fairly insignificant, but she was one of the more regularly featured women on our shows.

As part of the lead-up toward Hulk Hogan, we brought in Sherri Martel, who'd had some very high-profile roles working for Vince. We started using her in a very prominent way, building her as Ric Flair's eventual on-screen manager. One day Missy stormed into my office at Orlando. She demanded to know why I was using Sherri Martel instead of her, and basically made an ass of herself.

Missy Hyatt.

I want to be careful what I say here, because the bitch will come out and sue me again, but I had serious questions about how long she would last in the company. There wasn't much on camera that convinced me she was worth the effort. I have no idea what talent she really had. So for her to throw a temper tantrum because we'd decided to bring in another woman was just a little too catty for me to deal with. I decided on the spot to let her go.

Later that afternoon, I went out to meet my wife and kids in the parking lot, where they were waiting to go over to a barbecue we always had with the cast and crew after the show. Missy confronted me in front of my wife and demanded to know what I was doing and why I was doing it. I basically let her know I was done with her and didn't feel like getting into it any further.

Missy quickly filed suit, alleging sex discrimination. I believe she ended up saying in her complaint that while I was standing there talking to her, I reached across and fondled her breast.

Now, I'm capable of doing some crazy shit, but reaching across and fondling another woman's breast while my wife and kids are standing next to me is not one of them.

This was another one of the problems with Turner. In any group of wrestlers, there are going to be some who have a certain kind of mentality and lack of ethics when it comes to the way they do business. A few only care about the easiest way to scam a buck. Some, like the individual who was so proud that he figured out a way to steal plane tickets, don't mind committing fraud in the process.

Go figure.

Moving to Orlando

With the Disney tapings doing well, I suggested we think about moving our operations to Orlando.

There were a couple of reasons. One was the fact that Florida has no state income tax, so we all would have saved some money. Secondly, many of our freelance production people and wrestlers were already in Florida. If we relocated there, we would save on transportation costs, since we were flying them up to Atlanta for the Saturday show and other tapings.

At the same time, being in Atlanta didn't provide any production or promotion opportunities, and there weren't any strategic reasons for staying there. We were spending half our time in Florida anyway.

Big mistake, though.

I didn't realize the rest of the company wouldn't be as excited about moving to Florida as I was. I'm a bit of a gypsy, and to me, it doesn't matter where I live as long as my family is with me and I'm successful. But other people had roots in Atlanta, and homes in Atlanta, and they weren't excited about giving them up.

I didn't take that into consideration as much as I should have. I just stood up one day and said, "Guess what! We're moving to Disney World."

I assumed everyone would feel like me and be excited. Now I realize how they felt: *Wow, I'm not going to be able to work for WCW anymore. I'm going to have to find a new job.*

It didn't go over so well. And we didn't move.

Hollywood BS

Of course, when the dirtsheets got hold of my idea, they reported that I wanted to move down to Orlando because there were movie opportunities down there and Eric Bischoff would be one step closer to Hollywood.

That is so much bullshit.

It goes hand in hand with the rap that the only reason I was interested in doing something with WCW was that it would take me one step closer to Hollywood. Everything we did—from filming at Disney to bringing in Hollywood writers, stunt casting, you name it—was criticized as being somehow aimed at smoothing *my* path toward becoming a big-time Hollywood guy.

There is a grain of truth in the charge: I was looking at wrestling more from the point of view of Wilshire Boulevard than Peachtree Street. Our business was changing, and WCW had to change with it. But this had nothing to do with my personal goals—if I had wanted to be in Hollywood, I would have moved there in 1993 when I had the opportunity.

It's funny, but a lot of the things WCW did in 1994 weren't things *I* invented—they were things Vince McMahon had done first. The connection with Hollywood was a perfect example. In the 1980s he brought Cyndi Lauper, Mr. T, Liberace and others to events, integrating pop stars with wrestling. He came up with that idea, not me.

The fact is, it worked. It brought attention to the brand and got new people to sample the product. Some of them stuck around. That was my strategy, but it wasn't my invention.

The dirtsheet writers should have known better. But people would use anything they could to take potshots at what I was trying to do at WCW.

Suspension of Disbelief

Japanese Wrestling

I went over to Japan in 1994 to meet with representatives of the New Japan Pro Wrestling promotion. I went originally to find out how we could work more closely together. But the trip did much more than that. It fundamentally changed the way I thought about wrestling.

Wrestling isn't just popular in the United States. There are wrestling fans all over the world. American wrestlers can find themselves more popular overseas than in the States. Besides touring on our own in Europe, WCW had arrangements with Japanese promotions to capitalize on that popularity.

Me, Masa Saito, and Sonny Onoo at a traditional bathhouse.

The major Japanese promotions, All Japan and New Japan, drew fifty or sixty thousand people to their shows. Doing business with them gave us a way to offset our talent budget, which at the time was probably around $15 million. By subcontracting a group of performers for a high fee—"lending" them to the Japanese companies—we offset that cost significantly.

There were other benefits. Sending our wrestlers to Japan and elsewhere gave us an international reputation. Bringing their wrestlers to America—usually part of the exchange deals—did the same.

While WCW had done some business with Japan in the past, I wanted to expand that. I also wanted to mend some fences, since there had been disputes between our company and the New Japan promotion prior to my taking over.

It happened that the main American talent liaison with New Japan was an old friend of mine from high school, Brad Rheingans. Back in our younger days, Brad was a wrestler, and a damn good one—he made the U.S. Olympic team, though unfortunately for him it was the year we boycotted. Brad helped me smooth over past problems, and WCW was able to develop a very strong relationship with New Japan Pro Wrestling.

A Visit to Japan

When I set up a meeting with the New Japan promoters in early 1994, I hired Sonny Onoo—who'd invented and sold Ninja-Star Wars with me years before—as an interpreter and informal business and culture consultant. Sonny grew up in Japan and understood the business culture there. I knew that doing business in Japan for an American is quite extraordinary because of the differences in how we do business. He helped me really understand the Japanese mindset and negotiating process.

It was also enjoyable to go to Japan. You can go to Europe, South America, even parts of the Middle East, and it will feel somewhat familiar. But when you go to Japan, you can't even read the traffic signs. You don't have the slightest clue what people are saying.

The arena shows were inspiring. Sixty or seventy thousand people were watching wrestling. At the time, we were lucky if we could draw eight or ten thousand. I began studying and thinking about what was going on around me, trying to find elements I could bring back to WCW.

In Japan, a big dome show would typically receive major coverage in the sports pages and other media. Wrestling was treated like a legitimate sport, unlike here in the United States. Could you imagine seeing front-page coverage of a WCW or WWE Pay-Per-View in the *New York Times* or *USA Today*? That sort of thing was routine in Japan.

There was no way I could change that. That train left the station a long time before I got there.

The Japanese audiences also believed that the things happening in the ring were real. I couldn't change that back in the United States either—there was no way I could take audiences back to 1940 or 1950. But there was a psychology to the Japanese style that *could* be brought back and applied to our creative formula. Americans might not be willing to believe that everything about the match was real, but there might be a point where they were willing to suspend their disbelief—much as they would when going to see a play or movie and got caught up in the moment. If they were *allowed* to believe, *just for a moment or two,* they would enjoy the show more completely. And that would be the key to success.

Between Fact and Fiction

I realized then that pro wrestling needed to find a balance between showbiz and mystery—between the over-the-top entertainment that I believed in, and purely athletic contests where the ending does not appear to be predetermined. I wanted to find that sweet spot, where the audience believed—or at least responded as if they believed—that what they were seeing was real. Not the match necessarily, but the situation surrounding it.

I couldn't articulate it at the time, but I was thinking about trying to find a way to heighten people's suspension of disbelief. I needed to find a way to make what happened in the ring seem more believable, in terms of emotions if not facts. Suspension of disbelief had been ignored for so long in lieu of the other elements that go into pro wrestling that it was the one thing we could work on to heighten people's interest.

I knew we could never make the audience believe wrestling was real, but I knew we could do things that would make the audience go, *Wow. I know all that other stuff isn't real, but this, this must be real.*

If we could do *one* thing in the course of a two-hour broadcast that people thought was real, even if it was only for a moment, that made them suspend their disbelief, consciously or subconsciously, we would be more successful.

I started asking a lot of questions and watching the way the Japanese did it. I knew full well I couldn't import Japanese style. I was thinking more about attitude and philosophy. That could be imported to the United States.

On the Air

The Best Option

Even though I tried to cut back on my on-the-air appearances as my executive role increased, I soon found myself spending even more time than ever in front of the cameras. Quite frankly, I was the best option we had. Not that I thought I was that good—just the best option under the circumstances.

I became the play-by-play guy for the WCW Saturday-night show because I knew more about where we wanted to go and what we wanted to achieve storyline-wise than anybody else. It was easy for me to sell the direction of the match.

Everything I did, I did to change the perception of the brand. That required changing what people saw and heard on television, including the announcers. But my options were pretty limited. Our main announcer at that point was Tony Schiavone. Honestly, I wasn't that comfortable with Tony Schiavone because he was associated with the regional stigma we were trying to escape. He also had a radio face. That wasn't the image we were trying to project.

There really wasn't anybody available outside the company either. Wrestling play-by-play guys don't get nearly the credit that they should. It's a difficult art form. You have to operate under tremendous stress and pressure, and there just aren't that many people available to do the job. It's not like basketball or football or NASCAR where there are a lot of good announcers.

But Tony *was* a great play-by-play guy, which was why he stayed on air. He also happened to be one of the better producers I've ever worked with. Viewers saw him only as a personality, but he was working his butt off behind the camera. He was a detail-oriented person, calm under pressure, thorough and dependable. He had a work ethic second to none.

And by the way, he was a better play-by-play guy than I was. I just didn't have the baggage he did.

I didn't think of myself as a character. I would never have imagined that I was. If someone would have told me in 1994 what I was about to do in 1995, I would have laughed in their face.

Hogan vs. Flair

Hogan versus Flair was our focus in 1994. Their matches headlined our Pay-Per-Views, and remain among the most talked-about contests in wrestling history.

The first Hulk Hogan/Ric Flair Pay-Per-View in July 1994 at *Bash at the Beach* went well. A lot of that had to do with Ric Flair. Ric was very gracious when it came to the creative side of things. He did everything in his power to make Hogan feel comfortable. There was nothing selfish or self-serving about Flair's approach.

Flair won the second showdown at a *Clash of the Champions* special we did that August in Cedar Rapids, Iowa. But he didn't get the title because he won without a pin or submission, upping the stakes for their Pay-Per-View that fall at *Halloween Havoc.*

That bothered Ric a lot. I think he hoped to get the title with a clean win. He probably believed that since he did the job for Hogan in July, putting him over and establishing him, there should have been an automatic quid pro quo to return the favor. But I don't think that any of us seriously considered taking the title off Hogan that quickly.

It goes against any kind of long-term planning and logic to flip belts back and forth. You bring in Hulk Hogan, create all this hoopla, use him to get a lot of media attention, position him to be the guy who is going to move your brand forward, and then beat him sixty days after he gets there?

No.

Long-Term Thinking

That was one of the problems that I had with the short-term, month-to-month booking mentality, even when Ric had the book. People didn't think long-term. No one, except myself, Hulk Hogan, Bill Shaw, and probably Ted Turner, understood what it meant to have Hulk Hogan as our franchise player.

Ric looked at it from a performer's point of view—hey, I did the favor for you, you do it for me, and we'll have a rubber match, best two out of three.

The time between the August and October Pay-Per-Views saw my relationship with Ric Flair begin to spiral downward. Flair and Hogan's relationship also took a hit. The suggestion that Ric "retire" was partly to blame, even though everyone knew he wasn't really going to retire.

We had to figure out some way of increasing the stakes for the *Halloween Havoc* Pay-Per-View. One of the obvious elements that we could integrate into the story was the premise that if Ric Flair lost, he had to retire.

Let me say it again: Ric wasn't going to *really* retire. I don't recall specifically, but I probably suggested he go away for a while, take some time off, and take advantage of the "absence makes the heart grow fonder" factor. When you've played your character out for a long time, sometimes the smartest thing you can do for a character is to take it off television and bring it back three months later when it feels fresh again. But Ric didn't want to do it, and it became one of the more difficult scenarios that I had to manage.

Flair's Holdup

One of the things that made the angle more believable was the fact that Ric was in his mid-forties, which for most normal performers is knocking on retirement's door. Ric had his insecurities about that, which was only natural. Add to those the insecurities that he had relating to Hogan—the fact that Hogan came in and became the franchise player, to a degree displacing Flair as the franchise player—and you can understand how Ric became extremely insecure about his position.

I think Ric initially looked at bringing Hulk Hogan in as a big opportunity for himself and the company. Hogan made Ric's job as a booker easier. As a performer, if Ric was able to have matches with Hogan—even if he didn't win—he would benefit. But the rub came when Hogan wasn't interested in returning the favor by giving Flair the win in their next match. That's when Ric realized this was all about Hulk Hogan, and Ric Flair was a secondary talent. That was hard on Ric's ego. And that's understandable.

I don't think Ric thought that we were going to make him really retire. But he used the situation to negotiate a long-term contract for himself, using the *Halloween Havoc* match to, in effect, hold us up.

New Contract or No Match

Ric wanted a long-term deal. He agreed to go in the direction we wanted to go, provided we went in the direction *he* wanted. Which meant a multiyear extension.

Before the Hogan match, before his contract was due.

Ric wasn't necessarily interested in leveraging the situation for money. He was never really greedy when it came to money. I think he saw the situation as a way to get security, and that's what he wanted.

However, the way he went about it made me lose some respect for Ric. I understand holding out to maximize your leverage, but I personally would never do that myself. He played it to the hilt, right up to the very last minute. Even after we verbally agreed to terms, Bill Shaw actually had to bring a contract with him from Atlanta so Ric could sign it and could go on with the show.

Your Job Is to Perform

I come from a point of view where, if I'm an employee or an independent contractor and I take your money in exchange for my services, unless there is something written into that contract that gives me the ability to dictate how-where-when you're going to use my services, then my job is to show up and do what you ask me to do. I always had a problem with wrestlers who felt they should be able to take my money and then force a situation where I had to engage them in a conversation about how and when and why I wanted to use them.

That's not to say that I don't want to share ideas or exchange concepts or improve a scenario, but at the end of the day, the job of a performer is to perform. Decisions about using the performer are made by the person writing the check.

I'd been held up before Ric did it, and I was held up later on. The Honky Tonk Man tried to hold me up, and I kicked him out the door. There were a couple of guys who tried that technique, and it didn't work.

Ric Flair was the exception.

Randy Savage

Sometime in 1994, Bill Shaw, Bob Dhue, and I went out to check the competition at a house show in Phoenix. (Bob, who was still with WCW at the time, was excited because there was a great golf course at the hotel where we stayed.) I put on a hat and some glasses, real 007 stuff, bought our tickets, and sat up in the cheap seats like everybody else and watched the show. It was fun, and gave me a firsthand view of what Vince was up to.

It was at that show that I first saw Randy Savage perform in front of a live audience.

By that time Randy had been in wrestling for more than two decades. A former minor-league baseball player, the Macho Man first wrestled as the Spider in 1973 and had appeared with several promotions before beginning a long stint working for Vince in 1985. He'd had some memorable matches with Hulk Hogan and Ric Flair in the late 1980s and early '90s. In 1994, he started working as a color commentator, implying that his days as a main event talent were coming to an end.

Several months after I caught the show, Hogan called me up and said, "Hey, brother, I think Randy Savage is available."

I won't say Hogan pressured me, but he really did a sales job. He sold me on Savage. Not that it was too hard.

Savage wasn't very happy with what he was doing. Randy is a very proud individual, and, like a lot of performers, just wasn't ready to hang up his tights and put on a suit. He was much more interested in continuing to perform.

I talked to him over the phone. Then we met and worked something out. Randy was a spokesman for Slim Jim at the time, and I cut a deal for sponsorship with Slim Jim that offset the majority, if not all, of Randy's salary. We got Randy, if not for free, close to it. He went on to some memorable matches with Hogan and Flair, and did a memorable angle in early 1996 involving his ex-wife Miss Elizabeth, who "deserted" him for Flair.

Stealing talent

The Macho Man was the first of what seemed like a parade of WWE talent that would come to us over the next two years or so.

People have said that I was constantly looking for ways to hurt the WWE, and that signing wrestlers away from them was part of that strategy. That was not the case at all.

If the WWE thought that Randy Savage was valuable to their organization, they would have worked with him and come to an agreement with him. He was clearly unhappy with how he was being used, and given an alternative, it's not surprising he jumped to WCW.

My job was to build WCW. If people were available, and they were an asset to me, we would go ahead and sign that talent. It's no different than any other business or sport.

Hurting the WWE wasn't my motivation. I just wanted to make my company better.

Nearing the Black

A lot of great things happened in 1994. We figured out Disney. We brought on Hulk Hogan. At the end of the year, we got Randy Savage. We had Flair-Hogan matches that a lot of people in the wrestling community talked about for a long time.

There were still a lot of things we needed to fix, but we were gradually building the company. Any time that we stepped up, every time we took a risk, there was a return on investment. Ted Turner was starting to take notice.

By the end of 1994, we'd done enough to slow down the bleeding that I realized we could potentially turn the company around in 1995 and show a profit. No one prior to me had ever done that.

I knew that if I was the guy to show a profit, my stock as an executive in Turner Broadcasting was going to be pretty high. I also wanted to prove that Bill Shaw had been right when he took a chance on me. So the bottom line became my focus. I wanted to be the guy who did what no one else thought was possible.

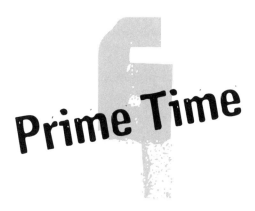

Prime Time

"He'll Understand"

Ted Turner & the Turner Men

In late 1994, early 1995, Ted Turner was Turner Broadcasting's alpha male. The company was really shaped in his image. It was very entrepreneurial, built as a unique combination of guts and vision. And it was growing. TNT and TBS were doing great. CNN was the recognized world leader in news. We owned the Hawks and the Braves, both of whom made it to the playoffs that season (the Braves won the World Series in 1995). We were acquiring New Line Cinema. A lot of great things were happening.

There was constant talk of Ted wanting to buy NBC or CBS. Every time all of us at WCW would hear that, we'd chomp at the bit. We knew how Ted perceived WCW, and we knew that, at the very least, we'd be given an opportunity to talk about using a network as a platform, even if it was just for a yearly special to help build the WCW brand.

At the time, TBS had a *Clash of the Champions* special that we would run in prime time a couple of times a year. That was our opportunity to put the best of our people out there in prime time. If we'd had CBS or NBC, our exposure would have been several times greater.

Even though I was a vice president of WCW, I didn't talk to Ted Turner on a personal basis at all. Once or twice I saw him at a company-wide meeting, but I never had any extensive dialogue with him. Quite frankly, I could have bumped into him in the hallway, and he might not have recognized who I was.

Harvey Schiller

Bill Shaw, and later on Harvey Schiller, were the ones who spoke directly to Ted Turner about WCW, and did so a regular basis. Harvey replaced Bill as WCW's head during a company restructuring in early 1995. I was very disappointed to lose Bill as my boss, but the move made a lot of sense organizationally. Harvey headed Turner Sports and was a strong leader. He'd been a colonel in the Air Force and had a military straightforwardness. He was a very impressive guy, physically and intellectually; when he came into a room, he instantly commanded respect.

Ultimately, I think it was a mistake to have WCW answer to Turner Sports—we would have been better off on the entertainment side. But it certainly didn't make any sense for us to be answering to the administration division where Bill Shaw was either. In any event, it wasn't my decision to make, and I didn't have a vote.

My first meeting with Harvey Schiller was very uncomfortable. Harvey didn't know a lot about wrestling. I think he looked at me and thought to himself, *This guy doesn't look like the corporate, buttoned-up executive that I like to work with.* Early on I'd been coming to work in a suit and tie, but as things went on I'd loosened up, generally wearing jeans and other casual clothes to work.

We were first and foremost a creative enterprise, and although we were all professionals, I felt the attempt to dress and act like our corporate peers kept us from thinking like entrepreneurs or people in the entertainment business. I was more interested in people's energy and creativity and work ethic than in whether they wore wingtip shoes.

At first, I got the impression that Harvey had no interest in WCW and that we were going to slide back into a situation where there was no real corporate support. But as I got to know him, I realized that his cold demeanor on the first meeting was just Harvey being Harvey. He didn't show much emotion, even when he was enthusiastic about something. We ended up working together fairly well.

If you didn't know Harvey very well, you didn't realize he had a great sense of humor. He was willing to poke fun of himself. And by the way, he was a ham. Two years later, I asked him to go on air for a bit and threaten to fire me. I barely got the invitation out of my mouth before he asked me where and when he should show up.

One bad thing did happen when Harvey was named head of Turner Sports and WCW was put under his control. Some of the people around me helping run WCW began returning to their old political ways, trying to position their wagons, so to speak, because they weren't sure how all this was going to shake out. We'd gotten away from that with Bill Shaw, but under the new regime we started to backslide.

One other thing happened when we reorganized—I became president of WCW. The truth is, I don't even remember the exact month, let alone the day or moment. We were doing so much then that things tended to blur together.

A Dollar Bet

Quite frankly, by early 1995, I had a little bit of a swagger. Things were turning around. There was positive press about us. And then, toward the end of the first quarter, I went through the projections for the rest of the year. I realized that if we made a couple more good moves strategically, we could turn a profit.

I voiced that opinion during a budget meeting. A short time later, I got a call from Bill Shaw, who introduced me to a guy named Harry Anderson. Anderson was one of the top people on the financial side of Turner. The way the company was structured, the accounting and legal sides of the business were autonomous. I had accountants in WCW, but they didn't report directly to me. They had told Anderson what I said. Anderson, curious about how a company that had lost money from day one could be nearing the black, asked Bill to set up a meeting.

We met in Bill Shaw's office. I walked Anderson through the numbers. He was friendly, but he was adamant—there was no way WCW could ever turn a profit.

I told him right in front of Bill Shaw: I will bet you a dollar that we will. And when I win this bet, you are going to get down on your hands and knees and hand me that dollar in front of WCW's employees.

Harry was probably four levels above me in the executive food chain. He got invited to meetings and parties that I never even heard about. He was a button-down member of the executive committee of Turner Broadcasting. I wore jeans and cowboy boots, had long hair, and showed up to work in a leather jacket.

He laughed, and accepted the bet. He was unconvinced that there was any way in hell that WCW could ever turn a profit.

Star TV

Sure I could turn a profit, I started looking at our international distribution.

International distribution basically means reselling footage you've already shot for use in the United States. Once you've shot the footage, you've basically paid for it already. If you can sell it again overseas, whatever you make is pure profit.

WCW had never been very strong in international distribution for a variety of reasons, including the fact that we didn't have recognizable stars. But now with Hulk Hogan and Randy Savage, we had names that people in Europe and Asia knew. I started turning up the heat on the international sales department to create more revenue. They found an opportunity with Star TV in China.

Star TV was aggressively buying up programming and paying fairly high dollar for it at the time. They made an offer big enough to put us in the black for the year. I've forgotten the details, but I believe it was our WCW Saturday-night show, which was our flagship at the time, and all of our syndicated product. I don't remember the number, but it was well into the six-figure range.

We wouldn't have made a great deal of money, but we would have been profitable, and that's all that mattered to me. I didn't care if we made ten dollars or ten million, I just wanted to see black ink.

I was absolutely obsessed with getting that deal. There was only one small problem.

Star TV was owned by Rupert Murdoch. Rupert Murdoch and Ted Turner hated each other. They had their own Vince McMahon–Eric Bischoff thing going on in the press, and it was ugly.

How could I do a deal with a company that was owned by Rupert Murdoch, and not have Ted Turner ask for my head on a silver platter? Or just take it off himself, for that matter.

I couldn't. I spent a month or two trying to figure things out. I knew I had to do the deal, but there was no way I could do it without taking it to Ted first. To do otherwise, to give content to Rupert Murdock without Ted's okay, would have been career suicide.

You have to remember, Ted valued content more than he valued dollars. He saw content as long-term dollars, and giving up content for short-term gain was not the way Ted did business.

Finally I called Scott Sassa, with whom I had a little bit of a relationship. Scott oversaw the television networks and had an enormous amount of influence in the company. He was a young guy, kind of a renegade, and a golden boy within Turner. Everybody considered him to be the heir apparent to Ted Turner. He was also a very cool guy. I laid out the situation for him.

"We have a chance to turn this company around, but I need your help. I need you to help me get this in front of Ted, and I need your support. I need you to go in and tell him, or help me tell him, why this is a good idea. Because if I go in there solo, I'm going to get shredded, and I won't get the deal done."

Scott saw the merit in it and agreed to accompany me.

What Do We Need to Compete?

The meeting ended up being myself, Scott Sassa, Harvey Schiller, and Ted Turner. I was a salesman before my wrestling career, and I knew exactly what to do. I honed my pitch. I tried to anticipate all of the objections and figured the best way to overcome them. I practiced laying out all the financial reasons for doing the deal, and countering the negatives.

I was nervous. I wanted the deal, and I'd never pitched Ted before; it was my first face-to-face meeting with him that really mattered. I was a little intimidated going in and sitting across from Ted, especially knowing that I was pitching something that was going to piss him off.

Finally, the time for the meeting arrived. We went in, I introduced myself, and began my presentation. I got, oh, maybe two and a half minutes into the pitch before Ted interrupted me.

"Uh, Eric, What do we need to do to become competitive with Vince?"

I had every answer for any possible question about Star TV and how we needed the deal to make a profit and grow the WCW brand. But I had *not* been thinking about being competitive with Vince. So when Ted Turner stopped me in the middle of my pitch and asked me a question I wasn't prepared to answer, I did what any good street fighter would do when he was about to get beat about the head: I tucked my chin to my chest, threw my fists up in front of my face to protect myself, and thought as quickly as I could.

Finally I blurted out, "Well, Ted, I think we need to have prime time."

That was the only thing Vince had that we didn't.

Ted looked at Scott Sassa and said, "Scott, I want you to give Eric two hours every Monday night on TNT."

You would have thought somebody cut Scott's tongue out of his head.

Scott looked at TNT as the coolest, slickest, most hip cable network going. Wrestling did not fit with the profile—remember, until that point we were on TBS, which had a much different image. I think as far as Scott was concerned, wrestling was for rednecks; it wasn't cool, it wasn't Hollywood. Scott was very happy to have wrestling on TBS, but he would never in his worst nightmare have dreamt that Ted would put it on TNT *in prime time*.

So Scott was in shock. And by the way, so was I.

Ted wanted to know how soon I could get a show on the air. I stuttered out, "I think I can do it by August."

"Great. Let's do it by August."

In order to buy some time, Scott pointed out that TNT network president Brad Siegel wasn't in the meeting. "Why don't we have a meeting next week and talk about it with Brad?"

Ted looked at Scott and said, "No. Brad's a smart young man. He'll understand what I want to do and why I want to do it. Let's just do it."

And that was the end of the discussion.

A Competitive Genius

Nobody asked how much it would cost or what impact it would have on the network. We had our marching orders. As for the Star TV deal, it was off the table. Ted expected us to focus on the new show—eventually called *Monday Night Nitro*—and make it work.

As we walked out of the meeting, I looked at Harvey Schiller, and he said, "Well, time to get to work." I looked at Scott Sassa, and he was still in shock. All he said was, "When Brad gets in tomorrow, you better go visit with him and figure this out."

I don't think Scott was pissed at me, but I'm sure if he had known this was going to happen, he wouldn't have gone into the meeting with me. Then again, I don't think anything would have changed: I think Ted would have told us to do it anyway, and Scott would have found out in a memo.

The impression I have of Ted Turner is that he's a genius in a lot of ways, and he's extremely competitive. He believed in WCW. And I think we had gained enough momentum that we were beginning to validate his beliefs. So when he started thinking about what it would take to get to the next level, going head-to-head with Vince was an obvious next step. I think he said to himself, *We've built this product; we're ready to compete. Let's compete.* I think it was really that simple.

Vince McMahon has his own opinions about what happened, taking it personally and claiming that Ted was out to get him. Maybe he was right—maybe there was something more malevolent going on. But I don't believe it. Ted just liked to take risks and compete, and very much believed in WCW. As far as he was concerned, taking WCW prime-time was a natural progression.

Better Than/Less Than/ Different Than

Pressure to Be Better

Going head-to-head with World Wrestling Federation would mean one of two things: we'd either rise to the occasion and be successful, or our failures and weaknesses would be obvious, and we'd never get a chance at it again.

I went back to my office and called a few people in—Craig Leathers, who was a director at the time, David Crockett, and most of my department heads. When I told them what had happened in my meeting with Ted, they were shocked as badly as I was. I'm not actually sure they believed me at first. Prime time had not been in our consciousness. We were already stretched to the limit just doing what we were doing.

But the more I thought about it, the more excited I became. It was a great opportunity for the brand, and for me personally. And I liked the pressure. I've always functioned well under pressure.

First thing the next morning, I went over to Brad's office, not knowing what to expect. I would have been angry and defensive if I'd had such a major shift of strategy happen to a network I was president of when I wasn't even in the room to voice an opinion. I anticipated a lot of resentment from Brad. To my surprise, Brad took a positive attitude.

"Look, this wasn't something I would have chosen to do," he said, "but if we're going to do it on my network, it's got to be great. And whatever it's going to take to make it great, I'll do what I can to support that."

The amount of enthusiasm and support Brad showed in that meeting wiped my doubts off the mat. It gave me a lot of confidence. I felt I had somebody at the network who really wanted to make it work.

It was a real pivot point. Up until that moment, just about everyone at WCW was shunned when they stepped into the North Tower, where all the company's top executives worked. We got the feeling many didn't even want us in the building. To have someone like Brad embrace us really gave me a lot of confidence.

In my career, the launch and success of *Nitro* is something I can point to and say, I did that. But I have to add that I wouldn't have been able to pull it off if it hadn't been for the vision of Ted Turner. And almost as importantly, the support of Brad Siegel.

I'm not trying to make an Oscar speech, but over the years Brad ended up taking a lot of heat for his involvement in the wrestling business, and it was undeserved. He supported WCW in every way he possibly could. A lot of *Nitro*'s success really had to do with Brad, and how he supported it. He gave us the tools to succeed.

Unpredictable

I grabbed all my department heads and said, *We're going to do this. We have a blank slate—how do we want to paint this picture?*

We spent days bouncing around ideas. I listened more than I talked. I wanted to hear what everyone was thinking.

Brad and I discussed doing some research to get an idea of what some of the audience was thinking. I'd worked with researchers before, and quite frankly, I found it to be pretty unproductive. The old saying that numbers lie and liars use numbers is even more true when it comes to research for television shows. Questions can be asked and research framed in a way that you can get any outcome you want—just as I'd done for the executives at Disney.

But Turner Broadcasting had an unusually talented research guy (I can't remember his name, unfortunately). He asked me about my goals for the show and what I wanted to find out. Then he came up with an approach to get into the audience's "head" in a way no researcher previously had. His idea was to create an equal balance of pro-WCW viewers and pro-WWE viewers, and mix in a certain percentage of nonwrestling fans as well as people who used to watch but didn't any longer. His only agenda was to try and help.

I've never believed that research is going to give you a blueprint or formula to make you successful. Too many people in the entertainment business have no real instinct for the business. They aren't creative people and don't really relate to the creative process. They are ad sales people, or business affairs people, or marketing people. They look at research more to provide an excuse or a safety net if a decision goes bad than as a tool to be used in combination with a truly creative process. But I do believe that if you look at that research and apply it against what your instincts tell you, it can be very helpful.

And that's what we did. The research dug below the surface. It was more about the psychology of why people enjoyed wrestling than about any one performer. The questions were things like: "What do you like about professional wrestling?"

The answer: "I like it when it's unpredictable."

"Unpredictable" and "spontaneous" popped up over and over. People like surprises, especially in wrestling. This may seem obvious now, but believe me, it wasn't then.

Different Than

After about three weeks, our creative discussions became unproductive. We started going in circles. There was no disagreement, but there wasn't much agreement either. So I went off by myself for a couple of days to think about the new show.

When I came back, I told my staff, "Here's what we're going to do. We have three choices: be better than them, less than them, or different than them. We can't be better than them. They have been around longer, have a lock on the audience, and are good at what they do. We don't want to be less than them, so we have to be different than them."

Everybody looked at me like: *Are you high, or what? What does that mean?*

At the time, WWE billed itself as the leader in family entertainment. I didn't think we could beat them at that. If we tried to be better than them at what they did, we'd need to knock things out of the park or be a miserable failure. On the other hand, if we admitted we weren't as good as them, we'd be losers from the start. Neither approach seemed very inviting.

"Here's how we're going to be different than them. Their show is taped. How can we be different than that? We go live."

I'd known early on that I wanted to do the show live, though I waited until the time was right to tell everyone. I worried it would crack a lot of people on the production side, who were uneasy enough as it was. I've always thought that something on live TV is more interesting than the same thing taped. It's hard for performers to be spontaneous when they're being taped. We'd also have trouble achieving the unpredictability and spontaneity that kept jumping out at me from the research on a taped show, since by the time we aired, word about what happened would have gotten out.

"All right, that's one," I said. "Here's another. Who's their audience? Who are they catering to?"

Their core viewers were kids. If you looked at their demographics at the time, that was their model. I didn't think we could go after the same audience and be better than them at doing it. So what were our options?

"If their audiences are kids, eleven to seventeen, we go after eighteen-to thirty-nine-year-old males. Let's make that our target."

"Hmmmm." Some heads in the room started to nod.

"How do their stories play out? What are the characters like?"

WWE's characters were over the top, basically live-action cartoons in animated storylines.

"Our storylines will be more reality based," I said. "We'll create stories that are more real to that eighteen-to-thirty-nine demo."

I wasn't suggesting that all of our characters make this radical shift, but I did want to do things that would focus our stories on an older demo.

The list got to be very long, but those were the key elements. And *Nitro* took shape from that.

Promote till You Drop

Pro wrestling philosophy dictated at the time that you have to cram the product down the audience's throat. Promote, promote, promote. *Tune in next week to see this . . . Call your local cable company and order this . . . Go to your local Ticketmaster and get your tickets now . . .*

That always bothered me. As a viewer, I hated listening to it. As a talent, I hated doing it. So I decided I was going to strictly limit the promos on the live show. I wasn't going to tell you this week what was going to be on next week.

You want to know? You'll have to tune in and find out.

That was a real departure—people just couldn't imagine why I wouldn't hype the next week's show. *How can you produce a wrestling show and not promote next week's main event match?*

When you look at a lot of successful television programs, you realize that they get you to come back not by telling you what's going to happen the following week, but by making you want to find out what's going to happen next. You follow the characters; you get hooked on the story. Every successful television series, whether it's a sitcom or a drama or a reality series, works that way.

My feeling was, if the show was live and we could create the sense that it was totally unpredictable, we'd create a show where the viewer never knew what was going to happen. If I could achieve that, I wouldn't *have* to promote what was going to happen next week. *Seinfeld* didn't. *ER* didn't. Viewers would tune in to find out.

My goal was to create a show that the audience would say, "Shit, I can't believe that they did that. What are they going to do next week?"

I knew it would work—if I could kick things off right. With the right surprise.

Blowing Down the Doors

Lex Luger

At some point while the show was being developed, Steve Borden—aka Sting—called me at home on a Saturday afternoon with something he wanted to talk about. Lex Luger had let him know that he was miserable and wanted out.

Here's Lex, at *Starrcade 1995*, taking on Mashahiro Chono.

I never really liked Lex much. He'd been at WCW when I first got there, before leaving to work for Vince. I hadn't had much opportunity to work with him face-to-face, but overall I thought he was an arrogant ass. He treated people badly and had too high an opinion of himself. And I never really thought much of his talent.

Quite frankly, he had fallen on his face. But whatever; his contract was coming due, and he wanted out. We were on the road a lot less, which meant it would be much easier to work for us. And he wanted to be in Atlanta more often, where he lived.

But between his lack of talent and piss-poor attitude, I had no interest in him whatsoever, and I told Sting that. Bringing in a guy like Lex Luger, a guy who in my opinion did nothing but bitch and complain and was a marginal talent at best, just didn't make any sense to me.

Sting really worked hard to convince me, saying things like, "Yeah, Lex can come off that way, but deep down inside he's a good guy and he really wants to make it work. He wants to prove he can be a part of the team."

Sting really sold his friend hard. And more out of respect for Sting than anything else, I agreed to take a meeting with Lex. I called him on the phone and said, "Okay, I'll meet with you, but I want no one, and I mean no one, to know about this, other than Sting and my wife, who's probably hearing me on the phone right now. I want no one, not even your attorney, to know you're talking to me."

In my mind, I was thinking that if I was going to do a deal with this guy, I wanted to use him as my shot heard around the world. Lex would be my surprise.

A Hard Bargain

There's a saying in our business: Telephone, television, tell-a-wrestler—news travels equally fast through all three media.

I didn't want anyone to know that Lex was coming over—*if* he was coming over. But I also thought that asking him to keep it a secret would act as a test to see how serious he was about being a team player. If word got out, I'd know he had leaked it.

We met in clandestine places, like Sting's garage. Lex would show up, then go up to the guest house above the garage. I'd come by about a half hour later and we'd have our meeting. It was like something out of a Bond movie.

After a few talks, I told him I was willing to give this a chance. But I was still very aware that I had to meet my budget, and I wasn't entirely convinced that Lex was being straight with me.

Lex was making—actually I can't recall exactly what he was making if I even knew at the time, but he was earning $500,000 to $750,000 when he'd left WCW a few years before. I couldn't afford that, at least not as a gamble. So I thought, here's the real test.

I told him, "All right. I'll give you a $150,000 a year. Take it or leave it.

"If this works out, if your attitude is what you say it will be, if you can fit in and be a part of the team, then we'll revisit it. I'm a fair guy. But you'll have to take the chance, because I'm taking a big chance bringing you back."

I didn't care whether he took it or not. I was of the frame of mind that if I could get him, great. Otherwise, I'd move on and figure out something else.

Lex was shocked. I think he was assuming I would welcome him back with open arms. He didn't hesitate, though. He was serious about coming back, even if it meant a short-term sacrifice and gamble on his part.

Surprise!!

Lex's contract literally expired at midnight the day before the first *Nitro* was scheduled to go on the air. Now somebody at WWE may have been asleep at the wheel, or maybe Lex just stayed off their radar screen—I wasn't on the other side of that, so I don't know. But whatever happened, no one realized what was going on. They thought Lex was still working for them.

But he wasn't. He finished working on Sunday night, September 3, 1995, then flew to Minneapolis, where *Nitro* was scheduled to debut at the Mall of America Monday night.

I didn't trust anyone in my own company to keep their mouth shut either. I was surrounded by people who had an obsessive-compulsive need to spew anything they knew to anyone who would listen.

To keep it secret, I had Lex make his own travel arrangements and get a room at a hotel in Minneapolis far from where we were staying. I had one of my security people meet him at the hotel and bring him over to the show at the last minute.

Lex literally ran onto the show about a half hour after it went on the air, stunning the audience. In their minds, Lex was a WWE guy. How could he be on WCW's new show? What was going on? What would happen next?

It was really, really effective. It set the tone for what I wanted *Nitro* to be.

Talent had jumped back and forth a lot in the past, but this was really the first time it had been done with no one knowing until the moment it happened. I can't tell you how effective it was. I'm sure Vince McMahon was in shock, but surprising him wasn't what I was after. I wanted the audience at the edge of their seats, and we'd achieved that right out of the gate. *Nitro* felt edgy—*different than any other wrestling show*—especially its direct competition, *Monday Night Raw*.

You could feel it in the air. At the end of that show, I knew we'd accomplished what we'd set out to accomplish.

Waterloo—*Not*

I took a lot of heat for doing the show at the mall. But I wanted this to feel truly special, and I couldn't really achieve that inside an arena.

Furthermore, this was the very first *Nitro* out of the box, and I wasn't sure I could put enough people in an arena to make it look good. The worst thing in the world that could have happened was to go into the Target Center in Minneapolis and only put 3,500 people in the arena. But holding it in the Mall of America, in the atrium, with three different levels of people looking down—kind of like the Roman Colliseum—that made it different, and better.

It worked. It just worked.

I did a bunch of interviews with newspapers and other media as we ramped up for the show. Much of my contentious relationship with the dirtsheet writers dates back to this time. Up until then, the writers, the critics, the inside community that didn't like me that much anyway, took a fair amount of joy from thinking that *Nitro* was going to be the thing that killed my career. *Oh, Eric Bischoff's insane. How can he possibly think this* Nitro *show would ever compete with Vince?* It went on and on and on. They had a field day predicting that *Nitro* would be an embarrassment to Turner Broadcasting and the end of WCW.

Now they had to eat crow, and they hated it. *Nitro*'s success proved just how little the wrestling "experts" really knew about the wrestling business. And I took every opportunity to point that out.

Quite honestly, I didn't know *Nitro* would be as successful as it became. I did think we would be competitive. But when the show was over, I knew in my heart that we'd achieved everything we'd set out to achieve—and more. And that's what I wanted— more.

The Monday Night Wars

Head-to-Head

Raw had been preempted by another show September 4, which was one reason we chose that night to debut. The next week we went head-to-head, starting a ratings war that would continue for years. The Monday Night Wars, as they came to be known, helped *both* WCW and WWE, bringing millions of new fans to the genre and changing the business forever. Prior to *Nitro* and the Monday Night Wars, *Raw* on USA Network netted Nielsen ratings in the 2.5 to 3 range. By the end of 1998, three years later, the combined audience regularly exceeded 8 or 9. That was a 300 percent increase in viewers.

Sometimes war is good.

We kicked butt that first week, drawing a 2.5 in the Nielson's to the WWE's 2.2. After that it went back and forth for a while, neck and neck.

From the beginning, I planned to be on *Nitro* as the main announcer—again, not because I wanted to be, but because I was the best option I had. I knew the edge and attitude I wanted to give the show, and it was easy for me to do. I became the face of *Nitro*, and relished the role.

I want to be careful how I say this, because I don't want it to sound like I'm putting myself over too much. But just about everything I had wanted to do with WCW was different than the way things were normally done. And it was successful. Because of that, I became almost intolerant of anything that was standard operating procedure when it came to producing, promoting, or building a wrestling program.

Clearly the goal now wasn't to become "competitive," it was to become number one. Over the course of the first *Nitro* show, I went from just wanting to be profitable to having the confidence that we could be number one in a television genre that had been dominated for almost fifteen years by World Wrestling Federation. Once I saw and felt the audience's reaction, I knew we were onto a winning formula.

That was an amazing amount of fuel for my fire.

It was also the beginning of my criticizing WWE on air. I positioned myself as a rebel—and WCW as the organization that was going to kick down the doors and command respect.

I wanted to turn up the volume. Way up. I was confident—if not overconfident. I wasn't aggressive—I was hyperaggressive. I'm pretty aggressive by nature—I'm aggressive in my sleep—but if I have momentum behind me like I did back then, I get hyperaggressive, and that's where my head was at. I smelled blood. Now I wanted the kill.

Pissing on the WWE Campfire

All the traditional thinkers around me cringed when I started criticizing WWE and Vince McMahon on the air. The people who worked for me were scared to death. They were afraid that what I was doing was wrong, because it was counter to what they had been taught: One never acknowledges the competition.

I not only acknowledged the competition; I pissed on their campfire.

The people around me were *so* afraid I had stepped over the line. They honestly thought Vince was going to pull some magic gorilla out of his hat while I was pulling rabbits out of mine. And some probably thought they were going to be put in a position where they'd never be able to go to work for WWE because they worked for WCW while I was in charge.

Some people have said that there was something personal between me and Vince McMahon, but that's bullshit. I'd only met the guy once, and he'd been a perfect gentleman, giving me a chance to try out for a job I wasn't qualified for. This was all about my desire to deliver.

In retrospect, some people have said that the WWE was in a weak position because of the steroid trial and the other problems Vince and the organization had dealt with during the early to mid-1990s. It's possible, I guess, but it had nothing to do with our strategy.

Nobody's going to believe this, but I didn't know or care about how they were being affected. I just paid attention to my own goals. I knew we were onto a formula that would work, and they were stuck in one that didn't. I was confident that Vince McMahon, based on everything I had heard, would dig in his heels and not react to anything we were doing. So I didn't worry about them.

Now, if I thought they would look at us and say, *Oh, wait, they're onto something—let's look at it and do it better.* Then I would have been worried. Ultimately, that's what they did—but it took them two and a half years of getting their brains beat out to really catch on.

Go Ahead, Try Our Competition

We usually knew what was going to happen on *Raw* ahead of time because their shows were taped in advance. We had no problem getting information on what had happened. We had various people whom we knew in the markets at the events who told us what had happened, but mostly the results were available online or in the dirtsheets where anyone could pick them up.

As part of my "screw the rules" formula, I began telling our viewers what WWE was doing on its show. I convinced Brad Siegel to let me start my show a couple of minutes before *Raw*, and I encouraged people to tune in to the competition because our show was so much better on every level, from production values to talent to storytelling, that I was confident people would prefer us. I *hoped* people would switch over—they'd see something very flat, and come back over to us for good.

It's like having two restaurants on the same corner, charging the same price but offering food of vastly different quality. If I have the better restaurant, I don't care if someone goes to the competition and tries it—they've just reinforced the quality of our product.

That's exactly what happened. Telling people what was going on positioned WCW as being supremely confident in its quality. I forced a taste test I knew we would win. I also started ending my show five to ten minutes after *Raw* went off the air (a strategy that WWE adapted and uses to this day) to achieve the same thing. And by breaking the rules, I reinforced the idea that we were the brash, take-no-prisoners bad boys of Monday-night TV.

New Audience

The dirtsheets and other media commentators at the time said we beat *Raw* by "stealing" their audience. We did certainly get a lot of *Raw* viewers, especially as the weeks passed. We also brought many of our Saturday viewers to Monday night. But looking back on *Nitro* from, as I like to say, 32,000 feet, it seems to me that a lot of what we did was develop a new audience.

WWE at the time had a core audience that was pretty young. We went after an older group, eighteen- to thirty-nine-year-olds, and we got them. The buzz we generated got a lot of new people sampling us. That's why I believe the majority of our growth came from an audience that hadn't been watching. It got to the point where ABC took out a full-page ad in the *Wall Street Journal* during the "up-fronts" (the period during the year when most ad sales decisions are made), trying to convince advertisers not to "Wrestle with Their Ad Dollars." This was because we were taking a big chunk out of *Monday Night Football*'s ass.

Among the other benefits of our television success, our house show business started to increase. We went from failing to draw five thousand people at an arena to drawing ten, fifteen, and twenty thousand people. It actually got to a point where people scalped tickets out in front of the arenas. The house show business, which had been losing money since day one of WCW's existence, became extremely profitable.

This period—from the moment Ted Turner threw Monday night into my lap, and for the next two or three years—remains the highlight of my professional life. There was no point where I felt anything other than elated. I felt there was nothing I couldn't do, nothing I couldn't achieve. I was working like crazy, putting in ridiculous hours, but it was all out of passion. The work I'd put in before had finally paid off. The risks, the sacrifices—even those cold winter nights with no heat when I'd fed my kids beans and venison while my cars were repossessed from my driveway—were all suddenly worth it.

To sit down and watch something like this grow before your very eyes was intoxicating. We went from being Turner Broadcasting's redheaded stepchild to being on top of the world.

Corporate Realities

Mr. ATM

Nobody in WWE would want to say, "God, Eric Bischoff and that crew down at WCW, they're more creative than us, they're smarter than us. They've got a better feel for the business than us."

It was a lot easier for people to stomach what was going on by saying, "Oh, those motherfuckers, they don't really understand anything. All they did was steal our talent and spend money. They didn't outsmart us; they outspent us. They have deep pockets. They have the resources."

Part of that was true. We *did* have financial resources that they didn't. But what was more true was that we knew what to do with it. We reinvented the business. That's what turned the tide.

Now, granted, I couldn't have gotten Hulk Hogan, I couldn't have gotten Scott Hall, we couldn't have gotten Kevin Nash—we couldn't have done the things we did at *Nitro* if we didn't have the money. We—Turner—also owned our own network; there's no question that was a huge advantage.

But there were some big disadvantages, too. As far as the corporate side was concerned, we were a pimple on a hamster's ass, despite the fact that Ted Turner liked us. For a lot of people at Turner Broadcasting, we were a lot more trouble than we were worth.

We had a high visibility when it came to lawsuits and injuries and issues related to violence on television. We attracted a lot of negative attention because of the nature of the business we were in.

We were constantly getting memos from the legal side of Turner Broadcasting trying to prevent us from making some of the same mistakes that had been made in the past.

Violence & Blood

WCW had a policy forbidding the deliberate use of blood at matches. In other words, guys weren't supposed to cut or "blade" themselves during shows, even though it was a time-honored technique for adding a little drama to the matches.

People would write in or call and say how terrible it was that they saw blood. Media reports about how AIDS could be transmitted through blood made the network sensitive to the issue. Turner Broadcasting's legal department said, "Look, it's an unnecessary risk. Don't do it."

Turner Broadcasting then tried to tell us that under no circumstances—even if it was an accident—were we to show blood. I thought that was stupid and overreacting, and wrote my own policy.

Personally, I was never a big fan of blood. Blood isn't something that makes people enjoy the product more. I think if occasionally it happens in the course of a match by accident, it happens. You show it. But if the match has so little drama that you're forced to cut your head open, you probably messed up earlier on.

Several of the wrestlers, especially the old-timers, were upset. Blood was part of the formula that they had grown up with. They felt that by not being able to do it, they were at a disadvantage. But I think it's overrated, and I don't see how not adding it into the storylines ever hurt us.

Sharing Production Teams

Another negative of being at Turner had to do with our production people.

Wrestling is a unique business. You can't put an ad in the paper and expect the best people to walk through the door with their résumés in hand. The talent pool just isn't that deep. This is true even for the midlevel production people. If you're looking for the best ENG crew to do a football game, you can find plenty of qualified people just by putting an ad in the trades, and find five or ten of the very best in the business. The same is not true in wrestling. Wrestling is a unique product even to produce.

Our problem was that most of the people producing our shows weren't WCW employees. They were Turner Broadcasting System crew members who did everything TBS did—the Hawks and the Braves, for example. We would get them as they became available.

Because of the status of WCW within the Turner organization, we didn't always get the cream of the crop. If the question was, *Are the Hawks going to get the A list or is the WCW going to get the A list, the answer was a no-brainer.*

That's not to say that we didn't have good people. But on any given week or month we might have two or three or four different guys doing the same job. They'd get transferred around based on the needs of the company. Oftentimes, we'd have cameramen posted on the ring corners who were phenomenal shooters when it came to basketball or baseball, but didn't have a clue about wrestling. Unless you've been around a wrestling ring for a long time, and you know how to anticipate what's going to happen, by the time you get your camera to the action, it's gone. And that made production challenging.

Not only did that remain a problem as we grew successful, it became more challenging in different ways. When we were that small company on TBS producing a weekly show in front of 750 winos in downtown Atlanta, our matches weren't that hard to shoot. But when you start producing complicated shows in front of 30,000 people in prime time, not having the best in the business becomes a real handicap.

The Downside of Success

When a small business makes the right moves and starts to grow, it can become a real American success story. But that success can bring problems as well, especially if the growth is too fast. The work that needs to be done increases exponentially. Mistakes that your customers might have overlooked or not noticed when you were small become major disasters when they're multiplied by a thousand. People who might have been okay at a job when there wasn't too much pressure may suddenly be in way over their heads when the screws are tightened.

We had a lot of the those problems as we became successful. A number were at least partially due to my lack of experience. Others were due to the politics that were so prevalent in the wrestling business. The culture of the business encourages backbiting, maneuvering to get ahead, and plain old foolishness. Layer that on top of a corporation with its own potential for political skullduggery, and it's a recipe for disaster.

One lesson I learned too late: when you buy out a company—or in my case, when you take over a company—it's often better in the long run to start from scratch, rather than trying to work with people who were part of the problem in the first place. We didn't do that, partly because it was hard to find qualified people, and partly because I believed I could rehabilitate some of the cancer that I inherited. But in hindsight, I really should have cleaned house when I took over the company early on.

I learned another very valuable lesson during this period: managing success is sometimes much more difficult than creating it in the first place.

Pulling the Trigger on Jesse & Steve

Firing the Governor

Ironically, I may be best known in some circles as the guy who fired Jesse Ventura and Steve Austin, two guys who went on to considerable fame after I let them go.

Jesse Ventura came into WCW from WWE as a color commentator in January 1992, when I was still a third-string announcer. At the time, he was a big star. He got a lot of attention. Every time he came into the CNN Center, he got the red carpet treatment. He was a big fish in a little pond.

When Jesse heard that Hogan was coming in, he started thinking about what that meant to him. As they say in the wrestling business, he started stirring the shit behind the scenes, badmouthing Hogan at every opportunity, talking about things that had happened in the past that put Hogan in a bad light.

Whether they were true or not true, in my opinion, was irrelevant. When a guy like Jesse Ventura, who was making a lot of money, started pissing and moaning because he was jealous—and no longer the biggest fish in our little pond—it really irritated me. It made me lose a tremendous amount of respect for Jesse.

The situation just kept deteriorating. It got to the point where Jesse would come in to do his work and literally pout like a child. He'd have a bad attitude and mope around the studio. He'd treat people badly, show up late, and just in general behave like a spoiled brat.

One day in 1995, I believe, we were between shows at a Disney taping. There was always a little downtime between shows, an hour or maybe a half hour. All of a sudden we couldn't find Jesse, who was supposed to be doing color commentary. We were ready to start taping—the crowd was there, Schiavone was at the play-by-play desk, the wrestlers were ready—but we had no Jesse Ventura.

Now mind you, this is a guy we're paying close to a half million dollars a year to basically work a day or two a week. By anyone's standards, that's a lot of money for a talent who doesn't have a lot of impact on the product.

We scrambled all over the place, looking for him while the audience and crew sat twiddling their thumbs. I finally found Jesse in another sound stage, sleeping in a dressing room.

I looked at him. He had three days' growth on his face and

looked like a wino sleeping on a park bench. I said to myself, *This is insane. This guy is running around, badmouthing Hogan, badmouthing the company, and walking around like one big dark cloud. I'm paying an entire production crew to suck air because this idiot is taking a nap in the middle of the day.*

It dawned me that I no longer wanted to do business with Jesse Ventura. The fact that all he did was bitch and moan when I woke him up confirmed it.

That's Steve Austin on the far left, not yet stone cold.

I didn't fire him, because he had a contract. I just quit using him and let his contract run out. I thought he was cancer.

Stone Cold Gone

Steve Austin was another guy I fired roughly around the same time.

The truth is, the best thing I ever did for Steve Austin was to fire him—though I assure you, my idea at the time wasn't to set him on the road to becoming a megastar.

Steve went through a lot, mentally and physically, during that time, and he came out of it—well, you know where he came out: he became one of the most famous wrestlers of all time. That says a lot about him as a performer, and even more about him as a man. My firing him—no matter whether I was justified or not—added a lot of fuel to an already competitive guy, but what he achieved was completely his own.

A lot of ink has been spilled over what happened—all of it wrong, at least from my perspective. Here's the real story.

Steve wasn't Stone Cold Steve Austin then. He hadn't developed or probably even thought of that character. But he was a pretty important wrestler in the WCW universe before Hogan came in. He'd been a tag team partner with the late Brian Pillman, and wrestled solo as "Stunning" Steve Austin, taking WCW's U.S. title in 1993.

When the word first broke that Hogan was coming to WCW, Steve came to me with a storyline that he wanted to work with Hogan. I don't recall the details now, but I do remember it had something to do with Steve being some kind of relative of Hogan's—Steve had a little bit of the Hogan hairline at the time. There was enough meat on the bone that I thought we could work with it. But I also knew that Hogan wanted his first program to be with Ric Flair. So despite the quality of the idea, there was no way it would work at that point.

I didn't handle the situation as well as I could have. I should have said to him, "Hey, Steve, here's what's really going on. I like your idea, and maybe we can work on it in the fall or early next year. Let's keep it in the hopper, and in the meantime, here's where we're going and why."

Had I done that, Steve might have had a better attitude. But I didn't. I just said something like, "Sure, let me think about it," or something to that effect, and let it go at that. Knowing Steve the way I know him now, he probably took that as a slap in the face.

Just like Jesse, Steve drifted into the bad-attitude category. Add to that some personal issues and injuries, and you have a guy walking around with a kind of pissed-off taste in his mouth.

Steve's contract was coming due, and we were negotiating a new one. I think he was making about two hundred or three hundred grand a year at the time. At that point, I wanted to keep Steve on the roster, despite the fact that he was out of action because of an injury.

"I'm Not Home"

Steve lived in Atlanta. Even though he was out with an injury, we wanted him to come in for an interview we were filming at Center Stage in Atlanta. He didn't show.

Given that there was some disorganization in the WCW at the time, it may have been that he didn't know he was scheduled for an interview, though I don't believe that was the case. In any event, I asked Tony Schiavone to give him a call and have him come in so we could do the interview. The idea was to keep the character alive on TV, even though he was out with an injury.

Tony came back and told me that he had talked to Steve's wife, who said he wasn't around.

Which would have been okay, except that Tony told me he heard Steve yelling in the background, "Tell that son of a bitch I'm not home, and you don't know where I am."

When I heard that, in my mind, Steve was gone. That just wasn't acceptable. When I got back to the office the next day, I said, *"Okay, send him a letter—we're done with him."*

I've been criticized for not firing Steve in person. Certainly Steve made an issue of it later. But given what Tony had told me, I didn't feel like I owed him any other type of response. Steve and I have since spoken about this. I have to admit, the way I handled it wasn't great, though given the same situation I would probably react the same way.

Within months of leaving us in the fall of 1995, Steve wrestled for Extreme Championship Wrestling, better known as ECW. He went from there to WWE, where he evolved into the Stone Cold Steve Austin character. You know the rest.

Of course, given what happened later, leaving the WCW was a blessing in disguise. Steve wouldn't have been able to become that rattlesnake character in WCW at the time. We had too many guys in front of him. But when he went over to WWE, there wasn't a lot of talent he had to rise above. Sometimes it's better to be lucky than good—and in Steve's case, he was lucky *and* good. He was lucky to be in a company that needed him at the right time. He didn't have to overcome a lot of politics and bs to prove that he was capable of doing what he could do.

Controversy & Trucks

900 Gossip

In the early and mid-1990s, WCW and WWE used 900 lines as a way of adding revenue and generating interest for the product. Fans would call up the numbers, paying by the minute for inside information that wasn't available elsewhere. This was before the Internet was really popular, remember, and the lines—some of them independent—were a source of supposed inside information.

"Mean" Gene and Sting.

They were also a source of controversy. In order for the 900 lines to be successful, they had to piss people off. So they were inherently a problem.

One of the 900-number deals we struck was with Gene Okerlund, the well-known wrestling announcer who'd come over to WCW. The deal let him share in the profits from the line. This meant that he had a self-serving reason to be controversial.

Overall, I didn't have too big a problem with that, but the talent often did. And sometimes we were criticized by people outside the industry. At one point in 1995 Phil Mushnick wrote a column in the *New*

York Post ripping Gene—and us—for plugging a story on the death of Jerry Blackwell with a tease along the lines of: *What famous wrestler just died?* When you called up, you had to listen until the end of the taped message, staying on the line for several minutes, before hearing the details. We drew a fair amount of complaints on that one.

I don't remember any of the incidents specifically, but there were times when the line threatened to get out of hand. I've always had a great relationship with Gene, but nonetheless, you give Gene enough rope and he'll hang you with it. Wrestlers and the crazy shit they do gave Gene a lot of material. Add to that the "scoops" he was able to create by, if not fabricating them, blowing things out of proportion—well, he rubbed a lot of people the wrong way.

But, at ninety-nine cents or a dollar-fifty a minute, the line and others like it were a great source of cash. And there were so many other things going on that were more important, it was hard to be sensitive to it—even though I fell victim to it myself from time to time.

It was uncomfortable, but at the end of the month I looked at how much money WCW made. *Okay. So I'm a little pissed off. Who cares?*

Monster Trucks

Sometimes when you try things that were never done before, you find out why—they're bad ideas. But I was willing to take that chance.

In our quest to do something different, we hooked up with a monster truck company in 1995. We integrated monster trucks into several skits and shows, including *Halloween Havoc 1995* where we drove—or appeared to drive—a monster truck off a five-story building.

That's *very* different. But the monster truck–wrestling connection didn't work.

The monster truck idea was part of a product integration strategy aimed at launching a licensing platform. The opportunity, when we were approached with it, made a tremendous amount of sense. But I made the mistake of proceeding with the idea before I had a definitive deal signed, sealed, and delivered. As I committed to the

idea, the people I was doing business with became more aggressive in pursuing their terms—they wanted too much from us. So much so that I lost interest pursuing it. The deal was no longer fair.

I learned a little about negotiating and leverage from that. I had taken the people I'd started negotiating with at face value from the beginning, and that was a mistake. They turned out not to be as fair as I thought.

To use a poker analogy—you just don't commit to the pot without knowing that you have a good hand. I'll never do that again.

Or at least, I'll try not to.

Wrestling with Peace

Ironies

Creating *Nitro* was such a major event that it tended to overshadow everything else that WCW did in 1995. But looking back, there were a lot of remarkable things that happened that year. One was our trip to North Korea.

The wrestling matches that we took part in were aired during the summer of 1995, right before *Nitro* went on the air. But we actually went to Korea in April. While the visit didn't make much of an impact on WCW, I can still recall it vividly. It was like visiting the far side of the moon.

By early 1995, we had rebuilt our relationship with New Japan. Antonio Inoki, a former Japanese senator and then chairman of the company, called me and asked for some help contacting Muhammad Ali, whom he had fought in a boxing-versus-wrestling fight in the 1970s. Ali had been recently part of a WCW event, and I was able to get them in touch.

Antonio Inoki is an interesting guy and a bit of an enigma. A successful politician, he served in the Japanese House of Council, which is similar to our senate. But he became involved in a scandal that killed his political career, forcing him to resign from his party leadership post.

He'd been a wrestler before going into politics, and in the mid-1990s he turned to wrestling to resurrect his political career. Inoki proposed to bring Japanese wrestlers to Pyongyang, North Korea's capital, as part of a peace festival.

Let's wrap ourselves up in the irony of that for a second:

Wrestling.

World peace.

Okay?

Actually, the idea was not quite as ironic or far-fetched as it sounds. Japan and Korea have always had extremely strained relations, going back just about to the beginning of time, when they would take turns pillaging each other's country. Things had been especially bad with North Korea ever since the beginning of the Cold War. Just as other sports have sometimes been used to thaw relations between different countries, Inoki hoped that wrestling could help bring the two old enemies together.

And if it worked for Japan and North Korea, he thought, why not add a few American wrestlers to the mix?

A Love for Travel

When I got the phone call and I was asked if we'd be interested in bringing some of our guys to North Korea, I have to tell you that, on a personal level, I was excited.

The one thing I liked about school when I was very young was learning about other cultures. I still remember the first time I heard about Marco Polo and the Silk Road trade route. Those things were fascinating. I would drift off in class, fantasizing about faraway places. As an adult, traveling and experiencing different things remained part of my nature.

So when I got that phone call and the opportunity to go to a place that is off-limits to Americans, I jumped at it. I said, "Absolutely, no problem."

I didn't discuss it with anyone. Didn't ask for permission. Didn't think about the fact that, as an American, I was prohibited from going to North Korea and spending money there.

I also just assumed that a lot of the guys would feel the way I felt.

Well, that came back to bite me in the ass. It turned out to be more difficult than I expected to get the wrestlers to come along. Hogan played with his Fu Manchu a minute, looked down at the floor, then back at me. "Hmm, brother. Don't think I can make that one."

Ric Flair didn't think it was a good idea, actually—but to his credit, he agreed to go along. Hawk, Animal, Chris Benoit, Scott Norton, and a couple of other guys agreed. We put together a pretty good team.

Best of all, Muhammad Ali agreed to come as well.

Permission? Who Needs Permission?

So how do you get State Department permission to visit a country that's an international pariah and that's officially at war with the United States?

The short answer is: You don't. You just do it.

The State Department wouldn't really know about our trip until we were there. We weren't going to fly directly to North Korea from the States; there was no way to do that. We would go to Tokyo, perform with New Japan, then get on a plane and go with them to North Korea. By the time the news reached the United States, we'd probably be back in Japan, if not home.

I went over to CNN and told some people I knew what I was thinking about. "What's the worst thing that will happen if the government finds out?"

They said, "Well, they might detain you. They might question you for a few days. They might hold you. They might fine you."

I said, "Okay, am I going to go to jail?"

If I was going to go to jail, I might have reconsidered. Maybe. But if it was just going to be a pain in the ass, I really wanted to go.

They said, "Nah, it's not really likely you'll go to jail."

So I gathered the troops, and off we went.

Psychological Warfare

We did the show in Tokyo with New Japan, then jumped on a North Korean military transport. It's a pretty short jaunt to North Korea from Japan, but nonetheless, we were on a military transport. It just changes the way you feel about shit from the get-go.

As we were getting ready to land, I looked out the window. The landscape absolutely amazed me. It was barren of life. It was a desolate desert. I live in the desert, but the North Korean desert looks nothing like the desert I know. I can't describe how desolate it was. I thought to myself, *My God, how does anybody live here?*

The people who met us were superficially friendly. They were very direct and professional. But I realized that in their minds, it was still 1951. They were still at war with the rest of the world. It was evident in everything we saw when we stepped off the plane.

The drab architecture, the way they looked at foreigners, everything.

The first thing they did was separate us into pairs. Sonny Onoo was with me, and we got paired up. We were assigned an interpreter who was actually a member of the North Korean secret police. She was supposed to stick to us the entire time we were there.

She asked us for our passports, which were immediately confiscated when we stepped into the airport. Passports are about as useless as tits on a boar hog in a place like North Korea, but taking them away let you know they were in control, not you.

Leave Our Women Alone

We got into cars and drove from the airport into downtown Pyongyang. Along the way we had to stop and pay homage to the dictator's father, Kim Il Sung, who had died the previous year. We were each given a flower to lay at the bottom of a giant statue of him in the center of the city.

Masa Saito is to my left.

nWo—gave *Nitro* the push it needed to beat *Raw.*

Ric Flair with Bill Shaw, just before *Halloween Havoc;*
he had *just* signed his new contract.

The Greatest—Muhammad Ali and our North Korean "interpreter."

My gals and my bike just before the Sturgis ride.

Sting, Scott Steiner, Miss Elizabeth, DDP, Ellis Edwards, and Big Bubba
getting lost on the way to Sturgis—
also know as the "thumbs-up-our-ass tour."

Gloving up George Foreman for a sparing session with Hogan.

Goldberg and Hogan, two of WCW's biggest draws.

Vince and all the boys have always treated me with respect.

That was weird enough, but what made it unnerving were all the North Korean cameras filming us. They were old-style cameras, the sort that haven't been used anywhere outside North Korea since, oh, 1930. They were filming this for propaganda purposes.

I'm thinking, *This is pretty fucked up.*

We got back into our cars and were on the way to the hotel. The interpreter turned around and said, "I must tell you. We have rules in North Korea. This is not America. You must leave our women alone."

I said, "Excuse me?"

"This is not America. In North Korea, you must leave our women alone."

"No problem. I'll be happy to do that."

We stopped at another monument, which looked like the Arc de Triomphe. Again, the newsreel cameras rolled. Our interpreter told us this was a war memorial that was put up to honor the tens of thousands of North Koreans who were incinerated by the Americans during the war—according to her, 52,000 in one night of bombing. I didn't buy it, but that wasn't the issue.

I didn't know what sort of reaction she was trying to get from me. I was aware of the cameras, and I thought to myself, the way I react is either going to make this trip interesting and positive, or interesting and negative.

I didn't want to appear sympathetic, but at the same time I didn't want to antagonize the North Koreans. For one of the few times in my life, I thought about how to react. I acknowledged what she said but kept my face as blank as possible. She asked questions about a particular bombing raid, whether I was aware of it. I said no, and just cut my answers to her questions very, very short. I didn't want my answers being edited in such a way that they could be used to somehow glorify the regime.

It was uncomfortable, but finally it was over. We went to our hotel, staying there for the rest of the night.

A Run of My Life

At the time I was running five to seven miles a day. I liked to run early in the morning, before I had breakfast.

The next morning I got up early, got dressed, and trotted out the back door of the hotel for my run. It was about 6 A.M., right before Pyongyang came to life. I had on these bright red sweatpants and a bright yellow sweatshirt and a black hat.

Pyongyang has enormously wide streets, even though there are almost no cars in the country. The streets are wide because they're designed for aircrafts if the airports are bombed. In the morning, starting about 6:30 or 6:45, they filled with North Koreans, all wearing their dark blue or gray suits, walking to work. These people were all really little, their growth stunted by the famines that had plagued the country for a decade or more by that time. I didn't see anyone over five-five the whole time I was there, and they were very frail and gray; so many of them looked close to death.

I was five-eleven and two hundred pounds. I looked like King freaking Kong to these people. And not only was I a westerner—probably the first and only one many of them saw in person in their lives—I was dressed in strange, bright red and yellow clothes. You cannot imagine the horror on these people's faces. They parted like the Red Sea as I ran through downtown Pyongyang.

I saw things I'd only read about up until then. Massive murals honoring the Communist Party workers were painted on the buildings. On the street corners, schoolkids gathered to sing nationalistic hymns honoring the state and Kim Jong-Il before going to school.

It was great until I got back to the hotel.

My Korean minder was fucking livid. She never imagined that I would get up at six in the morning and go for a run. She made it clear from that point forward that that would never happen again. Nonetheless, it was one of the coolest experiences I've ever had in my life.

Never a Bad Word

Having never experienced a Communist country, and especially one still stuck in the 1950s, I didn't know what to expect. I anticipated our rooms would be bugged and that kind of shit, but I had no idea of the extent to which it was true.

Scott Norton found out.

Now Scott is a great guy. He has this powerful, deep baritone voice that shakes the walls when he talks. He's about six-three, six-four, weighs three or four hundred pounds. Powerful guy. WCW fans will remember him wrestling with Ice Train as the Fire & Ice tag team around this time.

But Scott hates traveling. I think he'd rather take an ice pick to the rib cage than get on a plane. He can't stand being on buses because he gets claustrophobic. He's in the wrong business, because in our business, you have to travel a lot.

Anyway, soon after we got to Korea, Scott went to take a bath. The bathtub separated from the wall. Well, that started shit. He got on the phone—how he figured out how to use it is beyond me, since no one else could. He called his wife and bitched about everything: the room, the food, the secret police, North Korea in general. He mf'd these people all night long.

Clearly, there was someone listening in who could understand English.

When Scott came back to his hotel room the next day, the sheets were stripped off his bed and the room was turned upside down. No one would clean it or go near his room for the rest of the trip.

We were real careful with what we said and did after that.

One night we had dinner with some of the dignitaries, and were escorted out to watch a military parade. It looked like the films of the Soviet Union in the 1950s. At one point, someone whispered in my ear that the country's dictator, Kim Jong Il, was standing near us.

I wanted to turn around and look. But I thought, *You know what? This is one wacky cracker.* There were news stories about Kim

Jong Il at that time, detailing his tastes for young European actresses. They would make the mistake of coming over to "visit" and become semi-permanent "guests" of the state. I decided I'd just sit there and mind my own business.

The Wrestling

The wrestling in North Korea was amazing. The crowds were tremendous. The first night we had something like 170,000 people, and the next night 180,000. To be in a stadium with that many people was just unbelievable. I sat in a VIP dignitary section, and even from there, the ring looked like a postage stamp.

North Korean schoolkids put on an incredible show with banners before the main event, making it look like a giant dove was flying in a circle through the stadium. There were thousands and thousands of kids involved in the show, making different designs, from birds to flowers. Very impressive.

Then came the wrestling. I sat there thinking, These people have no idea who the Americans are. They can't possibly know who Ric Flair is, who the Road Warriors are, who the Steiners are. They don't have television. But they clap when they're supposed to. And they seem to be having a good time.

I wondered what they could possibly be thinking when they saw Ric Flair come out in his flowered, sequined robe as the *2001 Space Odyssey* theme blared through the speakers. I just kind of sat back and enjoyed it all.

Ali

I developed a pretty good friendship with Muhammad Ali on this trip. We didn't really get into any trouble for the trip, but I have to say, I would have been willing to go to jail just for that opportunity.

Muhammad Ali has a difficult time speaking because he suffers from Parkinson's syndrome, but his mind and his sense of humor are very sharp. On this trip, Muhammad told me that much of the "loudmouth Cassius Clay" that people came to know in the 1960s was due to the fact that as a young man, he used to go to the wrestling matches in Louisville and was fascinated by Gorgeous George. Muhammad emulated some of Gorgeous George's character because he saw how well it worked. Muhammad is a big wrestling fan and understood what it was all about.

Muhammad Ali is one of the very few people I've ever wanted to meet or get to know. I'm not really drawn to celebrities, despite what people think. I would have liked to have met Ronald Reagan, I would have liked to have met John Wayne, I would have liked to have met Abraham Lincoln. But other than that, I can't think of a lot of people who have really interested me—with the exception of Muhammad Ali.

I've always been a huge fan of Muhammad. As I've gotten older, I've come to understand what he stood for and the sacrifices he made during the 1960s and '70s. In many ways he's an unsung hero in American history, and I'm proud to have had a chance to spend time with him.

A year or so later, shortly after the 1996 Olympics, we met again while I was with my wife and kids in Japan. Muhammad asked me what I thought about him lighting the Olympic torch. I started to tell Muhammad that I thought it was a great moment. He stopped me in mid-sentence and asked me if I thought he embarrassed himself because of his hand tremor. I got tears in my eyes as I told him how excited I was while watching, and how proud I was for him.

Our Own Little War

Madusa

I've known Madusa—Debra Ann Micelli, who wrestled under the name Alundra Blayze in WWE—since 1987, when she started with Verne Gagne in the AWA. We'd been pretty good friends, actually.

So when she called me in the fall of 1995 and said she wanted to come over to WCW, I said, absolutely.

"And by the way, why don't you bring that championship belt with you?"

Madusa had just won the championship from Bertha Faye. She was pretty reluctant to do it; quite frankly, I talked to her into it. I'm sure to this day she wishes I hadn't, because it made it very difficult for her to go back to WWE later on.

Madusa came out on national television and walked over to the announcer's table. She gave her little promo, saying she was coming to WCW. All the while, she held her women's championship belt in her hand. When she was done, she dropped it into the garbage can.

To people outside the wrestling business, it was just another stunt. To people inside the wrestling business, it was sacrilege. Denigrating someone else's belt on national television was about as low a blow as you could deliver.

But, given that opportunity I took every advantage and ended up with a big ol' smile on my face. It was just another one of those in-your-face, fuck-you-WWE moves that I liked. It spoke to the attitude and aggression that I wanted our brand to have.

If I'd have thought about it a little more, I probably would have put the title on a fat little midget and called it the "other" championship, but I didn't think of it at the time.

Damn it.

I'm sure it pissed off the people in Titan Tower. But the funny thing is, you can see the moment on one of the highlights videos that WWE plays these days to warm up the crowd.

Time Warner

In late 1995, something was going on behind the scenes at Turner Broadcasting that would have far-reaching effects on WCW, though we didn't know it at the time. Ted Turner began talking with Time

Warner about selling a controlling share of the company to the corporate media giant.

The takeover of Turner by Time Warner—or the merger of the
two companies, depending on your perspective, I suppose—has
been documented in many places. Time Warner had been a large
minority stockholder for several years. Among the most onerous
provisions of the deal that brought Time Warner—and hundreds of
millions of dollars—to Turner was an agreement effectively giving
the corporation veto power over expenditures greater than $2 mil-
lion. Ted continually chafed under this and other provisions of the
deal. Eventually, though, he decided to strike a new deal that would
make the Turner Broadcasting empire part of Time Warner. The
merger went through in 1996.

Ted Turner remained a large stockholder of the combined company, and remained the day-to-day head of Turner Broadcasting—
and WCW's ultimate boss. But the boardrooms and executive suites
soon hosted battles far nastier than anything that took place on
Nitro. As a tiny division within a relatively small part of the company, WCW had no part in those fights. But like the rest of the corporate divisions, we had to live with the results.

I failed to recognize what the long-term implications of a merger
of that magnitude meant. It was one of my biggest mistakes ever. I
simply had no idea what the politics or nuances would be like.

When we heard about the merger talks, I took everything I
heard at face value. I still believed in Ted Turner, and I couldn't
imagine a situation where Ted Turner's opinion wouldn't matter a
heck of a lot.

I remember being invited to a Christmas party at Terry McGuirk's
home around this time, and meeting Gerald Levin, the head of Time
Warner, for the first time. He seemed like a nice old guy, even kind of
harmless.

Okay, so my people-reading skills were not up to this level of play.
Levin and Ted were patting each other on the back, and there

seemed like a lot of love in the room. I could never have imagined it was the beginning of the end.

In the Money

We finished 1995 in the black, the first time *ever* that WCW had turned a profit. Everything was working. We were firing on all eight cylinders. For the first time, we were no longer that bastard stepchild around the CNN Center.

If you recall, earlier in the year I'd made a bet with Harry Anderson about turning a profit. December 24 or 26 or whatever it was, we had a party for WCW employees at a little Mexican restaurant in downtown Atlanta. In front of three or four dozen WCW employees, Harry Anderson made good on the bet, getting down on his hands and knees to hand me the dollar.

Harry was a great sport about it. He had a fantastic sense of humor.

Bulletproof

Like I've said, by this time I walked around with a bit of a swagger. I took advantage of the political capital I had. Any time there was a political discussion or debate that put me at odds with someone on the corporate side of Turner, I would force that hand. More often than not, I won.

Maybe if I'd known what was going to happen, I would have played a more sophisticated political game. I wouldn't have been so aggressive. I wouldn't have taken as many risks, politically, as I did. I wasn't crazy, but I was confident, and it showed. If there were things that were important for my brand, my employees, I would fight aggressively, and I would fight dirty if I had to.

Not good in corporate politics.

But I wasn't thinking about that then. I was thinking, I'm Eric Bischoff. I've made this division profitable. I've had the head of finance on his hands and knees before me.

I had one of the highest-rated shows on cable. I could get what I wanted. In my mind, I was bulletproof. My stroke in the company shot through the roof of the CNN Tower.

WCW had had an amazing year—but 1996 was going to be even better.

Loose Cannons

Billionaire Ted

WWE was getting spanked. Rather than finding a direction that would work for them, they struck back in a number of ineffectual ways. Probably the funniest were the sketches aired on *Raw* starring a satirical character based on Ted Turner called "Billionaire Ted."

A lot has been written about the Billionaire Ted sketches, about how terrible the people at Turner thought they were. Supposedly WCW wanted to sue the tights off McMahon's wrestlers for them.

The truth is, we all thought they were kind of funny.

I felt a little bit bad, because it was a parody, and parodies are never complimentary to the subject. But at the same time, the skits didn't really hurt us. I thought they were a funny little attempt to get into the game and get competitive, but I knew they wouldn't be effective. WWE didn't have a clear understanding of why their audience had left them, and wouldn't acknowledge the fact that we found a formula that was successful. All they had left was to make fun of us.

It didn't bother me, and it really didn't bother Ted. We all thought, *Oh man, Ted is going to be hot.* I wasn't in the room, but Harvey Schiller told me that Ted laughed his ass off when he saw them. He thought they were funny as hell.

Legal Action

Billionaire Ted didn't scare me, and neither did threats of lawsuits and the flurry of letters that accompanied them.

Feeling under the gun, World Wrestling Federation had their lawyers threaten lawsuits for restraint of trade and other alleged commercial crimes and misdemeanors. They hoped—I guess—to try and scare us off. Again, they couldn't really figure out what we were doing, or maybe they couldn't really admit to themselves that we were smarter than they were, so they tried to scare us. They stirred the legal pot, hoping to rile the board of directors and shareholders.

Of course, lawyers being lawyers, any time we got a letter, our lawyers wanted to send one back. They had me write one that said, in polite legal language, stick it up your ass. Vince McMahon was obviously impressed with my prose; he read it on the air.

The kind of muck that was being thrown back and forth—they accused us of not having a drug-testing policy, for instance—defined the old expression, "The pot calling the kettle black." But things took on a life of their own, and eventually WWE filed a lawsuit. We countersued, just to show that we were not going to back down. To me, individually, and to the company, the whole thing was transparent and fairly silly.

Brian Pillman

I like keeping storylines secret. I knew it was next to impossible in my own organization to keep things secret. So there were times when I would work on a storyline with someone independent of everyone else, keeping it between me and him. Brian Pillman and his loose-cannon angle was one of the first.

Brian could be a very dark person to be around, depending on where his head was at, but he could also be a lot of fun. He had a great mind for the business. A lot of guys have a good imagination and can come up with ideas about how their characters can be used; only a select few can do that for other characters. Brian had that ability. He could look at other people and come up with ideas to enhance their character.

Brian and I had a good working relationship and a pretty good personal relationship. Brian came up with an idea for an angle where he would portray a character who might do just about anything at any moment, a character totally unpredictable, on the verge of snapping at any given moment, who might just be a little crazy.

I really liked the whole loose-cannon thing. It went directly to the philosophy of doing things differently and continually surprising the viewer.

By the beginning of 1996, Brian was playing the character not just when he was in the ring but outside as well. I remember once when we were in Las Vegas. We were doing the show at the MGM Grand, but I had a room at the Barbary Coast, where I could enjoy a little privacy coming and going without being seen by the people who throng the MGM. Everyone knew we stayed at that hotel, and they could stake out the elevators. Any time you came through, you had to make your way through hundreds of fans. So I would typically stay down the street under an assumed name.

One night my wife and I were at the bar having a drink. In walked Brian Pillman, acting normal and getting ready to check in. He glanced my way and must have seen me across the lobby.

He went showbiz immediately, causing an immense scene. This whole loose-cannon character came to life because he and I just happened to be in the same place. He knew what he was doing, and I knew what he was doing: furthering the image of himself as a lunatic, just in case someone happened to see us both there at the same time. I thought that was pretty cool.

Brian had a real ability to make the audience wonder if what they were seeing was real or not. That's part of the beauty of our business. A lot of the magic of wrestling comes from the blurring of the line between reality and show business. It enhances the suspension of disbelief.

Working the Talent

In early 1996, we decided we would take his loose-cannon character as far as we could take it—up to the point of me releasing Brian.

He would go over to ECW and badmouth me and WCW. At some point, he would come back.

We were going to use it, and go further than anyone had ever gone before. People would really believe it was true. That was our agreement.

Wrestling being wrestling, I knew there was a possibility that I was being worked. Releasing Brian let him sign a contract for more money at WWE; it also meant he might not come back. I was willing to take the risk, because if we could follow through on it, it would be a phenomenal storyline.

No one else was in on it, but as time went on, a few wrestlers figured it out. I know Hulk Hogan did. I remember I was doing play-by-play on *Nitro*, and something happened inside the ring. I don't remember what the incident was, but for some reason Hulk realized it was all a work. Hulk was pissed that I hadn't shared it with him.

My assistant, Janie Engle, came up to me during a break. She was white as a ghost. "Eric, Hogan just came up to me and said, well, he wanted me to tell you that you can go to hell."

He didn't explain why but I knew. Eventually the wrestlers were split about fifty-fifty on whether it was real or not. When I could do that to professionals, guys who were the most cynical in the business, I knew I was achieving my goals. If they didn't know, the audience didn't know.

The wrestlers didn't like it, of course, because they felt like they were being worked. But I didn't really care.

Was *I* Worked?

Brian left according to plan, and immediately began tearing me down on ECW—one of the many, many times that someone would use me to get over with an audience. He got a big hit there, and went from ECW to WWE.

Was *I* the one who was worked? After all, I'd let him out of his contract to go to the competition, where presumably he was paid more. Some people were definitely convinced I was.

I don't think so, though the truth of the matter is, none of us will ever know who was working who. I wasn't surprised that Brian signed with WWE. We'd already agreed to take it as far as it would go. Besides, it wasn't a blow to us, because we were well on our way, with a tremendous amount of momentum.

All the while he was at ECW and WWE, Brian called me, and we would shoot the shit and talk. We weren't good buddies or anything, but we would talk every six weeks or two months. In my mind, when we felt the time was right for him to come back, he would.

Unfortunately, Brian died before that happened.

Drug Abuse

I talked to Brian just a few weeks before he was found dead in a hotel room October 5, 1997. The media speculated about prescription pills being involved in Brian's death, but the coroner found that he had died of natural causes.

I guess because I thought of Brian as a friend, and the respect I felt for him, I wanted to support his family and let them know that—despite what the general audience might have thought—there was no bad blood between WCW and Brian. So I flew out to the funeral. On the trip and afterward, I reflected on what a terrible waste it was. He'd been so vibrant, so full of energy. He'd beaten cancer—Brian had been born with throat cancer—and now at thirty-five he was gone.

Brian's death provoked stories about drug abuse, despite the coroner's findings. Accusations of the misuse of everything from prescriptions to steroids to other illegal substances haunt pro wrestling and the sports and entertainment industries to this day.

There's no denying it's a problem. At WCW we had a drug test procedure in place. But as we've seen in sports from the Olympics to pro baseball, drug testing isn't perfect. The technology then was a lot less advanced than it is now. There were multiple ways then—as there still are—for individuals to avoid testing positive.

Steroids are a hot topic right now, but in my experience, the real issue isn't the performance-enhancing drugs; it's the prescription drugs. I know when I was at WCW guys would get prescriptions from doctors and then abuse those prescriptions. That's hard to regulate.

Off Help

When I came back from Brian's funeral, I gave a short speech to the wrestlers, suggesting we would help anyone who had a problem get help. I tried to encourage people to look at their own drug use, especially of prescription drugs. I didn't want anyone who needed help to be worried about losing their jobs if they tried to kick a habit. I made it clear we would give them whatever time they needed.

There were definitely people who had problems. They ignored me.

I want to be honest about this without beating up our business. In the entertainment business in general, performers—actors, musicians, athletes—are probably more prone to illegal and prescription drug abuse than your average citizen, because of the pressures, the lifestyle, and the personalities that are drawn to our business. People in the entertainment business are living life to the fullest. They're in the spotlight a lot of the time, even when they're not performing. That's a different kind of pressure than most people understand. People in the entertainment industry are prone to find ways to self-medicate that are not very healthy.

Pranks

Wrestlers are always pulling things, and sometimes you just have to laugh. Johnny Grunge once got into a bit of trouble for "borrowing" one of the company's production trucks. The word "stealing" may have been tossed around at the time, but it was just a prank. The truck, if I'm recalling this correctly, would have been David Crockett's responsibility, and apparently Crockett was the target of the prank.

David was a great guy, a real loyal person, and I owe him a debt of gratitude—he went all out to support me, going all the way back to the Disney days. He went to war for me, and he was a talented, talented person.

That said, he was pretty uptight, and a guy like Johnny Grunge stealing his truck—well, it was pretty funny.

Dirtsheets

Up until three, four, five years ago, the dirtsheets and the Internet sites would get some real, hard, deep inside information. There were times when I would come out of a meeting, and literally three hours later details of that meeting were online. And the same thing has happened to Vince at WWE. Shortly after I arrived in WWE, I remember we had a production meeting. Two hours later, details of that production meeting were on the Internet. And it drove Vince *crazy*. To the point where he threatened to fire anyone he thought was even communicating with these guys. I knew how he felt.

The dirtsheets had a real negative influence at WCW. There were a couple of top wresters who at one point used to leak a lot of information to Dave Meltzer, who still distributes the *Wrestling Observer.* I get a kick out of Meltzer's Web site. He leads people to believe by logging on to his site, you are going to get information on the headlines that he posts. All he really does is tease the reader with interesting headlines, while failing to deliver any real information. For that you have to buy the "news letter" that he brags "contains more than 35,000 words." The problem is, those 35,000 words are grammatically incorrect, run-on sentences that read like a fifth-grader wrote them. And most of the "news" contained in his publication is second-third-and sometimes fourth-hand information that is so far off the mark it would be comical if it weren't for the fact that so many people take it as fact.

Some of the people at WCW were smart enough to know that executives in Turner Broadcasting subscribed to the *Observer* so they could read it in the privacy of their offices and then appear as if they knew something about what was going on in the wrestling world. It was like someone reading the *National Enquirer* and thinking that they were current on world news.

Wade Keller was another editor the guys would feed. By building up a special relationship with these dirtsheet distributors (I have a hard time referring to them as writers), the wrestlers would make sure they were treated in a certain way in those publications. The executives would read the *Observer* or Keller's dirtsheet, and they'd see Dave Meltzer or Keller extolling the virtues of the moles that fed them information.

There was a lot of that kind of quid pro quo going on. The information was always one-sided and riddled with personal agendas.

What's interesting now is that because there's only one wrestling organization, and because Vince is more adamant than I was about leaking information and talking to these dirtsheets, the talent is much more paranoid about leaking information. So now what you get when you read these dirtsheets or anything online is a much more outside-the-camp point of view. Nobody's feeding these guys much anymore. The end result is, they're kind of pabulum. They're opinionated, but their opinions generally reflect the trends of the audience anyway, so it's safe opinion.

It's amazing how an industry that has grown as large as ours was influenced so adversely by what is nothing more than a group of nerds who probably couldn't get or hold a job doing anything else. It still amazes me that these goofs were able to influence people who would never even give them an interview for a legitimate job in the industry they wrote about.

Chris Benoit with Justin Liger.

Innovations

Cruiserweights

When people ask me about things I did that really changed the pro wrestling business, one I like to point to is the cruiserweight division.

WCW's cruiserweight division came about not just because I wanted to keep *Nitro* different from other shows, but because I wanted to keep some of its segments different from each other. I wanted quick-paced, athletic wrestling to quicken the pulse in the middle of the show.

When you get guys six-four, six-eight, and they weigh 250 and 300 pounds, no matter how good they are, they're only capable of doing certain things in the ring. The pace of that match is what it is. There were very few guys in the heavyweight category able to have the kind of fast-paced, athletic match I saw a lot of in Japan.

I started looking at New Japan and brought some of their wrestlers over to wrestle with guys like Brian Pillman. I also started looking for other wrestlers capable of having that style of match. That's when I became aware of wrestlers like Chris Jericho, Eddie Guerrero, Chris Benoit, and Dean Malenko. Eddie, Chris, and Dean all worked for New Japan Pro Wrestling in Japan. Masa Siato and Brad Rheingans recommended them highly.

Human Car Crash

I brought Dean, Eddie, and Chris in and told them, "Here's how I see you: I want you to be my human car crash. I'm going to use you in the middle of the show, right before or after the transition into the second hour. I want your matches to be different from the rest of the matches we see on the show. You guys are capable of having dynamic, fast-paced matches."

I don't think anybody in the wrestling business had called that division the cruiserweight division before. It had been referred to as "junior heavyweight." I didn't want to call anybody on my roster a junior anything. It worked okay for hamburgers, but not for wrestlers. I looked at boxing, and used their name for the weight class.

I loved the cruiserweight style. That's the kind of wrestling I like to watch—dynamic and fast-paced. A lot of the acrobatic stuff takes me out of the moment, but guys like Chris, Eddie certainly, Dean certainly—they were very fast-paced, yet credible performers. They were different than the heavyweights.

I wasn't the only fan. The cruiserweight division had a lot to do with the continued success of *Nitro*. I brought in Mike Tenay so we could talk about it on the air and educate the audience. Mike was a writer who was just a walking encyclopedia of knowledge. He was a real student of professional wrestling. He knew all the history and really studied the game.

Rey Mysterio.

It worked. It was different; it was exciting and high-flying. No one had ever seen anything like it before on this level. Clearly it existed elsewhere around the world, and in a very limited way in bingo halls around Pennsylvania. But no one had ever showcased this style of wrestling before at that level and with the consistency that I did.

Mexican Wrestlers

The cruiserweights also gave us a chance to give *Nitro* an international feel. Besides wrestlers from Japan, we were able to attract a lot of guys down in Mexico whom Chris, Eddie, and Dean knew.

There were some problems, partly because of the language barrier, and partly because of cultural differences. And there were the inevitable politics. Konan positioned himself as the godfather of the Mexican wrestlers. Konan was probably the worst person I could have chosen as a liaison, because he had his own agenda, but he was a popular and well-respected wrestler in Mexico.

There were often disputes over contracts, but the issue wasn't money—not directly, anyway. A lot of the Mexicans never really understood that, in many cases, their contracts didn't allow them to perform in Mexico. Rey Mysterio and a few others felt that they could, and that was a problem. We didn't want them risking injury. It's bad enough that we have to run that risk in our own rings and shows. But a lot of these guys wanted to keep up their career in Mexico.

Mexican wrestlers also had different attitudes toward masks than we did. In the Mexican tradition, once a wrestler donned a mask, he did not ever give it up. There were exceptions—plenty of them, actually—but the mask had a symbolic meaning among Mexican audiences that it just didn't have in the States.

Rey Mysterio's Mask

The mask became a big issue for Rey Mysterio.

I wanted Rey to be a character that kids could really relate to.

He had a lot of characteristics going for him. But he wore a mask, and the camera couldn't see his facial expressions. The expressions tell the story.

After Rey had been with us for quite some time, I knew his character could grow. Rey is a good-looking guy, and I thought taking the mask off would take him to the next level, make him a real superstar. But Rey, having been brought up in Mexico and having a different feel about the heritage of his character, balked. Not having grown up in Mexico, I didn't really understand it. I do now, but that said, I still think Rey was better off without the mask.

Rey's argument was, "Wait a minute, in Mexico, that's who I am."

"Yeah, but you're not in Mexico anymore, so guess what? You're going to lose the mask."

I actually tried to be more diplomatic than that, but it came down to push comes to shove. I had to stand my ground. He lost the mask in a Hair versus Mask match at *Superbrawl IX*, when Mysterio & Konan were defeated by Nash & Hall.

But losing the mask was hard on Rey. He didn't really embrace it. These days, he wrestles with it on in WWE.

Booking

By this time, Kevin Sullivan was our lead booker. Ric Flair hadn't worked out, and gradually Kevin assumed a bigger role in the committee in charge of the wrestling storylines.

Dusty Rhodes had brought Kevin in as an assistant booker, a kind of balance to his talents. Dusty knew that he was really good building up babyfaces. He also knew that to have a good babyface, you need effective heels. Kevin was one of the few bookers or wrestlers out there who really understood real heat and heels. Kevin was a little wacky, and some of his ideas were way, way out there, but he knew what it took to create real heat, and not just a Pavlovian response, which was what we had been doing up until that point—and quite frankly, what I see mostly today.

With the start of *Nitro*, I took a much greater role in booking. I felt I understood what the show needed, and had learned or absorbed enough to make it happen. The top third or so of the card was under my direction. Kevin and the rest of the booking committee took care of everything else.

Hogan as Heel

At the beginning of 1996, I began thinking a lot about Hulk Hogan as a character. His character, from my point of view, had played itself out.

I wasn't as dependant on Hogan as I was in 1994. Our contract required him to be used a certain number of days a year, and gave him a fixed amount for each Pay-Per-View. That was already in the budget and wouldn't be changed, one way or another. We'd already gotten our value from him, positioning our brand as a good advertising opportunity. I think we only had another three or four dates left in his contract.

But Hogan was a tremendous performer, and it made sense to try and do something more with him than just pencil him in. He was an enormous resource—if we could tap it.

The more I thought I about it, the more I came back to one idea. Hulk Hogan was one of the all-time great babyface characters. What would the impact be if he turned heel?

Handled correctly, it would be huge.

By this time I had a good relationship with Hogan on a personal level. So I called him and said, "Hulkster, what are you doing next Tuesday? I'd like to come down to Florida and run some ideas by you."

"Sure, brother. Come on down."

So I flew down to Tampa, rented a car, and went over to his mansion on the beach. We sat down, had a beer, shot the shit for a while, and got caught up. Everything was great.

Then I walked him through the idea that he might turn heel.

He stroked his Fu Manchu. He rested his chin on his hand and continued to stroke his Fu Manchu for what seemed like twenty minutes. Then he said, "Well, brother, until you've walked a mile in my red and yellow boots, you'll never really understand."

And with that, he looked at his watch and said, "I'm sorry, I've got to go pick my kids up at school."

He showed me to the door.

The Revolution Takes Hold

The War Within

Germination

itro revolutionized the pro wrestling business in many ways, changing the target audience, adding realistic storylines, creating more reality-based characters, emphasizing surprise as an important element to every show, and taking viewers backstage as part of the storytelling process—many of the things we take for granted today were done first on *Nitro*.

And if there was one angle that epitomized that revolution, that summed it up and embodied it better than all others, it was nWo—the New World Order.

Actually, the New World Order was a lot more than a simple storyline. It was a cult, a virus, a revolution. It was reality TV before reality TV was invented, or at least popularized. When the nWo wrestlers attacked WCW, they took the audience's real-life emotions and turned them into wrestling weapons. The audience rewarded us with some of the highest ratings cable programs have ever received.

Scott Hall

The seed of the idea was planted when I heard Scott Hall was interested in coming over to WCW.

Scott had worked with Verne Gagne in the AWA, teaming up with Curt Hennig. He'd left before I got there, but I knew his character. Scott had also been in the WCW for a short period while I was there. From there he went over to WWE, where I'd watched him as Razor Ramon. He was a tremendous performer, but he also had a reputation for stirring the pot behind the scenes.

Scott was friends with Diamond Dallas Page, who lived near me and who would occasionally stop by on a Saturday afternoon for a beer. One Saturday, Page came by and we started shooting the shit. He said, "Hey, I've been talking to Scott Hall and Kevin Nash. They're interested in making a move."

Nash, then known as Diesel, had also wrestled in WCW for a brief time before going over to WWE. While he usually played a heel, he had held the championship title for about a year, from late 1994 to 1995. He and Nash were good friends.

Page said they were miserable. They weren't happy with the politics, their pay—you name it.

By the way, that was no reflection on anything that was going on in WWE—at the time, I don't think anything could have made those two happy.

Anyway, they made it clear that they'd be willing to make a jump. Not knowing what the situation really was and whether I could trust them, I used Page as a go-between. The pitch was, "You come over here and you'll get a guaranteed paycheck, and you'll work less."

Compensation

As well as we were doing in 1996, WCW still did not have a great licensing and marketing business. In WWE someone like Nash or Hall could make considerable money from their cut of the licensing and merchandise. We didn't have that, which was one reason we had to continue guaranteeing contracts. In some cases, the amount was actually less than the performer might have made in WWE, but the fact that it was guaranteed meant a lot. We wanted to eventually build to the point where we could change our compensation plan to something along the revenue-sharing lines; we just weren't there yet.

Of course, at the time the WWE compensation plan really was: you got paid whatever Vince McMahon decided to pay you that day.

The fact that we were on the road a lot less—we had no plans to go beyond 180 days, while the WWE was on the road 250—was also a big draw. If you're a performer, you're thinking, I can make X working with WWE, but I'm on the road all the time, not spending any time with my family, and I'm breaking down. I can make X plus 10 percent and go to work for WCW and work half the time.

What would you do?

A lot of the guys who came over to WCW were attracted by the schedule, not the money. Most of the guys thought that if they stuck with WWE, they'd make more money in the long run, because of the revenue-sharing. But our lighter schedule was a real draw.

Despite what the WWE would like people to think—and despite what the dirtsheet writers loved to say—I didn't steal these guys. Any time talent went from WCW to WWE, nobody said Vince McMahon stole them. Whether it was Kevin Nash or Scott Hall or Vader or Ric Flair, it wasn't stealing if they left WCW. It was only grand larceny when someone left WWE for WCW—especially during this period.

Anyway, we ended up doing a deal with Scott Hall, and very shortly afterward, with Kevin Nash. I knew having them together represented a terrific creative possibility—but I had no idea what it was.

Disrespect

I looked at Scott and Kevin and said, "What's my story with these guys?"

The word had already leaked out that they were coming over. It had to, since they had to give notice. So I couldn't surprise anyone with it, the way I had with Lex Luger.

There was, however, anticipation, and the fact that both had been with the WCW before becoming stars in WWE. So I decided to build on that.

Scott came over on May 27, 1996. I picked him up at his hotel. We were in Macon, Georgia, for the show.

I wanted to get into his head and find out where he was at. I'd heard a lot of negative things about Scott, that he was a shit disturber, very problematic, very manipulative. Scott's chemical history was also pretty well known to just about everyone in the business. I knew I wasn't getting a solid corporate citizen.

The morale in our locker room was fairly high. For the first time, these guys were on the winning team. I'm not saying everybody was happy with every little thing, but for the most part the morale was good. I knew that. I also knew what a guy like Scott Hall could do if he was disgruntled. I had enough politics going on with Hogan and Flair.

On the drive to the show, I made it clear to Scott that if he was going to come in and turn the place upside down, I wasn't going to tolerate it.

Scott, to his credit, was very humble and assured me that wasn't the case. He meant it, at the time anyway.

I didn't share my plans with him, even then.

When we got there, I wrote his interview for him. I wanted people to say, *Holy shit, this must be real, because I've never seen anything like this before.* And I remember thinking, *God, I hope this guy can pull this off.*

My idea was for Scott to come down in the middle of a match, in a way that appeared to be spontaneous and unannounced. He'd walk down from the audience, grab a microphone, create a disturbance, and spout off. He was a rebel, pissed off, coming back to WCW with a chip on his shoulder.

The chip was that he had been disrespected at WCW. The company had held both him and Kevin back, and now they wanted revenge. They were the Outsiders. They had reached a level of stardom at WWE and decided to come back because they'd been disrespected.

That was the storyline, and Scott laid it out in his promo. He told the audience that he'd been disrespected and intended to fix that by kicking butt. He was coming back next week with his big friend—Nash, though his name wasn't mentioned—and they intended on taking no prisoners. He looked angry, and the audience responded as if he really was.

The beauty of the promo—if I may pat myself on the back— were the questions it raised. Who was coming with him? What would they do? How? What would the consequences be? What's their agenda?

That wasn't by accident. I'd figured out that the best way to tell a story was to get the audience to ask themselves, What's going to happen next?

If they wanted to know, they had to tune in and find out.

An Amazing Bump

Kevin Nash answered some of the questions the next week, just by showing up. Viewers were wondering how far we were going to take things, and the answer was, *Further than they thought.*

And I almost didn't survive it.

The bit began when, at *The Great American Bash* in Baltimore in my role as *Nitro* announcer, I stood on the stage and introduced Scott Hall.

"All right," I said in my most sardonic voice, "where's your big buddy?"

After they were banned from WCW events, Hall and Nash brought tickets, just so they could be thrown out.

Kevin Nash came out and yapped at the crowd. Scott punched me in the stomach to double me over, then Kevin hit me with a powerbomb.

The powerbomb started with Kevin grabbing me by the back of my head and tucking it down between his thighs. He reached over my back and locked his hands around my stomach, then flipped me up so I was basically sitting on his shoulders with my crotch in his face.

Now Kevin is seven feet tall. I was on his shoulders, so my head had to be a good nine or ten feet up in the air. To complete the move, he had to throw me off the stage, which itself is what? Five feet off the ground? And I was supposed to hit a target the size of a small mattress.

Great plan, except Kevin was completely blind. He couldn't see anything. If I missed the pad, I was going to hit concrete.

But we were well past the point of no return. He launched me blind. Fortunately, at the very last second he saw what he thought was the target and managed to twist me in its direction. *Most* of me hit *most* of the pad, and as much as it hurt, it was a hell of a lot better than the alternative.

Pad or no pad, the toss was a huge bump—figuratively as well as literally. By tossing WCW's boss so unceremoniously, the Outsiders had declared war on the WCW. In traditional wrestling terms, they were heels. But they were very *cool* heels, generating enormous heat for themselves—not least of all because a lot of WCW fans wouldn't have minded tossing me from the stage themselves.

Never Rehearse

Kevin had trouble finding the target when he threw me because we hadn't rehearsed the move. That was my fault—I don't like to rehearse, and don't whenever possible. I'm really superstitious about rehearsing things. I love the adrenaline rush, and if I rehearse something, I don't get the rush.

These days at WWE, they make me rehearse the trickier moves. Despite what people may think about Vince McMahon, he really does care about what happens to the people who work for him. Knowing I don't like to rehearse certain things, Vince has pulled me aside on several occasions and said, "No, you will rehearse this, Eric." And so I have. Reluctantly.

Injuries

With the exception of my perennial knee injuries and a few broken bones, I've never really gotten seriously hurt. Maybe that's luck. Or maybe it's because the things I've been involved in have been fairly limited. Even so, I've always had this feeling that I'm indestructible.

The broken bones may be evidence to the contrary. I was doing a WWE house show with Eugene (the character who was supposedly my mentally challenged nephew) at Madison Square Garden one time when he bodyslammed me. He followed that up with—well, I'm not sure what the move was, because by that time my eyes were closed. He ended up landing hard on my chest. Either because I'm not in shape anymore or because he misjudged, I cracked one of my ribs. It was more a nuisance than anything else. It didn't keep me from doing anything important. I didn't bother telling anyone at the time.

It made it difficult for me to cough or sneeze or laugh, but otherwise . . .

There was another incident in WWE with Kane, where he choke-slammed me off the side of the stage. Kane is one incredibly powerful guy. He brought me over to the edge of the stage and picked me all the way up.

One of the things you don't want to do as the guy taking that bump is reach down and try to find the floor with your hand. You want to take that bump across your back. Tuck your head in your chest so your head doesn't bounce, flatten your back out, roll your shoulders up a little bit, and take it all across your shoulder blades.

But being inexperienced and not having rehearsed it because I'm stubborn that way, about halfway down I started reaching for the floor. My hand hit first, and I fractured my thumb. Compared to what so many other performers have been through, these injuries are really not worth mentioning. But that's the point.

Now that I'm older and it takes me longer to heal, I've become a little more careful. Still, I'd rather get hurt than have a move look phony.

The Third Guy

Instantly Hot

The Outsider angle caught fire immediately. And as soon as that happened, the natural question was: Who's next? Who will the next person be to attack the WCW?

We spent four or five weeks developing the idea, giving hints and laying the groundwork. We planned to unveil the "third guy" at the *Bash at the Beach* Pay-Per-View in July.

I didn't know myself. It had to be someone *inside* WCW, but beyond that, I wasn't sure.

I decided to approach Sting, but I didn't know if he'd do it. Joining the Outsiders meant he'd have to turn heel, and Sting had always been a very successful babyface character.

Sting was receptive—not knock-me-over enthusiastic, but receptive. Everyone could see the power this storyline was developing. Just a few weeks old, it was already one of the most interesting stories in the last five or ten years. We began discussing how the storyline might develop. I talked to him a couple of times, in person and over the phone. No one else knew we were talking, not even Scott and Kevin. The identity of the third person had to be kept an extremely tight secret.

Hogan Checks In

About this time, I got a phone call from Hogan.

"Hey, brother, what are you doing? Come on out to L.A. I want to talk to you."

I hadn't spoken to him in months. He was out west working on a movie called *Santa with Muscles*, so I flew out to see what was on his mind.

Hogan sent a limo for me. It took me out to the mountains about an hour and a half from L.A. I got to his trailer about nine or ten. He'd just finished filming, and there was a cooler of beers and a couple of Cuban cigars—Montecristo No. 4's, I believe—sitting out. We kicked back and caught up on things.

"So, brother, who's the third guy?"

"Well, Hulkster," I told him. *"I don't know yet. I haven't made up my mind."*

"Well, I know who the third guy should be."

"Who would that be?"

"You're looking at him."

"Well, that's interesting, Hulk, but the only way that's going to work would be if you turn heel."

"Brother, I'm already there."

Hogan as Heel

Four or five months ago, Hogan had—gently—thrown me out of his house for suggesting he turn heel. Now, as he saw the Outsiders story unfold, he wanted to be part of it.

By this time I realized that Hogan was a master negotiator. I don't want to call him a manipulator, because of the negative connotations of the word, but if anyone can smell an opportunity and turn it to his benefit, it's Hulk Hogan. So I knew that as exciting as the idea was, there was a good possibility that another boot would drop.

We talked a bit. We weren't renegotiating the financial aspects of his deal, but because Hogan had creative control, I had to dance around a lot of what might happen story-wise.

We didn't really know how the angle would go. I thought it would be successful, but we couldn't be absolutely sure that it would be. If the audience shit on it, we would have to take it in one direction. If it went over, we'd go in another. And that had to be worked out in advance with Hogan, to make sure it would work. He also had a lot of questions about Scott and Kevin, and whether they were team players—valid questions, given their track records.

Would He or Wouldn't He?

Despite what he'd said, a large part of Hogan remained apprehensive. He had been a babyface for almost all of his professional career. To shed that persona, to shed the red and yellow, was a big step.

You have to understand, the red and yellow meant a lot outside the ring. Hulk Hogan is a good human being outside the ring. He's got a big heart. He's a guy who does a lot of work for charity. He knew that if he turned heel, all of that would be affected. A lot of kids buy into a character like Hogan or Sting. When you turn that good guy into a bad guy, you really do affect, in some small way, the lives of those children. And Hogan took that *very* seriously. He knew there would be a lot of Make-A-Wish kids, and a lot of the young people he worked with, wondering why Hogan was now a bad guy. They'd literally feel betrayed by their hero. For a lot of people, something like that wouldn't factor into a decision. But it was something Hulk was very concerned about.

Hulk also had two young kids at the time, and had to think about how this transition would affect them. As silly as that might seem to the outside world, what a wrestler does can have an immense impact on his family, especially young kids. Their friends don't understand the business, and no one can really explain it to them. Kids can be mean, and no parent wants to subject their children to things that are tough to deal with, especially if it's not necessary. Hogan already had more money than he could spend, so he didn't need to turn heel.

We discussed all of the implications daily, all the way up to Daytona where the Pay-Per-View was going to take place. Even then, I wasn't entirely sure Hulk was going to go through with it.

Sting

Being the team player and professional that he was, Sting stood there on the sidelines, ready to go if needed. It wasn't until an hour before the show—when Hogan showed up at the arena—that I knew for certain he was going to do it. I went to Sting and thanked him, saying how much I appreciated his standing by.

It was a tough conversation to have, because I knew that on some level he thought I didn't have confidence in him to pull it off.

But that wasn't the case. He could have pulled it off, and it would have worked.

It's just that Hogan turning heel was bigger. A lot bigger.

I think deep down inside Sting knew that. I think in some ways he might even have been a little relieved, because as willing as he was to take the chance, he knew what his character meant as a babyface, and turning heel would have been venturing into the unknown.

A New World Order

In a way my uncertainty over Hogan may have helped build the surprise. There had been no leaks because no one knew anything to leak. Kevin Nash and Scott Hall didn't know for sure who was going to be heel until Hogan showed up. And I didn't tell the announcers what was going on because they had a bad habit of foreshadowing what was going to happen. I wanted a real reaction out of them.

Walking around backstage, getting ready to go on, I felt electric. I knew it was going to work.

At this point, I had not even thought about what to call the conspiracy or organization or whatever it was Hogan was joining, beyond the Outsiders. That name wouldn't really work once he came over, but what would?

I walked Hogan through the match and the interview that he'd have to give afterward. He didn't like reading off scripts, so I didn't write anything out; we just went over the general direction so he could ad-lib.

As I was working through this dialogue with him, the name just popped into my head. I said, "Hulk, when you grab that mic, I want you to say, This is the beginning of the new . . . world . . . order."

The words kind of sprang into my mouth: New World Order.

New World Order.

new World order

Hogan claims the term was biblical. It may be. Maybe it was out there in political commentary: the first President Bush had spoken about a new world order a few years before. The general idea has been out there in different ways. But as far as we were concerned, it was spontaneous and unplanned.

As soon as I said those words, I realized they were going to work. They summed up everything we'd been doing, not just with the angle, but with *Nitro*. It was a new world order for wrestling. And the fans loved it.

An After-Sex Cigarette

A split second after Hogan made it clear he was the third man, I saw a fan throw a cup of Coke or Pepsi at the ring in disgust and anger.

I knew it had not only worked, but it had gone over big. Really big.

As Hogan filled the air with trash talk about Ted Turner and the WCW and what it stood for, people went *nuts*. They filled the ring with garbage. All the effort that had gone into keeping this thing quiet was worth it. The reality, the story, the anticipation, the surprise, the action, were all 100 percent right on the money. Viewers loved the war we'd created, and they were going to love it even more as the story continued.

When the show ended, I had the wrestling equivalent of an after-sex cigarette: I went back to my office, had my assistant bring me a beer, closed the door, and basked in the afterglow.

Elements of Success

Five Elements—SARSA

The nWo storyline evolved over time, but looking back at things now, it's a little easier to explain why it worked. It filled all of the important elements of storytelling—story, action, reality, surprise, and anticipation. That's the winning formula that we tried to follow on *Nitro*. We followed it unconsciously until I was able to articulate it for myself and then my staff, right around this time.

The Olympics were going on in Atlanta that summer. There was a lot of buzz in the press about the coverage. The previous Olympics had been a bust in the ratings, and I remember reading a lot about what NBC was going to do to try and turn that situation around.

Dick Ebersol was the executive at NBC in charge of the Olympics. He told a reporter for *USA Today* that the Olympics were going to be about story, action, and surprises. "Those are the elements that we are going to focus on to make the Olympics interesting," he said.

I cut the article out and saved it for several years, because it summarized exactly what we were trying to do. To keep the audience in that "sweet spot" where they were willing to suspend their disbelief, where they were guessing whether things were real or not, we needed a certain level of reality. Real life mixed in with the storylines, and angles blurred the distinction between entertainment and reality. When the line was blurred, the audience felt that anything could happen. And when they felt that way, they had to keep tuning in to see what the next thing was, the third man or whatever.

Our nWo third-man scenario made me realize there was another important element to storytelling as well: anticipation.

Most people underestimate the emotional value of anticipation, but I think it's the most important element of all. When you are a young child, you anticipate the holidays, your birthday, etc. By the time you're twelve or fourteen years old, you're anticipating your driver's license. It's akin to independence. The amount of anticipation that goes into that sixteenth birthday is immense. Then it's graduating from high school. Going off to college. Then turning twenty-one. And so on.

Does It Have the Elements?

Once I could articulate it for myself, I started preaching the formula to my writers. I called it SARSA: Story, Anticipation, Reality, Surprise, Action.

Not every idea can be equally strong in all five elements, but that's the goal. "When all five are there in a big way, we can live off that idea for two or three years," I would tell my writers. "If it has four out of the five, it's important enough to book into a Pay-Per-View. If it has three out of the five, it might get us through a week or two. If a story doesn't have at least three of the SARSA elements . . . I don't want to hear it."

My favorite question when a writer brought an idea to me was, "Where is it going next week?" I wanted the writers to have an arc—a beginning, middle, and end. We wanted a climax, a payoff for the audience—at a Pay-Per-View, if the story was good enough. Often I would say, *Tell me what you want to have happen a month from now and work backward.*

The formula worked really well. It became our mantra. I use it myself to this day.

Judging whether a story had SARSA was a gut thing. It couldn't be an exact science because some of it was subjective; I could kind of feel it when it was right. But another thing I did was check out how things were connecting with the crowds. I had a habit of finding places to hide during the shows, just watching our audiences. As time went on, it got more difficult to do this because I was so involved in the television show, but I could still do it at house shows. I'd watch the crowd and listen to what they had to say.

Hook and Drag

It wasn't an accident that the third-man storyline climaxed at a Pay-Per-View. Pay-Per-Views have been critical to the industry's business model since Vince McMahon took over World Wrestling Federation and took it national. Traditionally, Pay-Per-Views have featured the biggest matches of the year.

One of the things that we did on *Nitro*—and I took a lot of criticism for this—was put Pay-Per-View–quality matches on free TV. The stories that unfolded weekly on television—whether they centered on Ric Flair and Hulk Hogan, Kevin Nash and Roddy Piper, Sting and Randy Savage—always involved the top names. Did that take away from the Pay-Per-Views? I don't think so.

My theory was, people would pay for the quality of the story, not the talent in the story. I wasn't afraid to put Pay-Per-View–quality talent on free television—as long as we could provide a Pay-Per-View story the audience felt they *had* to see.

On the other side of that, I used a "hook and drag" strategy: we would take something from the Pay-Per-View and develop it on *Nitro* the following night. Instead of just wiping the slate clean and starting over from scratch after the story climaxed, we wanted to "hook" them at the Pay-Per-View, and then "drag" them into the next arc, continuing the story. I didn't want to feel as if I was starting over each and every month, because it was simply too much.

We couldn't do this on every story, obviously. But the nWo storylines often lent themselves to this strategy.

There was more to the Pay-Per-Views than coming up with "big" stories. The shows had to *feel* different from what was on free TV. And each Pay-Per-View needed a unique personality. We were also looking for ways to make them sponsorable, the way a major sporting event like a NASCAR race might be, so that we would increase the revenue stream.

Hogg Wild at Sturgis was born from those considerations.

Born to Be Wild

Sturgis

I've always been a biker at heart. When I was ten or so, I had a five-horsepower minibike I used to ride around the neighborhood. I bought my first motorcycle before I was old enough to drive, and I've owned at least one ever since.

Having grown up in the Midwest, I knew about Sturgis, the yearly motorcycle rally in Sturgis, South Dakota, which brings together hundreds of thousands of bikers from all over the country each August. I'd never gone—it was one of those situations where when I had the time I didn't have the money, and vice versa. But I knew about it, had read about it, and had always wanted to go. The timing just never worked out.

When we increased the Pay-Per-View schedule in 1995 and began looking for new and different ways to give these new Pay-Per-Views an identity, it occurred to me that it would be really cool to put on an event at Sturgis. I knew that there would be anywhere from 400,000 to 750,000 bikers there. More importantly, I knew there was an attitude and a demographic that would really give that August Pay-Per-View its own personality.

Just as I did with Disney and Hulk Hogan, I wanted to co-brand WCW with the biker image. The perception of bikers was that they are pretty edgy, aggressive, beer-drinking, fistfighting kind of guys. I thought that was an attitude that would serve WCW well, given the direction we were going with *Nitro*.

Sponsorships

I also saw Sturgis as a chance to connect with sponsors in a way wrestling had never done before. Sponsorship opportunities at certain levels seem obvious: there's a halo effect that comes with an activity that is associated with prestige. Rolex and golf, for example. But it's not so obvious on the opposite end of the spectrum, where wrestling—as well as motorcycles, for that matter—is concerned.

Advertisers looked at the sheer eyeballs associated with wrestling and recognized that it's a powerful way of reaching a mass audience. But they also looked at the audience—or what they *thought* was the audience—and didn't want to have their product associated with it.

The way to overcome that in my mind was to change the perception of wrestling. Wrestling will never be golf, but if you look at the wrestling audience and the NASCAR audience, you see a very close relationship. NASCAR had a great deal of success with blue-collar advertisers. Their target audience wasn't playing golf or wearing Rolexes, but they were making sixty or eighty thousand dollars a year, drinking beer, driving trucks, wearing Levis, and that sort of thing. That was our audience, too.

And that was the audience at Sturgis. Some people who hadn't been there were afraid of it, because of what they'd heard about the motorcycle clubs. But that wasn't really what it was all about. I've been to Sturgis now maybe ten times, and I've never seen so much as a fistfight. Despite the perception, the reality is, you have a bunch of middle-aged guys trying to relive a little bit of their youth. I'm not saying that there isn't a darker side of the event—and I'm sure law enforcement could point that out—but for the most part, it's just like a state fair for guys who like motorcycles.

I realized that "motorcycle culture" was already part of the mainstream. People saw it as edgy, which made it attractive. This was a couple of years before *Monster Garage* and *American Choppers*, two wildly successful cable shows. I saw the motorcycle phenomenon coming before a lot of other people did. I wanted to be the first one to plant my television "flag" in Sturgis.

I realized it might take a few years before the sponsorship deals opened up. And from an economic point of view, Sturgis didn't make a lot of sense, because we weren't going to get a gate. We couldn't charge for tickets. I also knew that, because of the very nature of an outdoor event, our production costs would be much higher than normal. Travel was also going to be a problem, because Sturgis is in the middle of nowhere. Hotels book up two years in advance, and rental cars are nonexistent; there are a lot of things that make producing an event at Sturgis difficult. But I thought in the long run, if we were able to maintain our presence there, as an annual event, the money that we would not make in traditional ticket sales would be more than offset by attracting advertisers and sponsors in the long run.

Of course, there were critics, and the whole idea of doing a Pay-Per-View at Sturgis was questioned by people supposedly "in the know" who were writing in dirtsheets and on the Internet.

That didn't bother me one bit. Anytime I did anything out of the box, the dirtsheets and some of the hard-core wrestling fans gave me flack. But I knew that none of these people had their heads inside the entertainment industry. The only thing they understood was what they had grown up with.

On the Road

The idea of the Pay-Per-View was an easy idea to sell to WCW, especially to a lot of the talent. Sting, Big Bubba Rogers, Diamond Dallas Page, the Sterner Brothers, Madusa—there were probably ten or twelve of us who all had Harleys and liked to ride.

I couldn't just show up with a ring and hope I could put on a wrestling event, so I went to the city of Sturgis, hoping to get support. I met with the city council and members of the rally committee responsible for putting on the event. They really rolled out the red carpet for us and made it easy to bring our monster of a production there. We arranged to construct an outdoor arena a block off Main Street.

Someone came up with the idea of shipping our bikes to the Mall of America, and then riding to the event. We'd film the ride across country, using it as part of the Pay-Per-View and for promotion.

And so we did. We had a press event at the mall, then jumped on our bikes and headed out. There were ten or twelve motorcycles, a couple of motor homes, a pickup, trailers, a truck with all sorts of miscellaneous parts in case someone broke down. We had crew members, mechanics, family—I brought my wife and my kids with me. It was a real adventure. The weather was hot and miserable, we got lost once or twice, and we ate a pound of bugs at eighty miles an hour. But at the end of the night we'd pull up at a hotel, meet at the bar, and just have a good time. It was quite the experience. We came together in a way that you just don't get in the course of your normal everyday business. A bond developed between Sting and me, the Stemers, Madusa, and the rest of the crew, thanks to this trip.

By the time we pulled into Sturgis, most of the outdoor arena was already set up. When I looked at it, I was really proud of what David Crockett and the rest of the crew had done.

Sturgis.

The afternoon before the show, a tremendous storm struck. We got hail that was probably an inch or an inch and a half in diameter, forty- or fifty-mile-an-hour winds, and a torrential downpour of rain. I was standing there looking up at all the rigging for the lights, and I thought, *Oh my God, all of this is going to come crashing down around me.* Fortunately, nothing came down.

Like the farmers say, if you don't like the weather in South Dakota, stick around for twenty minutes and it'll change. Sure enough, in twenty minutes, the storm was over. We went on to have a great show the next day.

There were no seats at ringside. We let anyone who wanted to ride their bikes right up to the ring. So we were surrounded by hundreds, if not thousands, of Harleys. When wrestlers were announced, guys revved their bikes, so you had this enormous roar as each event got under way. Pretty bad-ass.

Different, definitely different.

Dealing with Hogan

Not too long after Sturgis, Hogan and I were together in Denver when someone called him and said, "Hey, Vince McMahon is in town, and he'd like to talk with you."

Our contract with Hogan was coming up for renewal, and it was pretty obvious what McMahon wanted to talk about. Hogan looked at me and said, "I can't believe it. Vince McMahon is here and wants to talk to me about a deal."

"What are you going to do?"

"I'm going to go talk to him and hear what he has to say. But don't worry; I'm not going to do a deal with this guy."

I wasn't worried, but I was concerned. Hogan's heel turn had made him especially valuable to us.

In my opinion, the nWo would never have been the nWo without Kevin Hall and Scott Nash. Their attitude and personae were unique to the wrestling business and fit the architecture of the concept as if it was meant to be. That said, without the Hogan turn and the impact that had, the overall chemistry and angle wouldn't have lasted as long as it did.

I wasn't in a position where I could say that I could live without Hogan, even though Scott and Kevin were strong. But at the same time, even something as catastrophic as losing Hogan wouldn't have been so catastrophic that we couldn't have recovered from it. And I wasn't concerned about Hogan jumping over to WWE and maintaining that kind of persona—it wouldn't have worked without Scott and Kevin. There was no one for him to feed off, and as a stand-alone heel, he wouldn't have had the same impact. I didn't think WWE could use him effectively.

Hogan and Vince did talk, but I don't think their conversation could be considered a negotiation. And in the end it really wasn't hard for us to come to terms with Hogan on a new deal. If anything, it was much easier than the initial negotiations. The money was about the same, and the concerns and insecurities that Hogan had when he came over originally were gone.

Hogan tried to pretend that he was being a hard negotiator, but I knew deep down inside that he really didn't have many options. He was either going to stay with us or go someplace that he really didn't want to go. He'd told me multiple times how much he didn't trust Vince McMahon.

A lot of guys try to prop themselves up with accounts of how hard they are to come to terms with. But Hogan knew he had a good thing. He wasn't going to risk it for the unknown. That just wasn't his personality.

And we did have a good thing. As the Hulkster himself once put it, "Everything we touched turned to gold, brother."

Hall & Nash, a Creative Dynamo

I can tell you without bragging that no one else had anything to do with the nWo idea initially. That was out of necessity—not ego, not confidence. I couldn't trust any of the people at WCW. Word would have leaked out, and the surprise would have been ruined.

But after the nWo was born, Scott and Kevin really contributed the key elements of nWo's feel and attitude. I'd like to take most of the credit, but that would be a lie. Scott Hall and Kevin Nash had more to do with the attitude and tone of what the nWo represented than anybody.

Scott Hall was one of the most talented, creative people I've ever known in the wrestling business. When his head was on straight, he was an extremely creative guy. The problem, as we all know, was that Scott had demons that he couldn't overcome. But for a year, year and a half after the launch of nWo, Scott came up with a lot of great ideas. And Kevin fed off his energy.

Kevin and I both grew up in Detroit, at about the same time, and in neighborhoods that were close to each other. We had the same Detroit street mentality And a lot of what nWo did was consistent with the way we grew up. So when Kevin would bring something up, I related to it right away.

Spray-painting—tagging—opponents, for example; the attraction of being an outlaw, that sort of thing.

Beyond Scott, Kevin, and myself, there were a lot of people behind the scenes who made contributions. For example, we created the nWo graphic in 1996 by working with some graphics people down in Disney. They asked what I wanted the logo to represent. I talked through the general concept: they're rebels, counterculture, street thugs—everything the wrestling culture represents.

They came back to me with a couple of concepts. The one that jumped out was the now familiar black-and-white graffiti nWo logo. It went right along with the nWo attitude. It encapsulated everything we were trying to do.

The black-and-white video promos and vignettes that we began doing toward the end of 1996 were born out of necessity, not any lightning-strikes-in-the-middle-of-the-night inspiration. The first one we ever did came about because we needed to put Scott Hall, Kevin Nash, and Hulk Hogan together in a promo.

Hulk Hogan can be really, really good in a certain kind of interview. Kevin Nash can be good. Scott Hall is capable of being great. The problem is putting all three of those guys together, because their styles are very different. I knew it would be next to impossible to pull off a traditional wrestling promo.

So I sat back with Craig Leathers, one of my directors at the time, and said, "Let's do it differently than anything we've ever done before. Because we're not capable of doing a promo with these three guys together. It will turn into a twenty-minute clusterfuck."

We decided to do it in black and white instead of color, which was consistent with the message and attitude. We also wanted a piece that was more thematic than informational. We gave each guy their own sound bites, editing the promo together along the lines of a music video or underground documentary rather in the style of a traditional wrestling promo.

It was so damn good, and so damn different, that we knew it was going to work.

Finding My Inner Heel

A Gradual Thing

Often in life, there aren't really clear, defining moments or transitions. A lot of times, concepts are the amalgamation of days or weeks or months of conversation and collaboration.

It's always difficult for me to look back and pinpoint exactly where or how a certain storyline or angle was born. They evolve over time. You'll be at a meeting, and someone will throw out the kernel of an idea. Then someone else throws out something that changes the idea.

Which is how I, or rather my on-screen character, joined the New World Order.

I can be dishonest about it and blow smoke up my ass like so many other people do and make up a story, but the truth is, I don't remember where the decision was made or how it came about. We were looking for a plot twist, something that would shock the audience a little bit. Up until that point on camera, my character represented the traditional pro-WCW faction. I was aghast at the nWo invasion and everything the Outsiders did and represented. I was trying to fight them off.

When I revealed myself to be a part of the nWo in November 1996, the thinking was that this nWo cancer had gotten so deep inside the executive structure that they'd finally gotten to me. As the head of WCW, I was the ultimate turncoat, the boss who turned out to be part of the evil invasion.

In some ways, though, it was a very natural move for the character. The audience didn't like me that much anyway. I *was* the outsider, the guy who hadn't paid his dues. The decisions I made in power were counterintuitive and against conventional wisdom, so the fans who claimed to be insiders or purists despised me. I embraced that, turned up the volume on it, and made it work for us. I found my inner heel.

I knew people would say things like, "Oh, Bischoff just wants to be in the limelight and part of something successful." I knew there'd be personal attacks and barbs from the dirtsheet writers and some of the people in the locker room, who were quite frankly jealous. But I didn't care, because to me it just made sense. My career wasn't going to be defined by my character, but by how the company did. So I had nothing to lose, and everything to gain.

You can't have babyfaces without people the fans really hate. And they hated me.

Blurring the Line

I was in a fairly unique position for a character in pro wrestling, or any entertainment medium, frankly. I was Eric Bischoff, the president of a high-profile division of Turner Broadcasting and the executive producer of one of the most successful shows on cable television, playing Eric Bischoff the evil, self-serving bastard. I was running the real company and the fictional one.

It was confusing for people. It was certainly confusing for the limited intellectual bandwidth of the dirtsheet community, but it was equally confusing for people who thought they knew what was going on in wrestling but weren't quite sure.

That included a lot of executives at Time Warner. There were definitely people walking around who thought an absolute lunatic was running the company. They couldn't distinguish between reality and the fiction we had created.

It can still be a problem these days when I deal with entertainment executives on nonwrestling projects. But I've learned to accept it, and sometimes use it to my advantage, even in business. When I sense that I may be in the room with someone who may be confusing the character Eric Bischoff with the person Eric Bischoff, I point out in a fun way that there's a big difference between the guy on television and the guy in the room.

Hate Mail

With my on-air profile so high, I often got hate mail. Eighty percent was what you expected it to be—from people who were so out of touch that they were obsessive-compulsive about the wrestling business. There were also a number from fans espousing what they read online. You characterized that for what it was pretty easily.

But as the nWo angle continued, I started getting mail from people who were intelligent. They'd lost sight of what was real and what was not. That was exciting—it meant we'd really succeeded. I liked it, even though they were letters from people who wanted to kill me, castrate me, and burn me at the stake. If I could get people to that point, where they weren't differentiating between fact and fiction, they would tune in every week. And that happened more and more and more.

We had a referee named Randy Anderson. Randy got involved in a storyline. I can't remember exactly what it was, but I "fired" him one week as part of the story.

He came on the next week with his tail between his legs, dragging his kids along to confront me so I would feel sorry for him, and apologized. Randy was kind of a pathetic character. Let me rephrase that—Randy was a *sympathetic* character, with a beat-up, basset-hound look to him. You took one look at him, and your heart ached.

I let him tell his story and beg for his job back. I feigned that I was touched. I leaned down and said to one of his kids, "Tell your daddy—he's *still* fired!"

And he kind of moped away.

It did a lot for me as a heel, and it did a lot for the story. But a couple of days later, I came into the office, and Harvey Schiller had gotten a letter from a church group in Georgia in the community where Randy lived. They had seen what had happened, and taken up a donation for him.

I had truly found that sweet spot I was looking for after studying the Japanese product. I didn't convince anyone that everything they saw on our show was real. But more and more, people believed that my character and many of the others on the show were real.

Darker Side

There were some darker incidents, but nothing that hasn't happened to other performers, and nothing really very serious.

I don't want to come off like some streetwise tough guy, because that's really not the case. But having grown up in Detroit, I've always been able to tell when people were serious about fighting. I know when anger is serious enough that it becomes dangerous. I can tell when it is real, and when it's show. There is a big difference. A very big difference. And I can read it a hundred miles away

There were plenty of times when I'd be with Hogan and Nash in the ring, and I'd scan the immediate area around us, looking to see if anyone was going to jump in. Ninety-nine percent of the time, the audience's responses were fairly benign, jeering or booing or whatever. But every so often, I'd catch someone and look them in the eye and I'd know, if that guy had an ice pick and could get to me, I was in big trouble.

There was one time in Georgia, when I was doing my thing outside the ring, letting the crowd tell me what they thought of me. Out of the corner of my eye, I saw this guy coming from about thirty-five yards away. How he got that clear a shot at me, I don't know; clearly there was a security lapse somewhere.

I just stood there doing my promo, pretending I didn't see him as he came at me. Finally, he took a leap at me to tackle me. He had some steam on him. But while he was in midair, I bent my knees and ducked.

He went sliding across the arena floor, where the cops were waiting for him.

There were a few other close calls. We were in Newark, New Jersey. Hogan was playing his air guitar. I was in front of him, bowing down. As we were walking in, I saw a beer bottle arcing out of the cheap seats right at us.

I put my hand out and stopped Hogan. A full bottle of beer passed maybe six inches from my face and exploded on the cement nearby. Had that hit me in the head, I wouldn't be writing this right now.

Wild Blue Yonder

Sometime during 1996, I decided I needed to do something to take my mind off my work. I'm the type of the person who, when I get really passionate about something, will dream solutions to problems in my sleep. My subconscious never turns off.

While that's always worked well, by this time it had begun to take its toll. I was working seven days a week, ten, twelve hours a day—often more. I couldn't turn the WCW switch off. I knew I had to do something that would just allow me to stop thinking about my business, even if it was just for a couple of hours.

I hate golf. And anyway, most times when you're running or playing golf or whatever, you're still thinking about your business. But if you're learning to fly, you can't afford to think about anything else. You'll likely die.

I'd always been fascinated by airplanes—and maybe subconsciously, a little scared. The Detroit metro airport was located not far from the cemetery where my grandfather was buried. Occasionally, on Sunday mornings my grandmother and I would get on a bus and go to visit his grave. Then she'd take me to watch the airplanes take off and land. That probably started my fascination with flying.

And from the time I was a teenager, I had recurring nightmares where I'd be in an airplane and something catastrophic would happen while I was on approach. I'd be hung up in power lines or run out of gas, or something else would make me crash. I looked at it as a challenge—the only way I'm ever going to overcome this fear or nightmare is to do it.

I became passionate about flying, and still am to this day. Learning to fly, getting my pilot's license, my own plane, and then my instrument rating, were very intense and very effective as a release.

The Next Phase

Merging Our Futures

The FCC approved Time Warner's purchase of Turner Broadcasting in September 1996, roughly a year after it had first been announced. WCW was a tiny part of a company that cost Time Warner an estimated $7.5 to $8 billion in stock.

The merger didn't seem to affect me or WCW. Ted Turner still headed Turner Broadcasting, and the people I answered to remained the same. From my perspective, nothing had changed.

Or so it seemed.

I'd never been part of a corporate merger before, so I talked to someone early on about what to expect. He told me, Well, at first, you won't notice it too much. Then, somewhere in that first year, you'll notice that you're getting new rules and procedures that will subtly change the way you do business. By the end of the second year, going into the third year, you won't recognize the company you work for anymore.

Sure enough, by early 1997 people were telling me what I could and couldn't do. They all had good excuses, but that had never happened before. All of a sudden there were legal considerations about what could air and restrictions on whom I could hire. In and of themselves, they seemed innocuous at the time. But eventually, they began to add up.

The Scary Sting

A lot of *Nitro* in 1997 was about Sting—even though he never wrestled.

A lot of our wrestlers didn't like the nWo storyline. It was the first time they had ever seen heels cleaning the arenas with the babyfaces. The wrestlers kept wondering when they were going to get their comeback. But seeing the way the angle was going and how the audiences were responding, I wasn't anxious to let the babyfaces get their comeback too quickly. I wanted to milk it for as long as I could milk it. This was very disconcerting for a lot of the wrestlers who were used to a traditional formula.

On the other hand, once nWo started working, some of the non-nWo guys realized they needed to revamp their character. Sting was one of them. He'd been that highly animated character, with a platinum flattop, face paint, sequins, and all of that. He needed to update himself, get more of an edge. So we started exploring different options for that character.

Scott Hall came up with something he called "the scary Sting." He wanted Sting's character to have a little mystery about him, and danger. We never discussed it, but my guess is that Scott had seen the movie *The Crow* shortly before, because the connections between the lead character in the movie and what he suggested for Sting seem so obvious. They were both avengers, both mysterious, both out to right wrongs.

Sting embraced it. His character became an avenger, literally watching from the rafters, waiting for the right time to strike. The more the nWo succeeded in routing the WCW, the more he brooded.

An Evolution

Much like a lot of other things we had done that were not necessarily preplanned, we watched it evolve. Every week it became more and more apparent to me that we were onto something. Every week that went by where Sting didn't tell us what was on his mind, or why he was dressed in black—the more he didn't tell us, the more powerful and interesting he became as a character. I just let it roll.

All too often then—and even more so now—we in the wrestling business don't have the patience to let things build. We don't have the luxury of time to let a story or character build. But I took the chance with this. Much as I did with the nWo, I let it grow without forcing it in any direction. After a few months, it became clear that this was something we could sustain. It was powerful enough that it was no longer a question of whether we could keep it going, but of how did we want to pay it off?

I decided I wanted to pay it off with a Hogan versus Sting. We'd never seen that match. Now it made perfect sense.

Hogan was an anti-WCW character. The old-line fans didn't appreciate Hogan as a babyface, and liked him even less as a heel. Sting represented the last hope for the true, hard-core WCW fan.

By April or May of 1997, we'd decided to let it build toward *Starcade* in December. Then it became a question of keeping it fresh. That's why we came up with things like Sting rappeling down from the rafters and showing up with a vulture. All those crazy things we did, from Sting masks on the wrestlers to fake Stings in the audience, came from asking ourselves how we could make it different.

We got a better reaction from Sting doing nothing than we had from most wrestlers wrestling each week.

On Top of the World, but Not Quite Ready

Souled Out

Souled Out, the Pay-Per-View devoted solely to nWo we aired in January 1997, was another attempt at giving a Pay-Per-View a different feel. At the same time, I hoped to explore and possibly lay the groundwork for separating WCW into two separate brands: the mainstream or older WCW brand and the rebel nWo.

By late 1996 or early 1997, I decided to try to create two separate wrestling brands, nWo and WCW. Each would have its own roster of wrestlers and, eventually, its own show. That way, I could have my own war. Everyone had always fantasized about an event pitting WWE and WCW wrestlers—a Super Bowl, if you will. That was never going to happen. But I thought that, by creating two brands, I would get as close as possible.

By now we were so far ahead of WWE that they were not even really competition, at least not in my mind. I was a little full of myself, to say the least, but there was nothing coming out of WWE that led me to believe that they were going to be able to regroup at this point and challenge us.

And yet I knew competition was the key to our success. Us versus them was the formula that had gotten us to the top of the ratings. First, it was *Nitro* versus *Raw*. Now it was WCW as seen by the true-blue WCW fan, and nWo. I decided I had to maintain the audience's belief that nWo represented one style of wrestling, and WCW represented another. The clashes of those cultures and philosophies would sustain a tremendous story arc.

Because of that, *Souled Out* was designed to be the nWo's version of what a Pay-Per-View should look like. Everything about it was designed to reflect the renegade, counterculture anarchy that defined nWo. It had a stark, industrial feel, and we tried to do things in keeping with that. Instead of coming to the arena in limousines, for example, we rode in on garbage trucks.

The interesting story there is that it was about twenty-five degrees below zero when we filmed the trip in. It was snowing, bitterly cold, but we wanted to shoot it at night in downtown Cedar Rapids, and the only chance we had was the Saturday before the Pay-Per-View. It was cold as shit. Brutal. But it did set the tone.

Then there was the beauty contest. Everybody else celebrates beautiful women. We wanted to celebrate—uh, not so beautiful women.

Sometimes on different college campuses around the country, guys will have contests to see who can bring home the ugliest chick. And that's where the idea came from. We wanted to find the nastiest, gnarliest white trash we could possibly find. The women were in on it. We told them what we were doing. We said, "We're looking for some real women, wink, wink." A couple of them weighed two hundred and fifty, three hundred pounds.

As the leader of nWo, I was the one who got to pick the winner, crown her, and swap spit with her. At that moment, my wife sat back and said, "Oh, my God."

The buy rate on the Pay-Per-View was only .47, a drop off from

December's *Starcade*, which had hit .95. (The buy rate measures the percentage of possible cable subscribers who opt to pay for the program.) I won't deny that I would have loved higher numbers. On the other hand, I don't think our expectations were all that high, and the lower number was not a tremendous disappointment. This was the first time out for this Pay-Per-View, and anytime you're launching a new show, you can't expect the numbers to be stellar. The card—I forget the exact matches now—was okay, but it wasn't of the caliber we had at *Starcade*.

Even so, the numbers told me that we hadn't built the nWo up yet to the point where it could sustain its own weekly show. I felt that as strong as the concept had been up to this point, we didn't quite have the infrastructure in terms of story and talent to sustain it. And the buzz was starting to weaken.

Don't get me wrong, the audience was still into it. We were still selling out arenas. We were still kicking ass on television. But we weren't ready. I put off the idea of dividing WCW into two separate brands. The idea was good, but I had to slow the horse a little.

ECW & Paul Heyman

To hear Paul Heyman tell it, I was obsessed with his company, Extreme Championship Wrestling, around this time. According to some alleged histories of wrestling, both Vince McMahon and I took our best ideas from ECW. But the truth is, I didn't pay much attention to ECW at all. I couldn't even get it on cable where I lived.

ECW was a unique little company, with a nice little niche catering to so-called hard-core wrestling fans, but it was not the little niche that was interesting to me as a fan or, more importantly, one that had any sort of application to WCW.

I'm not sure what to say about Paul. He could be a chapter to himself. I first met him when he worked for Verne Gagne. Didn't like him then; didn't trust him then.

Creatively, I have a lot of respect for Paul. He's got a very solid and unique creative perspective. But he's got serious integrity issues that I have a hard time overlooking.

Big Bad Eric

Trying to keep ECW afloat with very little money—it eventually went bankrupt—Paul needed to get his people to work under pretty ridiculous conditions. He needed people who were willing to go to the extreme to execute the vision he had for ECW. Most of all, Paul needed people who would show up to work when they weren't getting paychecks.

One of the ways he did this was by painting a picture of how big bad Eric Bischoff and the almighty Ted Turner organization were doing everything they could to keep ECW down.

I didn't give a flying fuck about Paul Heyman or ECW. Every once in a while, I'd get a call from someone who'd say, "Hey, I haven't got a check from Paul Heyman in three months. He keeps telling me the check is in the mail, but it's not. I need to work. Will you hire me?"

I'd take a look at the situation, and maybe I'd hire them. That's all there ever was to it. Nothing sinister, nothing dark and evil. It was just business.

Paul would then turn the situation around. "There he is again, stealing our talent, trying to keep us down. They're afraid of us. We've got them on the run."

Nothing was farther from the truth.

But the Internet community and dirtsheets hung on it.

We were doing 5s and 6s on TNT; he was doing .5s on what was then the Nashville Network. We were putting fifteen, twenty, twenty-five thousand people in arenas all over the country: he was putting eleven hundred idiots in a bingo hall. His Pay-Per-View drew nothing. There was no reason to believe that we were on the same playing field competitively. But it worked for Paul. Or at least, he thought it did.

I remember one wrestler who wanted to come to WCW. Paul couldn't afford to pay him. The guy knew it. Paul knew it. Paul had some ridiculously loose contract that wouldn't have held up in court. Knowing Paul, he may have written it himself after the guy told him he was leaving ECW; I'm not sure.

This guy wanted to come over to us. Paul made a stink about a lawsuit. He knew, having worked at Turner, that all you had to do was say "lawsuit," and you'd get a check. Maybe a big check, maybe a little check, but you'd get something.

I didn't want to go through the bullshit. So I called him up and said, "Why don't we meet in Orlando? Let's see if we can figure out a way to make this work. Maybe we can have some fun here."

Paul came down. We had dinner. We couldn't see eye to eye. It wasn't bad, it wasn't hostile. We just couldn't make it work.

No one, including myself, knew at the time that there was a connection between WWE and ECW. No one knew that Paul was being subsidized by Vince McMahon. Paul was clearly speaking with Vince on a regular basis. And when he got back after our dinner, I believe he told someone at WWE that I was on cocaine.

Shortly after my meeting with Paul, during a deposition relating to a lawsuit between WWE and WCW, WWE lawyer Jerry McDivett asked me a series of questions about cocaine use. I thought, *Where the hell did this come from?* It was very odd. We'd had hours and hours of depositions, and nothing like that had ever come up. I didn't do cocaine and had no idea at the time why in the world McDivett was going in this direction. It was like asking me how many puppies I had set on fire that week.

Years later, I realized that Paul must have gone back and said, serious or not, "Oh, that fucking Eric, he's jacked up on cocaine." During our meeting, I'd excused myself several times to go to the restroom so I could take phone calls I didn't want to take in front of Paul. I guess he put one and zero together and came up with twenty-seven.

Do I respect him creatively? Yes. Would I work with him in the ring? Absolutely. Would I sit down and shoot the shit with him if we were sitting around an arena? Sure. He makes me laugh.

Do I believe he's so full of shit he believes his own lies? Absolutely.

And so do others who've worked with him.

Speaking of Characters . . .

Hulk Hogan called me one afternoon while I was at a meeting at the airport Marriott in Atlanta. He'd just gotten off the phone with Dennis Rodman. Rodman, the eccentric Chicago Bulls forward, was talking about doing a deal with the WWE. Hogan wanted us to grab Rodman instead.

"If I get you Rodman's number," he asked, "can you give him a call?"

Sure.

I ended up talking to Dennis's agent, Dwight Manley. I didn't ask him much about the WWE; it wasn't my concern. We ended up doing a deal pretty easily. I don't remember the dollar amount or the exact terms; it was probably in the area of two television appearances and a single Pay-Per-View, for something in the area of $1 million. That's a bit lower than was reported at the time.

Dennis was a very high-profile, very controversial character at the time. His basketball career was at its peak, and the Michael Jordan–led Bulls were in the middle of what would become an historic second three-peat as champions of the NBA.

If Dennis wasn't born to be a wrestling character, I don't know who was. He was an outrageous, over-the-top character. He attracted media attention wherever he went. He fit in perfectly with the nWo bad-boy image.

Dennis appeared at the *Bash at the Beach* Pay-Per-View that July, the first of several Pay-Per-Views that he did with us over the next few years. He was a pain in the ass to work with. Dennis is his own guy and pretty much operates in his own little world. Most of the time, that's inconsistent with the world around him. He doesn't like to conform to rules and regulations and structure and schedule—all the things that make the world go around. Getting him to train was problematic, and that limited what we could do with him. But he could also be a lot of fun, and in the end we were all surprised by how well he did as a wrestler.

Even though Rodman was a phenomenal athlete, wrestling is a whole different skill set and requires a good deal of training even for the more basic moves. While it looks easy, it's not. Professional athletes are often more confident than they should be in their ability to pick it up. There have been some exceptions. Karl Malone trained incredibly hard and performed exceptionally well.

Kevin Greene was another athlete who did a great job when he came on with us. Kevin was a five-time pro-bowl linebacker and standout with the Pittsburgh Steelers and Carolina Panthers. If I recall correctly, he was the NFL's third leading tackler of all time when he retired in 1999.

He poured himself into the training for our show, trying to be as good as he could possibly be. I had several conversations with Kevin, and he told me that wrestling was even more physically demanding than football. For a guy with that kind of world-class professional background to stand back and bow down to what these guys put themselves through says a lot.

A Million Bucks of Publicity

Some people criticized me for spending any money on Rodman. They didn't understand why a crazy basketball player—or any other nonwrestling athlete, for that matter—belonged in the wrestling ring.

They completely missed the point. And while the buy rate was pretty good—the event drew a .78 buy rate, better than *Slamboree* before it and Sturgis afterward—getting more people to tune in wasn't my real goal either. It's hard to measure any one element of a Pay-Per-View, but the thing that I was focusing on in hiring Rodman was the press attention we'd get. I knew hiring Rodman would create controversy—and controversy creates cash.

In those terms, the Pay-Per-View was a runaway success. If I had to buy the amount of press and coverage that Dennis Rodman got us, it would have cost me much, much more than what we paid him.

There was one added bonus, though it didn't appear on any balance sheet or business plan: he drank Hogan under the table. Rodman should get another ring just for that.

Bill Goldberg

Bill Goldberg was also a professional athlete before he came to us in 1997, though obviously he was in a different category than Rodman or Kevin Greene.

Bill had played for the Atlanta Falcons for a few years before injuries took their toll and he retired from the NFL. He knew a couple of the guys who worked at WCW and apparently told them he wanted to try wrestling. They had him contact me.

To be honest, it took me quite a while to respond. Bill and I might have traded phone calls once or twice, but because there was so much going on for me, I kept putting it off. Bill got real frustrated and said to somebody, I'm going to wait one more week, and then if I don't hear from Eric, I'm going to go do a deal with WWE.

I'm not sure who it was now, maybe Sting or Diamond Dallas Page, but somebody came to me and urged me to get back to him. I forced myself to find the time, and he really impressed me. Bill was a very likable guy, charismatic; he certainly had a tremendous look. I thought there was real potential there, so I hired him and put him in the PowerPlant for a couple of months.

Learning by Doing

You can only teach someone so much about performing within the confines of a gym or training facility. The real art in our business is the ability to connect with an audience and ultimately manipulate that audience's emotions. That's born from experience. You have to go out and do it.

We saw a lot of potential in Bill early on, and we wanted to collapse the learning curve. He had such a great look, and was *so* intense, that we wanted to get him out in front of people. So we put him out in the ring in what we called "dark" or "squash" matches. These were matches that weren't televised and took place at the arena right before *Nitro* went on. They were usually quick matches designed to rev up the audience and, more importantly, give the green, inexperienced performers a chance to get out in front of a crowd and develop their art.

I'd heard so many good things about Bill from the PowerPlant that I made it a point to watch Bill in the dark matches. I could tell he was going to be a star. People immediately identified with his character, a wrestler focused on stomping his opponent into oblivion as quickly and efficiently as possible. He got so caught up in who he was that the audience couldn't help believe in him as well. Bill got a tremendous reaction from the crowd whenever he performed.

That intensity was also one of the things that caused him ultimately to unravel, but that lay in the future.

Building Him Up

We had this great character, but Bill still didn't have enough experience in the ring to have much of a match with anybody. A great wrestling match is a tango or waltz that takes two people to really succeed. They both have to be equally talented. A Ric Flair or a Chris Benoit or a Triple H can have a great match with just about anybody because of their experience and their abilities. But those types of performers are few and far between.

It wasn't Bill's fault; he just didn't have enough experience yet. You can't give someone ten years of experience in six months.

But we *really* wanted to use him right away.

I don't know who came up with the idea—a lot of people seem to have taken credit for Bill's success over the years—but someone said something along these lines: "Let's have him go out, and do what he does best: let's have him mow through people as quickly as possible, and build that character. At the same time, we'll give him the experience to become a better wrestler."

And so began pro wrestling's famous unbeaten string, which would build and run through the following year. It was the first time, apparently, that a wrestler had a long unbeaten streak, and that such a streak was used as an angle. The audience gradually caught on, and one by one signs began appearing in the arenas with his record: 30–0, 42–0, 53–0.

Mistakes & Problems

Arn Anderson

From the launch of *Nitro*, WCW was on an incredible roll. It seemed we could do no wrong.

That's not to say that we didn't make mistakes. We did. I did. How I handled Arn Anderson's retirement was one of them.

Wrestling fans know that Arn was one of the Four Horsemen and was one of the best tag team wrestlers of all time. I have a lot of respect for Arn Anderson for a lot of different reasons. Did I think that Arn Anderson was a Ric Flair–caliber performer or a Hulk Hogan–caliber performer? No, I didn't. But I don't think it's fair to say that anybody really did. He didn't perform at that main-event level nationally. He didn't drive record buy rates or fill arenas. He was never a household name. But he was nonetheless a very solid and important part of the program. He was one of the wrestlers you need to have on your roster, in the upper third, upper 25 percent of your roster. He could go out there day in, day out, have great interviews, and perform in the ring. He had the talent and credibility to perform up to anyone's level or make a journeyman look like a seasoned vet. Not a lot of performers can do that.

In 1997, Arn Anderson suffered a neck injury that left him unable to perform in the ring. Arn was able to contribute in a lot of other ways after that, but as a wrestler, his career was pretty much over.

Once again, we took a real-life situation and wove it into a storyline. It was something we'd been doing since the start of *Nitro*, blurring the line between fact and fiction. It was the magic formula that made all of this work to begin with. But I didn't really understand the kind of impact this could have on certain individuals, and Arn was one of them.

Arn gave a retirement speech on *Nitro* August 25, 1997; the speech is still talked about as one of the most emotional in the history of the business. Arn had an ability to do an interview like no one else in the business. Add to that the real emotion of the situation, and it's not surprising that people in the cheap seats were wiping tears from their eyes.

The next week, WCW staged a tribute to him on *Nitro*. Midway through, nWo members began tearing into him, using clips from the speech the week before to make fun of him. Scott Hall and Kevin Nash had a ball with it.

The bit was highly effective. The audience related to Arn and showered Hall and Nash with abuse—which was the idea. But Arn's family was deeply hurt by it, and so was Arn. There were also bad feelings with other wrestlers behind the scenes who felt I went too far and disrespected Arn.

I've come to know and understand Arn much better since I started working with him in WWE. He's a very proud individual. Looking back at it, I asked too much—or most likely I didn't even ask. I just assumed and expected Arn would let us weave the reality of what he was going through into a storyline that would benefit others. I didn't take into consideration the emotional impact his forced retirement had on him and his family.

I thought if I was in his shoes, I'd do it, and therefore felt it shouldn't be an issue. The problem was, I wasn't in his shoes. I hadn't spent my professional life creating his character or legacy. Quite frankly, it's one of those things that if I had to do it over again, I wouldn't.

A Man of Courage

Arn's hard feelings toward me stayed with him for years. When I came into WWE, he was one of the people who turned white as a ghost when he saw me backstage for the first time. The look on his face mixed shock, anger, and fear—and probably some emotions I didn't even understand.

The first two and a half years I was in WWE, our relationship was very strained. I think on the surface we tried to pretend that we were moving on, but there was underlying tension and baggage between Arn and myself. Although we tried to ignore it, it was still there.

Arn went through some personal issues of his own while he was in WWE. He dealt with them with a great deal of dignity and courage. Afterward, I approached Arn and told him how much I admired him and the way he tackled things head-on in his life.

I think that was around that time we started to heal the old wounds. As it happened, Arn was one of the last people I said good-bye to when I got "fired" by Vince McMahon in 2005. I didn't know for certain if I'd be back, or when I'd have a chance to talk to him again. So I made sure I told him I appreciated the opportunity to work with him, appreciated the opportunity to get to know him better, and hoped that down the road we'd get to work together again.

Abuse of Power

As the head of nWo, my on-air character had an incredible reign of terror through 1996. He began to show signs of vulnerability in 1997, getting taken down a peg or two so the viewers would have some hope that he might finally be busted. Harvey Schiller even came on air and "suspended" me. It was a simple story, really. Someone rises to power, abuses that power, and appears to be unstoppable. Then something happens and reveals a flaw or a weakness, giving an opportunity for things to be reversed. Hope.

In real life, a reversal of fortune seemed unthinkable. Things at WCW were going extremely well. We were meeting and beating all of our financial targets. Harvey would tell stories about being on the golf course with other top executives from Turner, and all anyone wanted to talk about was WCW. *In a positive way!* I would get a phone call every Tuesday at three o'clock from Scott Sassa and Brad Siegel congratulating me on the ratings from the *Nitro* show the night before. We were high-fiving each other over the phone. I'd get calls from Ted Turner maybe once a month, saying how proud he was of WCW.

WWE wasn't real competition. They had their own style and appealed to a different audience. We were clearly different from what they did, and our audience loved what we were doing.

We were doing so well that no one, myself included, recognized the problems brewing. We were operating at the limits of our capacity, maybe even beyond. As much as I hate to admit it, I was going too fast. As hard as it is to create success, I would soon learn that managing it is even more challenging.

Horsepower Under the Hood

Part of the problem was personnel. We didn't have enough horsepower under the hood.

When I'd taken over, I didn't have the ability to go out and hire the best of the best as a support staff. For the most part, I had to work with what I had. Not only didn't I have the budget to go out and hire the right people, the unique nature of our business made it difficult to find the right people in the first place.

In the beginning, that was okay. We could make mistakes and survive them. Expectations were low.

As we became more successful, the mistakes we made were more noticeable. But everything we touched was so profitable, the mistakes didn't seem to have an effect. Our house-show business was going through the roof, our Pay-Per-Views were doing very well, and we were developing licensing and marketing platforms. All of the revenue streams showed tremendous growth, so it was easy to overlook mistakes. It was only as the load became heavier and the stakes became higher that the mistakes began taking a very noticeable toll.

We needed more mental horsepower to keep up with our success, and we didn't have it. If I had to do it all over again, there would be a laundry list of people I'd have fired early on, because they were unqualified for the positions they were in. For whatever reason, whether it was a soft spot in my heart or because I thought I could get them on board, I didn't can them.

Despite my reputation, I never really enjoyed firing anybody— particularly people who had been in the business all of their professional lives. In many cases, they didn't have anywhere else to go.

And in some others, it was easier to keep them around than to rock the human resources boat.

There were individuals who worked for WCW overseeing our live event promotion who weren't up to the job. Gary Juster, in particular, was in my opinion the most ineffective, untalented individual I've ever had the misfortune to work with. He'd been with the company from day one, but his only claim to fame was being a great politician. He was a protégé of Jim Barnett. The only real skill Gary developed was being an ass-kisser. But he occupied a position that was critical to our success—or lack thereof.

Sharon Sidello bounced around from marketing to Pay-Per-View. She was very intelligent. She impressed me from time to time, but overall I don't think she had the kind of vision to grow her department to the extent she should have grown it. She didn't have the horsepower and presence. Moreover, her relationship with Ole Anderson tainted her point of view. She was constantly positioning for more power, but couldn't make things happen in the areas where she had control. I debated often whether I should keep her on staff, and in retrospect I wish I hadn't.

We also had our own unique challenges because we were part of a large corporate structure. Accounting and legal did not report to me, and it was sometimes difficult to manage them because they had their own agendas and points of view. In terms of checks and balances, I understand and agree with the structure. But I wish I had had someone working directly for me who could have done a better job interfacing with those two departments than I did. I didn't really have the time to do a good job. Even if I had, I didn't have the personality, and I wasn't really interested.

Hiring Freeze

We were growing and needed more people to handle the work. The increased revenue would have justified a larger payroll. Why didn't I go out and hire more people?

I couldn't. There was a companywide hiring freeze. Even if I had the money for a position, I didn't have the ability to go outside the company and find someone to fill it. I had to take someone from inside the company. I soon discovered that the only people available were on the bubble—they were either earmarked for termination from the jobs they already had in other departments of Turner or had put in a request to be transferred to another division.

I wasn't allowed to "steal" people from other departments either. They had to be thinking of quitting or, like I said, about to get fired; then human resources would send them my way.

Turner's merger with Time Warner had led to pressure for more revenue, lower costs, greater profit. That applied to everyone, not just WCW. Things were tight in 1997. They would get a lot worse in 1998 and then 1999 as Time Warner ramped up for its merger with AOL.

For us, the squeeze came with *Thunder,* the Thursday-night show we added in 1998.

Yet Another Show

This Isn't a Joke

Right after the Sturgis Pay-Per-View in the summer of 1997, I took a short vacation. I was beat, and I needed time with my wife and kids. We'd recently bought some property up in Wyoming, so we decided that after the event we'd rent a van, drive up to the property, and spend some time with the kids.

About halfway there, I got a phone call from Harvey Schiller. "Eric, how are you? Congratulations, great Pay-Per-View," all the yada yada yada stuff.

"By the way," he added, "I just got out of a meeting with Ted. Because of the success of *Monday Nitro* on TNT, Ted wants to launch a show on TBS."

"Harvey, I'm on vacation, I'm not going to let you piss me off." I thought he was kidding. "I'm not taking the bait. Come up with another joke."

"No, Eric, I'm serious. Ted wants to do this."

"Harvey, no matter how hard you try, I'm not going to take the bait."

It took him several minutes to convince me he was serious. The new show, which we eventually called *Thunder*, was supposed to be another two-hour live event broadcast every week in prime time.

I thought to myself, My God, we're already operating at 110 percent capacity. This *has* to be a joke.

EBITDA

We had a big meeting with Brad Siegel, TBS, and other people at Turner Broadcasting. It was the first time I heard the term "EBITDA": Earnings Before Interest, Taxes, Depreciation, and Amortization.

The term, which is a way of measuring profitability, has been around in accounting circles for a long time. But it really came into vogue in the 1980s and '90s during corporate takeovers and mergers. The emphasis on EBITDA led to wholesale layoffs in many industries, since the easiest way to increase profits in the short run is by cutting expenses, and the biggest expense in many industries is salaries. Of course, that's a very short-sighted approach, since it can be difficult to sustain a business and almost impossible to grow without adding more employees. Looking at EBITDA instead of thinking about ways to grow the company can choke a business—as many corporations, AOL Time Warner in particular, would eventually discover.

I was to hear about EBITDA a lot over the next few years, as the Time Warner corporate mentality gradually strangled Turner's entrepreneurial culture. What EBITDA meant in this case was that no one wanted to do anything that would increase their division's expenses—like contributing toward the costs of a new wrestling show.

They were concerned that their "profit centers"—whether TBS or TNT or Turner Sports or whatever—had good numbers at the end of the year. Their stock options depended on it.

Ted had mandated that we were going to have *Thunder* on TBS, but he hadn't specified where the money for it was to come from. Before the merger, this wouldn't have been as much of an issue. Mandates rolled downhill from Ted Turner, who expected his people to figure out how to implement them. He kept people focused on the company as a whole. But now the corporate culture had changed, and everyone worried about their own division. We knew what the mission was, but no one wanted to pay for it.

The additional production expense in running another show was huge. Another *Nitro*-like show would call for another forty or fifty people. I'd have to hire fifteen to twenty new production people alone. I had no idea where to find them, since I couldn't hire from outside the company.

And then there was the talent. If I used just the wrestlers I already had in another two-hour show, I'd overexpose them. I'd also run the risk of watering the stories down to the point where they wouldn't be significant any longer. And that assumed that I didn't run them down to the point of sheer exhaustion. Another show meant I had to add on-air talent and writers or bookers as well.

The cost to produce the show would have run somewhere between $12 and $15 million a year. TBS, in theory the buyer and beneficiary of *Thunder*, refused to pay it.

The Power to Say No

It's possible that I had the power to say no.

Maybe if I had said, *"No, Ted,"* we wouldn't have gone through with it. Maybe if I said, "This decision will have a long-term negative impact on *Nitro* and WCW," I could have stopped the train. But I didn't.

I didn't think I was in a position to argue against anything Ted wanted. He didn't call and say, "Hey, Eric, do you think we should or shouldn't?" Had I gotten *that* message, I would have been happy to give Ted all the reasons why we shouldn't. But that wasn't the situation. I wasn't given an opportunity to vote; I was given an opportunity to do what I was told to do.

Brad Siegel pulled me aside and said, "Eric, this is a mistake; don't walk the plank on this one. Don't step out there if you're not a hundred percent sure. This is a mistake." I wish I had taken Brad's advice at that time.

I didn't want to disappoint Ted. And I was overconfident that I could make it work. I was willing to risk my career doing it.

I tried to find the funds by expanding WCW's operations and growing our revenue. I went back to my staff and said, *"If we increase our house show business by twenty-five or thirty percent"*—I forget the actual number—*"what will that do to our revenue?"*

The number that came back was big enough to almost cover the projected cost of producing the show. Adding another hour to *Nitro*—taking it from two to three hours—we'd get even closer. TBS came up with a small amount of money, though they were still basically getting *Thunder* for free.

Rather than saying no, I'd figured out a way to pay for it.

Positioned for Failure

I wasn't looking at it clearly, but WCW was being positioned for failure.

A division that didn't live up to the expectations for EBITDA was in trouble. Knowing now that there were still people with an agenda to make WCW go away, I should not have taken on the responsibility for financing *Thunder*. It not only stretched us beyond our capacity but weakened our finances.

The new emphasis on EBITDA was not the only change going on above me. Ted Turner was slowly but surely being neutralized by the Time Warner executives he'd sold his company to. He'd always been WCW's strongest booster. With him out of the way, those who wanted to get rid of the company would have an easy time of it.

I didn't realize any of that then. I thought Ted was still the captain of the ship. He said, This is what I want. Being the good sailor I was, I said to myself, *Okay, if no one else is willing to make this work, I will.*

It buried us.

Too Much

Bret Hart & the Montreal Screwjob

Bret Hart

It was during the preparations for what became *Thunder* that I got the green light to get Bret Hart. We needed another one or two very high-profile pieces of talent for the new show.

Bret began wrestling in 1976. By the 1990s, he was one of the biggest stars in the WWE. A native of Calgary, he had an immense following in Canada, where he had the status of a national hero.

Bret's contract with WWE had come due in 1996, and he and I had had a conversation around that time, feeling each other out. Contrary to what was reported at the time and has been repeated ever since, we never got into serious negotiations. We met in Los Angeles and hit it off personally. The chemistry was good. But I don't think he was really serious about coming over, and I didn't really need him. Bret ended up signing a large multiyear deal with Vince McMahon.

Less than a year later, Bret made it clear that he was available. I can't speak to what happened with Bret and Vince. Different reports have claimed that Vince gave Bret his blessing to talk with us because WWE had financial problems at the time. I really don't know any of that. All I know is that Bret and I put together an agreement very quickly.

Montreal Screwjob

There was no secret that Bret was coming over to WCW. The fact that Bret was WWE Champion posed real problems for Vince. He wanted Bret to lose the title before coming over to us. Bret didn't want to lose the title in Montreal. I wasn't there, so I don't know, but according to what's been published, Bret and Vince worked out an agreement that would have let Bret hold on to the title during a match in Montreal; he would hand the title to Vince on a live *Raw* show the following day.

But if that was the agreement, Vince changed his mind. At the Montreal show, he had the referee quick-count Bret out, awarding the title to Shawn Michaels. The episode was filmed and aired on the documentary *Wrestling with Shadows*, and became known to most fans as the Montreal Screwjob.

It's possible that Vince thought he couldn't trust Bret—or more accurately, couldn't trust me.

I had given Vince every reason in the world to believe that I would exploit the situation to my maximum ability and denigrate WWE in every way possible. I'm sure he thought I would have Bret trash the title in much the way I had Madusa trash the women's championship on national television. But that wasn't the case.

Had Vince known what Bret and I had really discussed—and more importantly, what the legal division at Turner Broadcasting told me I could do and couldn't do—Montreal never would have happened. At the time we were involved in copyright and trade-mark litigation with WWE, and the legal department of Turner

Broadcasting didn't want to add fuel to the fire. They made it clear that I had to work within certain parameters—and those parameters did NOT include anything close to trashing WWE titles.

I was cool with that, because at that point it didn't really matter. We had clearly positioned ourselves as number one, and I didn't need to pull the kind of stuff I had back when Madusa came over. But Vince didn't know that, and I don't think anyone could have convinced him.

In fact, while we were settling our contract terms, Bret came to me and said, "What's going to happen if Vince wants me to lose the match in Montreal?" I told him it didn't matter.

"The audience is sophisticated enough to understand what's going on. Your win-loss record is really not that important. How you end your relationship with WWE is not important. Do whatever you feel you need to do. If you need to lose in order to shake hands and part company as friends, go ahead and do that."

Vince McMahon had nothing to fear, and ultimately the Montreal incident was unnecessary and unfortunate.

Or maybe not. Maybe it ultimately played itself out, and everyone made money off it. But I know firsthand that it had a pretty big impact on Bret.

Not the Same Bret

When Bret got to WCW, he was not the Bret Hart that we had watched in WWE. I think the incident with Vince McMahon took a tremendous toll on him. Or perhaps Bret never really felt at home in WCW. Either way, he never quite regained his passion for the business.

As much as I like Bret and respect him, there was a real lack of passion and commitment. I kind of understood it, though it was hard for me to relate to his sense of betrayal. For me, it was about the outcome of a wrestling match. As underhanded as it *may* have been—italicize *may*, because I'm still not sure it was all that it was supposed to be—at the end of the day it was just a wrestling match. None of it is real anyway. I have a hard time understanding why a wrestler takes something that is fiction to heart, though many do.

I was hoping that Bret would get used to being in WCW, and would kick it back into gear. But it didn't happen.

Oh, Canada

Part of it was that Bret felt he let his fans down. There's a different culture in Canada. They view their national celebrities as national heroes. That's not true in the United States. We don't think of them as uniquely American celebrities. In Canada, they're *Canadian* celebrities. And if they migrate into the United States and meet with success, they become national heroes because they've succeeded in America. Canadians are so proud of other Canadians that it's almost obnoxious.

I've tried to figure it out over the years. One reason, I think, is that Canada isn't really an independent country.

Sure, technically they are, in the sense that there's a border and they have their own laws. But otherwise they're totally dependent on the United States. Their economy is completely dependent on ours. Their army and their navy are nonexistent when it comes to being able to actually defend their country; they rely on the United States to do most of the job. If you look at the demographics of Canada, a large percentage of the population lives within a hundred miles or so of the border. Why do you think that's the case? So they can get the hell out of Canada as often as they can!

When you add all of that up, there's a certain sense of inferiority. So any time you have a Dan Aykroyd or a Celine Dion or a Bret Hart or a Wayne Gretzky, Canadians tend to hold that person up to a level that those of us in the United States just don't understand. Even though the first thing most of these people do is move to the United States.

Bret was a national hero to Canadians. When I first heard him say that, I thought, *Man, that's a little wacky. That's taking the whole self-promotion thing to a whole 'nother level.* But the fact is, it's true. So what happened to Bret in Montreal had a much bigger impact on him than it might have had for another wrestler.

Passion

After Bret came to WCW, a lot of people criticized us for not using him the "correct" way, as if there's a "correct" way to use someone like Bret Hart, or any wrestler. There is no set formula that is absolutely tried and true and proven. It's all subjective. The greatest part of it depends on the creative powers of the artist himself.

You can have the best-written screenplay, with the best director, the best sound track, and the best supporting cast, and if your lead actor really doesn't feel the part, chances are that movie is never going to be what you want it to be.

I think in some part, that was the problem with Bret. Regardless of how we used him, there was never the passion and the commitment to the role that could propel him.

Steve Austin is a perfect example of a guy who had been cast in certain roles that he didn't really relate to, such as the Ringmaster. I'm sure he gave as much as he could to those roles, but they weren't Steve. When he became the rattlesnake, when he was allowed to be just Steve Austin, it was a character he understood. It clicked. For a lot of reasons.

When things hit big, there are always a lot of reasons why they work. But Steve's passion was a major reason.

Eric Bischoff, Vince McMahon, Steven Spielberg, an independent film director that no one's ever heard of—we can only do so much when creating a role for someone. It's really up to the performer. He or she brings life to the role.

I'm not suggesting that we had the best ideas for Bret Hart. But regardless of our shortcomings, Bret came to WCW with baggage because of Montreal. He couldn't shake it. It was all he talked about. Constantly.

A Screwjob of Our Own

Sting & Hogan at *Starcade*

We went into *Starcade*, the December 1997 Pay-Per-View, knowing that we had a hit on our hands. We'd been building the Sting character for a year, leading to the inevitable confrontation with Hogan. The anticipation was intense. It was a classic babyface vs. heel confrontation with our own cutting-edge spin: an edgy babyface, Sting, taking on a good guy gone vicious, Hulk Hogan.

But for the first time since the very early matches, Hogan and I disagreed over the outcome.

The way we'd built it up, Sting should have been the clean winner. But Hogan was underwhelmed with Sting, and balked.

I didn't really see his point of view. I had a hard time reading between the lines with Hogan because he didn't come flat out and tell me what his issues were. But I think Hogan was disappointed with Sting's preparation. Sting was clearly out of shape. He looked like he hadn't seen a gym or a tanning bed in six months. Up until that time, Sting could get away with that. He'd show up at the arenas and do his act wearing his black trench coat and his face paint; he didn't actually wrestle.

This is me reading between the lines here, but I think Hogan figured, "Hey, wait a minute. We built this guy up for six months. He hasn't even bothered to stay in halfway decent shape and looks like he's been living in a cave." In Hogan's mind, that was a letdown.

Sting was a difficult guy to communicate with. He wasn't a hard person to do business with—don't confuse those two. Sting was very honest and for the most part straightforward, but in dealing with Hogan he kept his cards very close to his vest. There was a lot of—call it "diplomacy." They kept feeling each other out.

I don't think Sting really trusted Hogan. I think the lack of trust was somewhat well founded. There was some of it that wasn't, but a lot was. Sting had spent all of this time building up this character, and I think it was important to him that the payoff be decisive and one-sided—and in his favor. He wanted the win to have creditability, boosting the character as we went forward.

Hogan, on the other hand, felt that Sting hadn't really committed, or he would have shown up in better shape. Therefore, he wasn't that eager to have the match finish the way Sting wanted it to finish.

The way a wrestler wins or loses can be as important as the result. Losing a match on a disqualification, for example, is viewed far differently than losing on a submission. It's not just a matter of ego. It has implications for future storylines and the characters involved.

Of course, Hogan had creative control over the outcome of his matches. So I was caught in the middle.

We came up with a finish that mimicked what had happened to Bret Hart in Montreal. Sting would lose, or seem to lose, on a quick count by referee Nick Patrick. Bret Hart would rush in, shouting something along the lines of, "I'm not going to let this happen again." He'd toss the crooked ref from the ring and set up Sting to flatten Hogan with a scorpion deathlock. It wasn't the finish Sting wanted, because it wasn't clean, but it seemed like a decent compromise between two powerful pieces of talent.

A Flubbed Ending

The ending did not go the way it was supposed to. Literally millions of fans saw a count that was anything but quick. Replays make it pretty clear that Sting was legitimately counted out.

Which meant that the one who was screwed was Hogan, not Sting. And it undercut everything we'd been building toward.

To this day, I'm not sure why Nick Patrick's count didn't go the way we planned. It may have been one of those things that just happens in a live event. I didn't think he had done it on purpose, as some people suggested; I would have fired him on the spot if I had.

Quite frankly, the only thing I could do at that point was try to figure out a way to fix it the following day. We focused on the controversy—we replayed the tape of the count on *Nitro* and claimed Hogan had won—to justify a rematch and keep interest in the storyline. But it was immensely controversial, and put a bad spin on what should have been a wildly successful angle and Pay-Per-View.

Getting My Ass Kicked

That *Starcade* also marked the first time that I actually wrestled in a match. It was an inauspicious debut.

By that time my on-air persona had evolved to the point where he had enough heat that he could benefit a babyface. I felt it was time to share some of that heat.

I didn't want to get myself involved in a very high-profile matchup. I didn't have enough confidence in my ability, and I didn't want to put myself out there in that way, but I thought it was safe for me to step into the ring with Larry Zbyszko.

The match itself was actually Larry's idea, and I agreed right away. I thought a few people would think it was interesting to watch me get my ass kicked.

I knew Larry from my days in the AWA. We had good chemistry together. I also knew he'd spend the time to work with me so I wouldn't embarrass myself or him.

Unfortunately, while we were rehearsing a few days before the match, I blew out my knee. I fractured a bone at the top of the joint. It sounds worse than it was, really. It wasn't even that painful, but it swelled, and I couldn't really put much weight on it.

We had to adjust quite a bit because of it. Not that it mattered much to the outcome of the match—Larry had his way with me, and would have even if I'd been in perfect shape.

It was still a tremendous amount of fun. I'd gone out and created emotion by running my mouth, but this was a different way to get a reaction.

Nash's "Heart Attack"

That *Starcade* was also notable for something that *didn't* happen—the match between Kevin Nash and Giant. Nash's absence set off a flurry of speculation and rumor. A lot of people believed—and probably still do—that Nash simply boycotted the Pay-Per-View because he didn't want to lose to Giant.

He probably didn't want to lose, but that wasn't why he didn't show.

When his head is on straight, Kevin is one of the most creative and talented people I've ever met in the business. He doesn't have anything close to the personal problems that Scott Hall had. But Kevin did have a tendency to withdraw when Scott went off the deep end. He went off the deep end in his own way.

This was our first experience with a personal issue of Kevin's that has plagued him from time to time. His dad died of a heart attack when he was very young. At the time of *Starcade*, Kevin was getting to the age where his father had passed away, and I think his own mind he was afraid he might follow in his footsteps. So from time to time, when he had a little heartburn or a funny feeling in his chest, he would overreact.

That Saturday when I arrived in Washington for the Pay-Per-View, I got a call that Kevin was in a hospital in Phoenix and undergoing tests for a heart attack. Because of some of the stunts Kevin and Scott had played in the past, my first reaction was that it was Kevin's way of not having to show up to work. But I picked up the phone and eventually found out that Kevin was truly in the hospital undergoing tests. As angry and disappointed as I was, it was a legitimate scare.

Of course, a lot of people jumped to the conclusion that Kevin was playing games. It wasn't true, though given the bad feelings that were starting to cycle through the locker room, it wasn't surprising that they thought that.

Starcade closed out 1997 by scoring a 1.9 buy rate, our best ever. WCW had peaked, though we had no idea at the time.

Seeds of Destruction

Thunder Debut

Thunder's debut on Thursday night, January 8, 1998, scored a 4.0 Nielsen rating, said to be the highest cable debut of all time. But the success was mostly due to *Nitro*. Our Monday-night show was at its peak, and it was relatively easy to drag that audience over to TBS and cross-promote the show. I wasn't surprised it was successful.

The show did better than most cable programs, hovering in the low 3's over the next year and a half. But the ratings were always well behind those of *Nitro*. Quite frankly, *Thunder* just wasn't a great show. We attempted to give it a different look and feel than *Nitro*, because it was so important to be different. We put different talent on the shows at first, but we knew that couldn't last; we simply didn't have enough top talent for both shows. And nWo wasn't strong enough on its own to give it *Thunder*. The show ended up looking dark, and didn't have the energy *Nitro* had. We didn't do a good job of making it *different*, so it became *less*.

Discontent

The politics and the egos among some of the talent began to wear pretty thin soon after *Thunder's* debut. I brought Bret Hart in specifically because I needed more talent for *Thunder* and our expanded schedule. But bringing him in and paying him the amount of money that I had to pay him created a whole new set of problems with a lot of the other wrestlers. They didn't like the fact that a newcomer was making more than they were.

Adding more house shows only made morale worse. It contradicted one of the basic rules I'd followed in making WCW profitable. One of the draws for talent had been the fact that we put on substantially less shows per year than WWE. The better quality of life had been a big motivator, a reason for wrestlers to join us. Now we'd taken that away.

I tried to split up the wrestlers and rotate the schedule, but the load remained much heavier than it had been. Wrestlers weren't the only ones who were stretched either. The production people, the office staff, and the people in our support positions also had to do more. Some complained and were generally uncomfortable, even though they soldiered on. It was more a slow burn than an explosion.

Besides *Thunder* and the additional house shows, we expanded *Nitro* to three hours. There was no additional expense doing that, because everybody was already there. Whether you do a one-hour show or a three-hour show, 95 percent of the costs are the same. But the problem was, the expansion meant we had to fill the extra forty-four minutes with content. That helped overexpose the talent, watering down the impact of a lot of what we were doing.

Then, just as the pressure on WCW was building from within, WWE figured it all out.

Real Competition

Mike Tyson

I remember being in Los Angeles sometime in December 1997 and getting a phone call from someone who said, "You'll never believe this, but Vince is negotiating with Mike Tyson to appear on *Wrestle-Mania*."

At the time, I kind of went, *Eh, whatever.* I didn't think they could get a deal done. Mike was pretty hot, and the price tag pretty high. It was apparent from everything we were hearing that WWE had a hard time keeping the water coolers in the building, so finding the money to pay a guy like Mike Tyson seemed unlikely.

I also didn't think they'd know what to do with him once they got him. Everything they'd done until that point stuck to the tried-and-true WWE formula: animated characters, stories designed for a very young audience. In the past, celebrities on WWE had more or less just showed up. They added their aura to the product but didn't really get involved in the storyline in a meaningful way. Simply bringing in Mike Tyson without adjusting their formula wouldn't make much of a difference.

Then at the very end of January 1998, when I was down in Kissimmee, Florida, I got a phone call that told me how they were going to use Tyson at the upcoming *WrestleMania.* Austin and McMahon were going to be involved, and the angle was much more realistic than anything they'd done before. In fact, it felt very much like what we were doing in *Nitro.* Only better.

I remember hanging up the phone and going, *Hmm, if that's what they're going to do, that's going to change things.* They had figured out our formula, and were willing to use it.

Stone Cold & Shooting the Bird

Looking back, the storyline itself was relatively simple but extremely effective. WWE developed a feud between Stone Cold Steve Austin and Vince McMahon. Vince wanted to bring Tyson in as a world-class athlete to shake things up. Austin took exception. All the buzz around Tyson upped the excitement level exponentially. Even to this day, as I go back and look at it, they set the angle up beautifully. They wove in enough reality to get the audience to that important point where they would suspend disbelief. To this day, when I see it, it feels real.

This wasn't a storyline that appealed to a twelve-year-old kid. This was aimed at young males in the workforce, people who'd be upset at being passed over for a promotion, people who'd resent their boss, who had something to prove. It appealed to fans who wished they could spit in their boss's eye.

One of the keys to the angle's success was Vince McMahon's decision to put himself out there as the owner of the company, something he hadn't been willing to do until now. And they couldn't have picked a better guy than Mike Tyson to give their show an edge. Tyson had edge, he was dangerous—times ten.

The Pay-Per-View helped Steve Austin launch his bad-ass, rattlesnake character to the moon. Everybody wanted to see a wrestler stand up to Tyson and put him in his place, and there was nobody better to pull that off than Steve Austin.

Once I saw the tape, I knew we were in deep shit.

End of a Run

WrestleMania XIV gave *Raw* an immediate bump in April 1998, helping end our run of eighty-something weeks in a row where we'd beaten them head-to-head in the television ratings. But despite what the media claimed, no one at Turner or Time Warner panicked.

Our numbers were still very solid. Our revenues were still very solid. We were still growing and meeting all of our projections. In the real corporate world—as opposed to the world of dirtsheet writers—as long as we met our projections and forecasts, no one complained about anything.

Internally, those of us at WCW were concerned. We were in a real fight, and we hadn't been in one in a long time. It put some pressure on us, but we weren't pulling our hair out, going around crying, "Woe is me." In some respects, we embraced it. In many ways, I felt it was healthy and would help grow the business.

And the truth of the matter is, it did. Where the total Nielsen share in 1997 might have been around 7, as the WWE came on, the share ran close to 10. Instead of us having a 5 and them having a 3, they had a 5 and we had a 4, or we had a 5 and they had a 5. The bottom line was, more people were watching wrestling than ever before.

I didn't want to be on the short end of the stick. My ego was too big and my pride was too powerful. But I wasn't looking for something sharp to slit my wrists with.

Ric Flair

Just as we found ourselves in a real fight with the WWE, Rick Flair went AWOL. His absence from the ring in April 1998 led to a bitter dispute. Because of it, he didn't wrestle for several months.

Ric has been vocal in his point of view. He contends that he gave proper notice and was entitled to take the time off. While I don't want to *not* talk about the controversy, I also don't want to take cheap shots at Ric Flair, or even give people the impression that I am.

In my opinion, he was in breach of contract. Obviously, we have different views of what happened.

The contract was very specific. There was no ambiguity. It didn't allow Ric to pick and choose when he was to perform. There was a procedure in place to follow if anyone wanted time off. In my opinion, Ric didn't follow that procedure.

What happened next was unfortunate. Ric wanted to prove a point, and I had to prove a point. He drew a line in the sand, and I felt I had no choice but maintain my position. If I allowed Ric or anyone to decide when and where they could show up to work at that point, I would have had a massive problem. To this day, I would do the same thing.

Pages from Our Book

WWE Invasion

Just in case no one realized that the World Wrestling Federation had latched on to our formula, they launched D-Generation X, a group of wrestlers who could have been nWo's third or fourth string. Then D-Generation X—usually known as DX—tried to "invade" WCW, showing up at our events and corporate headquarters. It echoed nWo's "invasion" of WCW a few years earlier. It was probably more amusing than anything, but it left no doubt that we now had real competition.

Ironically, the decision I made to fire Syxx—Sean Waltman—in early 1998 inadvertently helped the angle. Quite frankly, firing Sean was one of the biggest favors I did for WWE at the time.

Sean Waltman, Kevin Nash, and Scott Hall were like the Three Amigos, thick as thieves and inseparable on-screen and off. They stuck together and watched each others' backs. Sean was able to take advantage of his friendship with Kevin and Scott. In many ways, Sean was lucky to even have a job.

Don't get me wrong. Sean had talent, and was a great performer when he was sober. The problem was, those periods were few and far between. But even then, he wasn't very articulate and didn't have the ability to do a promo that well. His role in nWo was perfect for him. He didn't have to say all that much. He relied on his looks and his work rate, which at the time ranged from good to amazing, depending on what his chemical balance was.

In late 1997 or early 1998, we'd come to a verbal agreement with Sean on a new contract. We agreed on terms and sent the written contract to his manager, Barry Bloom. We also started paying him under the terms of that agreement.

A few months later, someone from my legal department told me

Sean hadn't signed the contract, and I called Barry and said, "Let's get this thing signed and get it out of the way."

And I was hit with, "Well, we want to talk about the terms of the deal."

That pissed me off to the point where I fired Sean immediately To me, that was just a sleazy way to conduct business, and I've been exposed to a lot of sleaze.

There were reports at the time that he was released because he was injured, but he wasn't. He wasn't even fired because he was an average talent with an above-average paycheck. He was fired because we had agreed to a deal and, rather than fulfilling his obligation, he tried to renegotiate. It wouldn't have mattered to me if he had a broken neck, cancer, AIDS, typhoid, and the first domestic case of the bird flu virus—I still would have fired him. He wasn't worth the pain in the ass he'd become.

DX

The timing was great for WWE and DX. Sean signed with them and brought the renegade, bad-ass nWo attitude and credibility with him. He cut his promo on me, criticizing me on air and claiming that Scott and Kevin wanted to quit WCW as well and come with him.

Like I said before, he wasn't the first guy to use me to get over. Still, he did it very effectively. From an artistic point of view, it was perfect.

DX would not have had the impact it had were it not for Sean. It was more about coincidence and circumstance than talent. It may have been a blatant rip-off of nWo, but it worked. The fact that they had balls big enough to come over and show up at CNN Center and WCW headquarters only made it cooler.

Part of me said, *I wish I'd been able to do that.*

The truth is, we'd thought of doing the same thing with nWo. Scott Hall, myself, and a few others had talked ad nauseam about it back in 1996. We'd sketched out a raid on Titan Towers—WWE's headquarters. We'd even thought of buying tickets to WWE events, making sure we were in the "hard camera" side so we'd be seen.

There were several drawbacks to the idea. For one thing, the nWo cast would have had to skip a *Nitro* show to pull it off. More importantly, we were on the receiving end of a lot of litigation from WWE. Invading WWE would have given our corporate lawyers massive coronaries.

Once the nWo angle went over with the crowd in a big way, there was no reason to do it. We stopped talking about the idea, at least seriously.

While the creative side of me dug the DX invasion bit, the business side of me said, *Okay, now what do we do?*

The answer was to take it up a notch or two—or ten.

Calling out Vince

After DX "attacked" the CNN Center in May, I went on the air and put it back in their faces.

"Sean, you come out to WCW headquarters when you know I'm not there. You're calling me out and talking about what an evil bastard I am. But the truth of the matter is, you're nothing but a puppet. You're doing Vince McMahon's work."

I took a piss on Sean and then said, "If Vince has a problem with me, maybe he should step into the ring with me. We'll settle our conflicts like men."

We had a Pay-Per-View *Slamboree* coming up in Worcester, Massachusetts, and I invited Vince to meet me there. I knew it would create a tremendous amount of controversy and probably get under Vince's skin. And from what I've been told, I succeeded.

I went backstage, and all the wrestlers were kind of cheering me on—"Hey, whoa, that's cool, I can't believe you did that," and that sort of thing.

I thought it was great until Hogan came up to me and said,

"Brother, you realize what you've done? He's going to take this seriously. There's no way he's not going to come and try to kick your ass."

And I said, "Great. It'll make one hell of a Pay-Per-View, no matter how it turns out."

I continued calling Vince out on television in the week or weeks before the Pay-Per-View. I turned it up pretty heavy, goading him and making fun of him.

I fully expected Vince to show up. We had security waiting outside at all the exits. They had explicit orders that if Vince or any WWE representatives showed up, they were to be escorted to the locker room and ring posthaste, no questions asked.

Paul White, better known as Big Show, came to me just before the match. "Boss, what are you going to do if this goes bad?"

"Paul," I said, "as long as it doesn't look as if there's going to be any long-term permanent injury, don't get involved."

I was fully prepared to get my ass kicked. I didn't think I would—my kickboxing skills were still there, and I thought I could work the ring. But there's always that chance. I'd had my ass kicked so many times before in my life that getting my ass kicked on a Pay-Per-View of this magnitude wouldn't have bothered me a bit.

Unfortunately, Vince didn't come. His daughter Stephanie was graduating from college that weekend. Whether that was the reason or whether Vince had decided he wasn't going to take the bait, he didn't show up. If he had, it would have been the most talked about event *ever.* It would have helped both promotions.

Were We Stale?

Over the second half of 1998, WWE won the Monday Night Wars, the head-to-head competition in the Nielsens, more and more. There were a number of reasons.

One was that we had gotten stale. *Nitro* had been around for a number of years. We'd done a lot of crazy things that had never been done before. In raising the bar as high as we did every week, we'd made the audience expect more. We overdelivered for two, two and a half years, until finally we couldn't meet their expectations.

But we were also held back by a number of other factors. One was WWE's lawsuit, which was slowly wending its way toward resolution. It wasn't because we were doing anything illegal, or had been prior to their suit. It's just that the lawsuits forced another layer of corporate involvement in WCW, dampening what we could and couldn' t do.

Suddenly, corporate legal started watching WCW and what was going on in the shows. They started dictating what we could and couldn't do. Not wanting to undermine their case, they shied away from any angle that attacked WWE or even mentioned it. An nWo counterattack against DX at Titan Towers, for example, would never, ever have passed muster. At a time when I needed to take the gloves off and get more aggressive than I had ever been, I had one hand tied behind my back and the other handcuffed to my desk.

Ideally, we'd have gone down to Titan headquarters. Ideally, we'd have had a fistfight in the parking lot and taped it. We would have showed up at a WWE event and caused as much shit as we could possibly cause. We'd have done any number of things other than just laying back and letting them have their fun.

From a creative point of view, it was the beginning of the end.

Feeling the Pressure

We felt the pressure not just from competition, but from the large expansion of our house show business, the addition of *Thunder*, and the decision to add a third hour to *Nitro*. Our infrastructure—or lack thereof—showed the strain. Trying to turn things around that summer, I let my vice president, Nick Lambros, go.

Nick had come over to WCW from the Turner legal side a few years before. I'd been looking for a good, strong legal guy to oversee the business side of WCW, and when Bill Shaw referred Nick to me, I signed him up.

In the beginning it was a good move. We got along great. He had a good handle on the business side of things, where he brought experience and aptitude to the management team. But our relationship eventually started to go downhill. Nick was a lot more political than I was. I think Harvey Schiller also felt more comfortable with Nick, because he was a button-down executive and I wasn't. I think Nick sensed an opportunity to get close to Harvey, and Harvey acted accordingly.

By 1998, it was my opinion that Nick was no longer as committed to WCW as he was to using WCW to climb the Time Warner corporate ladder. That became apparent to me on a couple of different occasions. Over a period of a few months I saw Nick furthering his own career rather than doing what would have been in the best interests of WCW.

I would complain that there were a lot of things that needed to be done—licensing, marketing, and merchandising, for example—but were somehow not getting taken care of. Whenever I dug into why this was happening, I would find a stack of things on Nick's desk that hadn't been touched. Finally, I had to make a decision to let Nick go.

It was a tough, tough personal decision. I liked Nick a lot. In the very beginning, he and I were very close. He was all about WCW and the brand. He was very much a partner and a big asset. But as things deteriorated and the pressure got worse, Nick became a liability.

The reaction at first was positive—but ultimately, I think it was an indication of what some of the people who were working below me were really all about.

The minute I let Nick go, the people who reported directly to him came to me and told me what a great move it was, how supportive they were, how they had always hoped to report directly to me. Now they would be able to solve all sorts of problems and get a lot of work done.

My initial reaction was, *Wow, I guess I made the right decision. I wish I had acted sooner.*

In retrospect, I was watching a lot of very insecure and unprofessional people trying to save themselves. They weren't necessarily being honest with me or themselves. They were just taking advantage of the situation to save their jobs or further their careers.

Is it unusual? Probably not. Do I wish I would have recognized it for what it really was? Yes.

The Real Reason (Men Commit Crimes)

Some personnel issues that year were pleasant to deal with. Sting's movie was one of them.

Sting was taking acting classes and was very much interested in becoming an actor. I supported that. I think performers need to expand their horizons to become better performers. Sometimes it's a lot of easier to develop your talent through other forms of entertainment.

I found I could improve my own ability as a performer by doing live radio. For some reason, learning how to paint pictures and connect with an audience via a microphone helped me on-camera. I also did some acting on television; during my time at WCW I appeared on *The Jeff Foxworthy Show* and *Arli$$* on HBO. I found that working off a script in an environment I wasn't used to made me a better performer at WCW. So I encouraged other people to do the same.

People on the periphery of the wrestling business took that as "Eric Bischoff aspiring to be a Hollywood guy." That's not true. Eric Bischoff aspired to be a better performer and encouraged others to do the same.

At some point Sting came to me and told me his acting coach had a small production company. "We want to do an independent feature called *The Real Reason (Men Commit Crimes),*" he said. "Would you"—meaning WCW and Turner Broadcasting—"underwrite it and fund it?"

It was a very small budget. Sting was someone who, relatively speaking, was underpaid at WCW. But he never asked for more money, never asked to renegotiate his contract. He always lived up to his contract and did it with a real positive attitude. So I took the proposal to Harvey Schiller, and I said, "Look, here's a guy who's been with the company through the good times and the bad times. Everybody else at his level is making significantly more money than he is, just because of timing issues with his contract. He's got a great attitude, and he's not asking for a raise. But he is asking for some support. Is it worth it to give him some support?"

Harvey agreed that it was.

The movie came out at the end of 1998, and I was listed as executive producer. It wasn't part of a move by WCW or myself to branch out into movies, though some writers claimed it was. If anything, it could be considered as bonus compensation to a guy who truly deserved it.

Head to Head

Hogan and Goldberg

I was getting onto an entrance ramp in Marina Del Rey one day that summer, on my way to the Los Angeles International Airport, when I got a call from Hulk Hogan. We were fighting *Raw* head-to-head, and had a major event coming up at the beginning of July at the Georgia Dome.

"Brother, I know what to do."

"What is it, Hulkster?"

"Put me in a match with Goldberg. Let him beat me for the title."

I went, *Whoa*. It was completely out of left field.

When I hung up the phone, I thought to myself, What's this going to cost me? I thought it was one of those moves where I'd get a call from Hulk's attorney twenty minutes later: "Well, if you're going to do that, you have to write him a check."

It didn't end up costing me anything. And the match was one of the highlights of 1998 and still remains a contest that wrestling fans like to talk about.

Goldberg was on fire, riding his incredible unbeaten string. His victory over Hogan solidified his status as one of the top wrestlers in the game. The tremendous audience response helped Hogan as well, but WCW was the main beneficiary, with a healthy boost in the ratings and a victory that night head-to-head with *Raw*.

The match was definitely Pay-Per-View quality, but we'd put Pay-Per-View quality matches on free TV before. We felt it was okay to blow things up on television, giving them away for free, because by doing that we would build our audience over the long term, getting more people to sample the program. And in this case, it helped build Bill Goldberg's career in front of the largest possible audience.

Of course, I was criticized in the dirtsheets. But at that point if they criticized me, it usually convinced me that I was doing the right thing.

Jay Leno

Shortly after the Hogan-Goldberg match, I was up at my ranch in Cody, Wyoming, hosting a family reunion when I got a message that a Gary Consadine of NBC had called. He was an executive producer at *The Tonight Show,* and the message indicated he was interested in doing something with Jay Leno and WCW.

I assumed they wanted one of the wrestlers on the show. I turned it over to our PR department and went on with the family gathering. A day or two later, I got another call from my office, saying, "No, no, no. Gary wants to talk to you. He wants to do something with Jay wrestling in the ring."

I didn't have any idea what they wanted to do, or what I might be interested in, but I liked it immediately. It was a great opportunity. I went right out to L.A. and talked to Gary and Jay. It was clear from the get-go that they were wide open.

I came up with an idea that called for Leno to make fun of Hogan in his monologue. He'd do it one night, then the next, and then the next. Just rip on Hogan. On the third night, Hogan and I would come out of the crowd and threaten to kick his ass. From that point, a Pay-Per-View grudge match would be a foregone conclusion.

Leno loved it.

We did the bit at the end of the month. Hogan and I came down through the audience and jumped up on the stage. We didn't inform a lot of people in advance, including the security guards, who at first were more than a little concerned. I'd told Jay that we had to make it feel real, and he kept it as serious and as real as it could possibly be. We had a yelling and shoving match, then threw Jay and Kevin Eubanks off the set.

I walked around and sat down behind Jay's desk, put my feet up on Leno's desk, and introduced my guest for the evening, Hollywood Hogan. We had our own little interview, and it was a hell of a lot of fun. It was a great way to launch the angle.

Ripping Off Leno

Over the next few weeks, Jay faxed his Friday-night monologue to me, and I repeated it on *Nitro*, usually word for word. I even built a set that looked just like the *Tonight Show* set. I tried to pretend I was the funniest son of a bitch on the planet. He got pissed off that I was stealing his jokes, and the war of words escalated into a tag team match between Hogan and myself and Jay and Diamond Dallas Page at Sturgis that August.

I picked Diamond Dallas Page for the match for a couple of reasons. For one, the angle was sheer entertainment. I didn't want to pair Leno up with a Sting or Ric Flair or Bret Hart or Goldberg; I

didn't want their credibility to be diminished. Page was at a point in his career where that kind of a rub with Leno and Hogan would only help him, and the entertainment-only nature of the event wouldn't hurt him.

As much as it will hurt Page's feelings when he reads this, I never saw him as a guy who would wear the championship title and lead the company for long periods of time. For a short period, yes, but he wasn't a Sting or a Ric Flair in terms of status.

But at the same time, I knew Page would put a lot of time in and do whatever he had to to make Leno look good. Page had a tremendous work ethic, and a great deal of ability.

We all rehearsed the match for a little over a week before the Pay-Per-View. We set up a ring not far from the *Tonight Show* and worked out every day after Jay finished with his show. Jay worked really hard. He was very committed and took it seriously. He wasn't necessarily the most athletic person you'll ever meet, but he didn't let that stop him. He was head and shoulders above all the celebrities I've worked with, except maybe Karl Malone and Kevin Greene, in terms of attitude and professionalism.

The match was designed to showcase Jay, and it did. Page bounced around the ring, and his athleticism and skill made us all look good. It was a great event from an entertainment and brand point of view. Not surprisingly, the hard-core audience panned the event.

Jay kicked my ass good, but by that time everybody was kicking my ass.

Communicating

At the Sturgis Pay-Per-View in 1998, Hogan and Kevin Nash got into a discussion about the direction of WCW. Kevin felt that Hogan was using too much influence, negatively affecting some of the storylines and the other wrestlers. Hogan felt that Kevin and Scott Hall had their own agendas that were not in the best interests of anyone else. And by the way, both of those views were shared by a lot of the other wrestlers.

Rather than backstabbing each other, which was the case with so many wrestlers, Kevin and Hogan said, "Okay, we have a problem. Let's hash it out."

There were reports later that they had an argument. I was thirty feet away. It was about as calm and rational as any discussion I've seen any two people have.

I was glad. I wanted them to be honest with each other. If they could be honest with each other, I believed they could begin to trust each other. And if they could trust each other, many of the problems they had with each other would probably go away.

The problem with people in general is that when they're not communicating, there are problems. That was the big issue there. Nash and Hall had their sphere of influence and core of support among the wrestlers. Hogan had his own core of support. It was important that they work out their issues. Their talk had a positive effect on the company. It became easier to move storylines forward. And I wasn't hearing both sides bitching about the other.

The Beginning of the End

Bullshit

The most important thing that happened during the run up to the Sturgis Pay-Per-View had nothing to do with Jay Leno. It had to do with his monologues.

One Tuesday morning after a *Nitro*, I got into the office and found a note on my desk directing me to attend a meeting over at Techwood, the original campus of Turner Broadcasting. I went right over and found myself in a room with a dozen people, most of whom I'd never seen before. I sat down, and they proceeded to tell me how WCW was going to be positioned from that point forward.

The first thing I thought was that someone was playing an elaborate joke. But it just kept going on, and getting stranger as it went.

Standards and Practices?

One woman stood up and introduced herself as Terri Tingle. She was the head of standards and practices.

While I had heard the term used before and knew what it meant, I had no idea why she was talking to me. No one in the history of WCW had ever interfaced with a department called standards and practices.

She proceeded to tell me that the Jay Leno jokes were no longer appropriate.

Now in retrospect, it occurs to me that the political jokes in the monologues may have been what caused the trouble. This was July 1998, at the height—or depth—of the Monica Lewinsky affair. Everybody was making fun of Bill Clinton, including Jay Leno. It was no secret that that Time Warner was filled with Democrats, and it may have been part of the issue. I would get "very persuasive" e-mails any time my "voluntary" contribution—which was "suggested" based on a percentage of my salary—to the Turner Political Action Contribution was late. But at the time all I could think of was the fact that I was telling jokes that were suitable for broadcast television. You would think that if it was okay for NBC, it would be okay for cable.

In my gut, I knew this was *way, way* upside down.

The Way the World Really Is

Not only did Tingle tell me what jokes I could use, she proceeded to tell me that from that point forward, I was to give her all of the scripts for my shows two or three weeks in advance so that she would have time to review them prior to their airing.

No way, I told her. Number one, we didn't use scripts per se.

"We have outlines and formats with bullet points and production directions. This isn't *Gone with the Friggin' Wind*."

You have to understand where my head was at. I was thinking, *Well, this is bullshit. I'm just going to stand up and jump up and down on people's chests until they decide they don't want to do this anymore. I'll force the issue, and we'll sit down in front of Ted and figure this mess out.*

Little did I know that Ted Turner was losing control of his own company.

We kept going. I ripped them apart, one by one. They told me what I should do, and I told them what I thought of their suggestions. Finally a guy at the end of the table—it's a small world, so I'll say I've forgotten his name—stood up and said: "Here's how we're going to position WCW in the advertising community."

Now remember, WCW had no control over how its advertising was sold. Ad sales were handled by the Turner advertising department, and it was completely out of our hands. That was bad enough. Now they apparently felt that since they were selling the ads, they had a right to tell me what the show would be.

My show, he said, was going to be targeted toward children and families.

That's when lights went off in my head and I started to see colors.

Flipping Off the Crowd

We were still on solid ground ratings-wise. Financially, we were doing very well, meeting all of our revenue projections.

At the same time, though, our personnel were stretched beyond capacity. WWE had gotten very aggressive, closing the ratings gap. Steve Austin was flipping off crowds and chugging a cold one in the ring at the end of his matches. They were doing all this sexual stuff to get the male audience—*our* audience—to switch over.

And now I have this thirty-something woman asking for nonexistent scripts and telling me I can't use jokes that have already aired on network television. And I have a guy—with a straight face—who wants me to target kids and offer family wrestling.

It was the most absurd thing I'd ever heard of.

I started sweating, literally. I saw the control of my show slipping through my hands.

When my friend in advertising got done telling me how and why WCW was going to be positioned as a kids' show, I said, "Excuse me, Advertising Friend. What's the name of my show?"

"Uh, *Nitro*."

"What night of the week does it air?"

There was this uncomfortable, awkward moment of resounding silence.

My feeling was that not only did no one in the room have the faintest clue what we were doing, they didn't even watch the show. Their silence proved my point.

But it probably wasn't the smartest thing to do from a political point of view.

A Line in the Sand

There was no way *Nitro* was going to be turned into a family-friendly hour after everything we had done. It was the most asinine, absurd direction that anyone could have suggested.

I knew I either had to fight or just walk away.

I almost walked away. I should have. I went home after Sturgis and told my wife I had made up my mind that I wasn't going back.

Ultimately, I changed my mind. To this day, that is probably my single biggest regret.

At that moment, WCW was still such a cash cow that I might have been able to fight the fight. By walking away, I would have drawn a line in the sand that *might* have caused them to back down.

But that's not my nature. My nature is to fight—I'd generally rather fight than have sex, on any given day. Good fights are harder to come by.

I also felt that I had a contract, and an obligation to fulfill it. There was nothing in the agreement that gave me the opportunity to quit because I didn't like the working conditions.

I felt that by quitting, I would be letting down Ted Turner—and, whether it was true or not, Bill Shaw. They were both men I greatly respected. It would have been an unprofessional thing to do.

Last but not least, I'd built my life around the wrestling business. Quitting the WCW meant leaving wrestling for good. I certainly didn't expect I'd be welcomed in WWE with open arms. I wasn't ready to walk away from pro wrestling.

Team Player

So I stuck around.

I went around being as openly antagonistic and difficult to work with as anyone could possibly be. I called bullshit when I saw bullshit. I pulled no punches and didn't even try to pretend I was toeing the company line. I honestly thought that at some point I'd end up in front of Ted. At that point, I thought, everything would be resolved in WCW's favor.

The more I resisted, the more difficult I made it for myself. They became more and more aggressive. They knew something I didn't know—Ted wasn't going to step in.

Time Warner was being restructured. The people in positions in Turner Broadcasting who had never wanted WCW to be successful in the first place were now calling the shots, and making decisions for all of the divisions in the company. I was probably one of the first on their hit list.

Only later did I realize that the meetings that had led up to my ambush at Techwood had probably been going on for four to six months. The decision to confront me may have been sped along because of the Monica Lewinsky jokes, but it had obviously been coming for a while.

The image I'd had of a rebel—which, quite frankly, I played up and exploited from time to time—had worked well in the Turner entrepreneurial environment. In the new corporate structure it was a handicap. They wanted corporate committee clones, not mavericks.

Things went like this for several months. I didn't realize, really, that I wasn't going to get to go in front of Ted for several months. I couldn't get past Harvey Schiller, and Harvey couldn't get past the committee of Turner executives above him.

Without a Parachute

Up until the summer of 1998, Harvey had always fought for WCW. But now he was no longer willing to fight. He was more interested in his own political agenda than any problems that I had. Harvey wanted to be president of Turner Broadcasting, and he was willing to throw WCW under the bus—at least temporarily—to achieve that.

Without having Ted to fall back on, and with no support from Harvey, I was flying without a plane, let alone a parachute. It was brutal. Week to week, we fought. I'd get into yelling and screaming matches with standards and practices over the phone. They would demand things that just weren't practical or even possible.

Have you ever heard of George Carlin's list of things you can never say on television? Imagine that list times a hundred. That was the list standards and practices gave us of things not to do.

But that wasn't the half of it.

"Some of the things you're not allowed to do aren't on this list," Terri Tingle told me. "So if you want to do anything we might be offended by, you have to call us up."

I know it sounds pretty funny, but I'm not exaggerating. That's how insane it was.

Over on *Raw*, you have Mae Young giving birth to a hand. You've got Sable taking her tits out of her top. And I'm being told, "Here's a list of a thousand and one things you can't do. And oh by the way, if it's not on this list, call me before you do it. Now go out and get 'em."

Budget Cuts

The wrestling police were bad enough. We also had to deal with bean counters gone wild. Finance took a look at our EBITDA—damaged by *Thunder*—and decided it wasn't good.

"You have to cut your production budget. We've got to reach twenty percent growth in all of our divisions, and the only way you're going to do that is by cutting all of your costs. So slice, slice, slice."

The cuts hit our promotion budget hard, undercutting our ability to drive interest in the brand. Marketing and promotional expenses seem easy to cut, because they're not fixed costs, like rent for example. But in our business, marketing and advertising get us to the dance. If you don't market your product, it dies very quickly.

We went from 160 miles an hour, flying down the center of the track, to being told we couldn't use tires anymore.

"And damn it, get out there and win that race!"

That's how ludicrous it was.

Remember, in three and a half years, WCW had gone from a company losing 10 million a year to one that netted 40 million in profit in 1998. But we were supposed to cut back.

Toeing the Line

I could either toe the line and do as I was told, or I could sabotage my superiors. While I fought the powers-that-were privately, publicly I had to do my job. I had to carry the message back to WCW and put it into effect.

I couldn't tell the talent everything that was going on. I couldn't say, "Look, guys, gather round. I know what we've been doing the last couple of years and what we've done. I created the formula, and you guys made it better. But here's what we're going to do: think *Sesame Street*."

I tried to be as positive as I could. A lot of the wrestlers, the creative people, and even some department heads protested. They were concerned that the momentum that we had created with our programming was going to be lost. They saw that we were now going in the opposite direction—and they knew it was wrong. The proof was in the numbers—Nielsen ratings, buy rates, asses in seats. They all pointed out that what we were going to do wasn't going to work.

My job now was to stand on a soapbox and espouse the company line. I had to look everyone in the eye and tell them this was the right strategy.

I was a hypocrite.

I knew what I was telling them was wrong. It was bullshit.

My choice was either to quit, or toe the company line. And I chose, unfortunately, to stay.

My morale went into the toilet. The talent began to unravel. WCW started to fall apart.

Entrepreneurs Not Needed

Ultimately, AOL Time Warner became the largest unmitigated disaster in corporate history. WCW wasn't the only victim, but it was one of the first. The serial mergers that created the company—Time merging with Warner, then Turner, then AOL—plowed under a lot of lives.

The corporation failed because it became exactly the opposite of the company that Ted Turner built. Turner Broadcasting was built on vision—and risk. Ted was willing to risk failure to achieve phenomenal levels of success.

Gerald Levin claimed he wanted to merge with Turner to inculcate Time Warner with the Turner entrepreneurial culture. Guess what? It worked the other way around. All of the entrepreneurs Ted had attracted became paralyzed either by fear or their own greed and concern for stock options.

That's all anyone cared about, their stock options. Whatever they could do, whatever they could say—whatever they could *not* do or say—to protect those almighty stock options, they did. Or didn't do.

The atmosphere became one of paralysis. Decisions weren't made, boats weren't rocked. Standard operating procedure was to form a committee to name a committee that would appoint a group to study a problem, then report back to an advisory committee to make a presentation to the original committee. It was like working for the federal government.

Shit Storms

Unraveling

As time went on, it became clear to anyone who worked with me that emotionally I'd thrown in the towel. I told people that if things didn't change, I was getting out.

That was the cue for several individuals to make political hay. Some of the political animals around me realized that I had gone from a guy with the Midas touch to someone who had no control over his own company. They began angling for power—or simply survival. They weren't interested in saving the company; they were interested in trying to save their asses.

The dirtsheets began filling up with backstage gossip and rumors of what was going on behind the scenes. Wrestlers and staff leaked a lot of information, sometimes to benefit themselves directly, sometimes just to stir the shit. In their twisted minds, they thought the dissension would benefit them.

The dirtsheets pointed out all the things that were going wrong with WCW. Some of what they wrote was true, though they didn't understand the reasons why. They took the position they'd always taken: Eric Bischoff was not the guy to run the company.

So much of what they wrote was, at the very best bullshit and speculation. Some of it was intentionally misleading and inappropriate information fed to them by people hoping to fulfill their own agendas.

Among many other things, someone gave the media information on what we were willing to pay talent whose contracts were being negotiated. This was all confidential information prepared by an attorney. If we'd had the time and the focus, we not only would have fired the people responsible, but prosecuted them as well.

Was I angry?

Yeah.

But the leaks were just one more thing. The real issue was the shift in the way the company was operating, and my lack of ability to do anything about it. WWE began beating us in the ratings week after week, and there was nothing I could do to stop it.

I don't want to come off like I had all the answers. I didn't. By this time, I had *no* answers. I didn't have a rabbit in my hat. I didn't even have a hat. There were so many things going on around me and that company—and the other companies and divisions in Turner and Time Warner as well—that there wasn't one thing that could stop the spiral.

Scott Hall, Human Train Wreck

It was at this same time that Scott Hall's personal problems became acute. Anybody who could read knew about it. His name appeared in police blotters almost as often as wrestling reports. His alcohol abuse problems were hard to miss.

Scott had been in treatment once or twice. When he got out, he was good for a few weeks, then spiraled back again. By the fall of 1998 he was basically unmanageable. His wife, if she hadn't filed for divorce, was about to.

Roughly about this time, Brad Siegel came to me and asked me if would hire his niece, Emily. She had done some work in television and was hoping to have a career in the field. I said, sure.

Big mistake. You bring an attractive young woman who's the niece of a president of a division of Turner Broadcasting into that shark tank, and trouble is sure to follow.

Scott immediately latched on to her. He thought that by getting close to her, he'd somehow be able to protect himself from me. That just added to the chaos and mess. They both ended up creating all kinds of internal problems.

Halloween Havoc

Talk about your shit storms.

Our 1998 *Halloween Havoc* Pay-Per-View ran about fifteen minutes over the time allotted. A large portion of the paying audience went dark and missed the end of the match. As bad as that was, the fallout from trying to fix it was even worse.

Matches go longer than they should for any number of reasons. Wrestling isn't a science. When you send a wrestler out and say, "Okay, you have ten minutes to get your match in," sometimes they get it to within thirty seconds. Sometimes they go five minutes over. At a Pay-Per-View where there's eight or nine matches, if four or five go significantly over, you end up going into your main event short of time.

The main event is the reason that most people buy the Pay-Per-View, and it's usually supposed to go twenty or twenty-five minutes. So you're faced with a tough situation. If the match ends when it's supposed to end—say after only seven minutes—it leaves a very bad taste in the mouths of the consumers. On the other hand, if you go over, you run the very real risk of losing your satellite time. Unless you've made prior arrangements, you go off the bird when your time is up.

I don't remember exactly what happened at *Halloween Havoc,* but I assume that the earlier matches ran over significantly. At some point, we realized we had a problem, and we scrambled. We got hold of the Pay-Per-View companies and explained what was going on, asking for more satellite time. For the most part, we were given reason to believe that we had the additional time.

The Pay-Per-View industry wasn't as sophisticated back then as it is now. For whatever reason, while some of our customers ended up getting the signal, the majority did not. Most of the people who had bought the Pay-Per-View never saw the finish.

Bad Choices

We had basically two choices.

One was to find a way to use the fact that the show was blacked out in a storyline. That was a very, very bad choice, because we'd be basically taking our customers' money, not delivering what we promised, and then telling them that we did it on purpose for a storyline.

Bad to worse situation. Not an option.

The other choice was to replay the finish on *Nitro*. This way everybody who bought the Pay-Per-View could see it.

When that was presented to me as an option, I thought, *Well, at least everyone gets what they paid for.* It seemed to be the most reasonable thing to do. I made the decision—or I should say, I recommended to the Turner committee running things above me—to run the finish on *Nitro*, and we did.

The problem with that—and frankly, I didn't anticipate it—was that not only did the people who bought the Pay-Per-View see the ending, everyone who *didn't* buy the Pay-Per-View saw it as well. Those who paid their $29.95 or whatever said, "Hey, why should we pay for it when everyone else is getting it for free?"

The argument wasn't entirely valid, because the Pay-Per-View included a lot more than that final match. But disgruntled viewers made their point in a mass letter-writing campaign, e-mails, and phone calls.

Unfortunately, there was no way to put the ending back out there just for them. Refunding the money wasn't an option either. Typically, 60 percent of the Pay-Per-View fee went to the provider. WCW got only 40 percent. If we were forced to refund the fee, we'd be giving back more than twice what we'd received. It was a *big* number.

The collective committees that ran WCW at the time went, "What a disaster." It reinforced their desire to get rid of WCW, and helped strengthen the various committees' stranglehold over us.

The Pay-Per-View was my responsibility, and running over was my mistake. But did we do the best we could do under the circumstances? Absolutely.

The match had a 10.2 share during that quarter hour of *Nitro*, a tremendous rating, but no one cracked champagne over that one.

Out of the Tower

Among other mistakes that affected WCW that year was the relocation of WCW's headquarters away from the CNN Towers and the rest of Turner Broadcasting. But it was a mistake that I, and everyone else at WCW, had no part in.

When Turner acquired the new NHL franchise for the Thrashers, space had to be found for the team's headquarters. Harvey Schiller, who was on the fifteenth floor, wanted it close to him. The organization was kind of a crown jewel for Harvey. The only option was to move it to the floor below him—where we were.

We were told to find office space outside the CNN Center.

That kind of thing ordinarily doesn't bother me. I can work out of the back of my car as long as I have all the tools I need. But I think a lot of people felt it was a slap in the face. Employees who had survived the redheaded-stepchild era, who'd been embarrassed just to walk through the CNN Center with a WCW ID badge, felt it was a real insult. They'd lived through the bad times and could be openly proud of their association with a division that was making money and generating positive press from the likes of the *Wall Street Journal*. Now they were rewarded by being told they weren't important enough to be in the building.

Morale took another nosedive.

In retrospect, moving furthered the idea that we didn't belong in Turner Broadcasting. When you lose direct communication with your peers and no longer have easy access to them, they consciously or subconsciously perceive you to be less than them. It has a variety of impacts.

Add to that, the place we moved to was a cesspool. It was a former factory and warehouse in one of the worst parts of town—which says a lot, because there are a lot of worst parts of town in Atlanta. There were no windows, and the carpet smelled like mold.

We made the best of it. We cleaned it up and painted the walls, but it was not the kind of place where you showed up for work every morning and said, "Oh, man, am I glad to be a part of this."

You'd say, "Man, this place still smells like sewage."

Angles

If Jesse Can Do It

Having lived in Minnesota as long as I did, I found it odd that Jesse Ventura, who's kind of an outspoken, apolitical figure in every sense, could somehow get elected there. I think a lot of it was mostly his timing. The political dysfunction of Minnesota coincided with the popularity of professional wrestling, and he happened to be the right guy in the right place at the right time. Our success turned Jesse into a cult hero among a large part of the voting population of Minnesota. Jesse was smart enough to figure out a way to tap into that and exploit it while people who were more focused on traditional voting blocs had neutralized themselves.

Shortly after the election in November 1998, Hulk Hogan declared he was going to run for president. It was fun to laugh about, but it was so transparent and unoriginal that it didn't have any legs. We dropped it after a few weeks of laughs.

Burying the Hatchet in My Head

The conflict between the WCW and Ric Flair ended in the fall of 1998 with an agreement that brought Ric back to work. As soon as we settled things, we wove the conflict into a storyline arc, generating heat between Flair and myself.

It was natural. Ric Flair was still regarded as the traditional NWA/WCW guy. Viewers saw me as anything but.

Ric had spun the story to make me look like an evil villain and a power-hungry zealot. I was more than happy to take advantage of that. It fit the formula and made a lot of sense. Once we got business out of the way, we were happy to use it to benefit the company. We shook hands, drank a beer, and it was like we had never had a problem.

The storyline built until, at the end of the year, I met Ric for a match for control of the WCW. Ric's son Reid got involved in the story. He was very young at the time, but he was a really cool kid—still is. I think he was fourteen at the time, or maybe even younger. Ric had started him as an amateur wrestler, and he was a big kid for his age.

I got a big kick out of working with him. He'd heard Ric spout off about me, but he didn't let that bother him, or if he did, it didn't show. He was polite and a hard worker. It was fun watching him get into the ring for the first time, with ten or fifteen thousand people cheering him on. I think I let him take me down and run me around the ring a little bit. He got a big kick out of it, and I got a big kick out of it.

We had to give the audience something more than just Ric kicking my ass to make the showdown feel special. So after he whipped me, Ric shaved my head.

I think everyone in the audience would have loved to have been wielding the blade. They were living vicariously through Flair, humiliating me.

As if being shorn wasn't bad enough, we made a big deal out of my silver roots. I'd started turning gray when I was twenty-five, and by 1989 I was probably eighty-five percent silver. But I'd been dying my hair since 1985, and no one had ever seen me silver on camera. Preparing for the match, I'd let the roots grow up a quarter of an inch, and when Ric shaved me I literally looked like Pepe Lepew, the Warner Brothers skunk.

Nash and the Book

I think Kevin Nash might have been the one who came up with the storyline. By that point, I'd given him the book. I was pulling back as far as I could creatively.

I'd lost my passion. I was so disillusioned and bitter and betrayed about everything that I didn't have the desire to wrap my head around stories. In all the pressure of the situation, I couldn't think of anything that excited me. I knew that meant I couldn't come up with anything that would excite the audience either. We needed a fresh mind.

Kevin stepped up. He'd always been pretty creative, and he was the best person we had internally for the job. But he wasn't a booker. With all the strong points he had, he remained a performer first, and thought like one. He also had to work under all of the ridiculous restrictions handed down from above, which made his job even harder.

People criticized Kevin for using the position to get himself over. I don't agree with that at all. If a performer is also functioning as the head writer, and the head writer knows that he needs to find a performer whom he can trust for a difficult part, who will he go to first?

Himself.

It's unfortunate, but natural. I think Kevin wanted to be a success. There was a lot of discord in WCW at the time, and he knew that if he used himself in a difficult situation, he'd show up and give it one hundred percent, without bitching. That goes a long way when you're working under that kind of pressure.

Asses in the Seats

The Turning Point That Wasn't

Since the demise of WCW, people have tried singling out one or two things as the reason that WCW ultimately went under. They look for a simple turning point in the road to disaster.

Just about everything we were allowed to do at the time didn't work, so it's pretty easy to go back and look at certain things and form a revisionist point of view that says, See? If they hadn't done that, this wouldn't have happened.

One of the most popular—if that's the right word—of these pseudo turning points is the incident on the January 4 *Nitro* when Schiavone told the audience that Mick Foley was about to win the championship on *Raw*. The show had been taped a week before, so we knew what was going to happen.

Giving WWE endings away was something we'd done from the very beginning, though the dirtsheet writers seemed to have forgotten that at the time. They thought it was new, and a sudden fit of pique on my part. There were stories that I was angry with WWE about some slight, imagined or otherwise. I wasn't.

People did switch from our program to theirs, at least according to the Nielsen ratings. I don't think it really mattered a bit. By that point, the tide had turned so significantly that us talking about one match didn't matter.

Foley, while at WCW. He's wrestling as Cactus Jack in '94.

Mick Foley

Mick Foley and I have a good relationship. At least, I think we do. Mick may have a different opinion. He came up to me one day after one of his books was published, "Oh, man, I really apologize. I hope you didn't take anything I wrote personally."

I said, "Mick, I didn't take it personally because I didn't read it."

I still haven't. Probably should. But to my recollection—and granted, it's been ten or fifteen years ago now—my relationship with Mick Foley was never bad. I liked him, and his family. He has a beautiful wife and what has always seemed to me to be a great relationship with her.

The biggest issue that Mick and I had when he was in WCW was his propensity to do things that were dangerous to himself. He felt he needed to do these insane, high-risk stunts in order to advance his character and get to the level he wanted.

When I heard that his ear was ripped off in a ring accident in Europe, I wasn't surprised. I was disappointed for him. Sorry it had happened. But not surprised.

Fortunately his hair's always been long enough to cover up the ear that's no longer there, and he chooses to walk around with half of his teeth missing, so I don't think it had any psychological effect on him. It was just another case of Mick being Mick.

I was never a big fan of that kind of high-risk crash-and-burn performance. But as the guy running WCW and responsible for the people who worked for me, it was just too much of an exposure. If we were to allow him to do some of the things that he wanted to do, they'd be on my conscience as a person, forget the corporate liability.

What I tried to do was say, *Mick, you can't go as far as you want to go here.* And that was one of the reasons that he left and went over to ECW. Because I was this rising star that people hated, Mick kind of used me to get himself over. By burying me, using my character as a tool to be the babyface, he got himself over.

That ECW crowd lived on the Internet. Ninety-eight percent of the audience were the kind of guys who stock shelves at Kmart part-time. The Internet and ECW were the only social lives they had.

But they loved the crazy shit that Mick did. And when Mick came out and said, "I left WCW because Eric Bischoff is an asshole"—the roof blew off.

It was an automatic way to get himself over as a character. And then before you know it, in the minds of a lot of people, it was all true.

NBC

The real turning point for WCW came in August 1998, when I lost control of my company and its future. But even by the end of the year, you couldn't see it in the ratings. You couldn't see it in the financial books. You couldn't tell by the number of people coming to events. But our fate had been sealed.

I didn't want to accept that, but the NBC fiasco that took place during the end of 1998 and beginning of 1999 left no room for doubt.

At the time, the NBA and its players were involved in a labor dispute. NBC ended up with some holes in their programming schedule. Gary Consadine called me, and I flew out to L.A. to discuss some ideas for a special. It was a fantastic opportunity; WCW had never had a prime-time special on one of the big three networks. We could use a special to bolster our image and reposition WCW, growing our audience just at the point where the ratings were really starting to slip.

We came up with an idea that we called the *St. Valentine's Day Massacre.* The special would end with Dennis Rodman and Carmen Electra getting a divorce in the middle of the ring. Everyone else has weddings; we were going to go the other way!

I got the green light from NBC and went back to Harvey Schiller for his approval right before Christmas.

"Harvey, here's what we've got. We can do a two-hour special on NBC. It's prime time. It's a great way to reposition ourselves and do something out of the box—bigger than and different than WWE. What do you think?"

Unfortunately, Harvey was no longer in a position to make that kind of decision on his own. He had to take it to a committee of Turner execs. I got a call back right after the first of the year from ad sales. I was told, "Yeah, that's a great opportunity, but we don't want to do it."

Ad sales.

Ad sales!'

They apparently felt that by putting our brand on NBC, we would put Turner salespeople at some kind of disadvantage.

I was fucking livid.

Anyone who knew anything about building a brand and running a business should have recognized that a prime-time special is one hellacious opportunity. Worse, they didn't even call me as soon as they'd made their decision, dragging matters along until well after the first of the year. I had to put off the NBC people, which of course didn't make them particularly happy.

It still pisses me off.

Off the Books for Good

The only way to explain that decision is this: there were people at a very high level in the Turner/Time Warner organization who absolutely did not want WCW to succeed. They did everything they could, from early 1998, to lay the groundwork for WCW's failure, so they could get WCW off the books.

They couldn't do that when Ted Turner was in firm control, but by now his grip had slipped.

They couldn't attack WCW directly, either. They had to play the corporate game, waiting until the time was right. As Machiavellian as that may sound, I can't think of any other reason why such a great opportunity was sabotaged.

Fresh Perspectives

A Trip to Paris

This was one of the most miserable times of my life.

What I really needed was to be as far away from WCW as I could be to gain perspective. During the late winter and early spring of 1999, I stayed away as much as possible. I still had responsibility for the division *on paper*, but I cut back as much as possible—no more seventy-hour workweeks. I did a lot less travel, and disengaged emotionally as much as possible.

One good thing did happen to me in early 1999; I took my daughter Montanna to Paris for spring break.

She was a high school student at the time, and very interested in French, which she'd been studying since the sixth grade. Going to France was something she really wanted to do, and it was an opportunity to spend time with her that I'd rarely had since taking over WCW.

My son and I share a lot of similar hobbies and interests. I like to ride motorcycles; most young men like that as well, and he's no exception. I took him hunting and fishing with me from the time he was five. We'd fly out to Wyoming and fish together, hunt together, just do a lot of things together.

I didn't have a lot of those kinds of bonding opportunities with my daughter. Fathers and daughters are just different. But when she expressed an interest in seeing Paris, I thought that was a great opportunity for us to do something together. It was one of the first times in a long time that I put her before everything else.

We had a wonderful time. We had a great guide who really knew Paris very well. She took us to parts of the city that tourists rarely see, explaining the culture and history. But most importantly, I got very close to my daughter. We still make an effort to carve out father-daughter things.

Mishmash Set

In April 1999 we unveiled a new *Nitro* set. It was part of a broader TNT initiative to revamp the brand. It started as an attempt to freshen up our look, but ended as a new-retro tech stale mishmash clusterfuck. It was a perfect example of the old saying that a camel is a horse created by a committee.

A guy by the name of Jay Hassman, our vice president of marketing at the time, headed up the redesign. It was a collective effort that included focus groups and test marketing. The result was a perfect example of what happens when corporate committees try to handle creative.

Some things, particularly things of a creative nature, have to be done only by people who have a demonstrated talent or instinct for creativity. When you involve noncreative people in a committee environment, the result will inevitably be muddled. Committee decisions are made by consensus and compromise, which is not the way creative decisions need to be made.

It was typical of what was going on at Time Warner at the time. Everything was created by committee, and everything was compromised. None of WCW's creative people had a say in the redesign. By then, from Harvey Schiller on down, we had little input in our company.

Nitro Monologues

At one point in May I started doing monologues on *Nitro* that spoke frankly about the fact that we were no longer on top in the ratings. I took a fair share of the blame for that, and asked the audience to give us a chance as we tried harder. The monologues acknowledged my dual role as a performer and as the head of the company, and were an attempt at breaking the "invisible wall" between the audience and the performers.

Pro wrestling fans have a voracious appetite for information. That's one of the reasons the parasitic life forms that call themselves writers and editors have been able to make a living off dirtsheets. The wrestling audience loves inside information. Many fans are more interested in what's going on behind the scenes than what's going on inside the ring.

These spots were my attempt to recognize that. I felt that by avoiding talking about what was going on with the ratings or not acknowledging it, we would further antagonize that fan base. I thought that if I came out and said, "You're right. We suck. But we're going to fight, so give us a chance," we might get one.

The spots didn't have an impact, though. By that time, the audience had already voted with their TV remote. We'd gone from *Nitro* doing 4s and 5s while *Raw* did 2s and 3s to *Nitro* doing 2s and 3s and *Raw* doing 4s and 5s. The disparity between the two brands was clear. Viewers had embraced what Vince was doing—cutting-edge shows aimed at adults, with plenty of titillation—and had rejected what we were doing, a weak show aimed at being more "family-friendly" and handcuffed by the "vision" of corporate clones who didn't know what night we aired. No amount of contrition or explanation was going to change that. People liked the competitor better. They voted with their remotes and gave a landslide victory to WWE.

WWE had conceded that the formula we'd invented was better and embraced that formula. They took our formula and did it bigger and better. For Steve Austin to stand up and flip off the audience, then chug a can of beer in the middle of the ring—that was a bold, bold move. They turned the volume way up.

By that point, we probably couldn't have turned things around without going to extreme measures. Even now, the only thing I can think of that might have worked was to turn the volume up even higher, get even more outrageous and more real. But that wasn't going to happen. It wasn't even a fantasy.

Tragedy & Dissension

Owen Hart

In the spring of 1999, Bret Hart began generating some interest with a new storyline that had him pretending to quit WCW. In March, he challenged Goldberg to a showdown in Toronto and was speared for his trouble—only to reveal an iron plate under the hockey shirt he was wearing. He denounced WCW and walked out. Bret continued the angle over the next few weeks, at one point telling the Canadian press that he now had "more time to watch the Calgary Hitmen" in the hockey playoffs. A lot of fans and most of the media bought the storyline as real.

Bret was scheduled to go on *The Tonight Show* May 24 to continue the angle. I forget the details now, but somehow Jay Leno's interview on that Monday-night show was going to launch the next phase of the storyline. Bret and I planned to meet in L.A. the Sunday night before the show. We would work out the details of what we wanted to accomplish, and then I'd introduce him to Leno.

I got into L.A. a few hours ahead of time Sunday and was watching an NBA game when someone called me to tell me that Bret's brother Owen had just died at a WWE Pay-Per-View. He'd fallen to his death during a stunt where he was supposed to rappel down to the ring.

I was shocked, and I didn't believe it.

A couple of months before, as a twisted practical joke, one of the wrestlers in WCW had made a prank call claiming that Bret's father had passed away. I'd been informed and told Bret he needed to call home. Bret did so, finding out that it wasn't true at all.

It was a pretty disgusting joke, or rib, as the wrestlers liked to call it. So you can imagine what went through my mind this time. I had no doubt that the person who called me thought it was true, but they could have been easily fooled as I had been earlier in the year. So I placed three or four phone calls to people I knew I could trust. They confirmed that Owen had really died.

Bret was already in the air on his way to meet me. I knew I had to go to the airport and tell him.

As it turned out, I wasn't the first one to tell Bret. He was on an Air Canada flight, and when the news broke, some people at Air Canada gave the information to the captain of the flight, who had it passed along to Bret.

I met Bret at the airport and could tell by the look on his face that he already knew. I spent several hours with him, trying to console him as best I could. Then he went home. It was a tough time for Bret.

I canceled the deal with NBC. There was just no way I could ask Bret to go on the air. We also canceled a bit on *Nitro* where Sting was supposed to rappel to the stage. We were confident that his stunt was safe—we'd been doing it for a long time and had all sorts of precautions in place—but we wanted to be sensitive to the situation.

Even though he wrestled for us a few months later, I don't think Bret ever really came back from his brother's death. He was injured during *Starcade 1999* and soon after retired.

There are a lot of things I like about Bret. I was happy to see him up on the stage at the WWE Hall of Fame inductions at *WrestleMania 22.* It was a step in the right direction. Bret is carrying around a lot of baggage, and I hope he finds a way to lighten that load. Whether his issues with Shawn Michaels or Hulk Hogan or Ric Flair are real or imagined—or maybe a little of both—there's a time when you just have to let those things go. Those issues are in the past; no one can go back and change anything. But the future, the opportunity to share moments like Hall of Fame dinners and the other events that happen from time to time, are in valuable. People in the sports entertainment industry, especially those select few who have performed at the levels of Bret Hart, Hulk Hogan, and Shawn Michaels, share something that is special. They can find a lot of joy and laughter in the positive memories and experiences if they just put some of those past issues aside. I hope that happens some day.

I haven't talked to him in years, but I think if I saw Bret on the street today, we'd probably hug, go grab a beer and a steak, and talk about what could have been.

Goldberg's Contract Dispute

By this time, Barry Bloom represented a lot of the talent we had contractual trouble with, including Ric Flair. So maybe it wasn't a coincidence that we had problems with Bill Goldberg during the spring of 1999—even though he was signed for a long-term contract.

Barry had been a pretty good friend of mine at one time. I'd even encouraged wrestlers to use him as an agent. My thinking was that they were going to have a lawyer or manager anyway, and I'd much rather them have someone who understood the wrestling business. But by now I'd lost a lot of respect for Barry. The issues with Flair, the attempt to renegotiate Sean Waltman's deal after we had already reached an agreement months before, and a host of other similar issues made it clear that Barry was just another parasite trying to suck as much blood from WCW as he could. It was no surprise that Bill wanted to renegotiate his contract even though he had plenty of time left on the deal. It was standard operating procedure for Barry Bloom's clients. I think after Barry had accumulated a number, of wrestlers, he got greedy.

Barry came to me in the late spring or maybe early summer of 1999 and said Bill Goldberg wanted to renegotiate his contract. I said, Well, sure, come to me a year and a half from now, and we'll discuss it. He has a lot of time left on his contract.

I was willing to bonus Bill because he'd taken off as a character. But their response was no, they wanted a new deal. It pissed me off, and put me on the defensive. Once I'm on the defensive, I tend to look for an offensive solution. And all that did was escalate the situation. It went back and forth between us and got stupid.

Then Henry Holmes got involved. Henry was Hogan's attorney and had a reputation for being very aggressive. I'd had a lot of experience with Henry. We'd had ups and downs, but overall had a pretty positive relationship. Barry, knowing that Henry had a lot of success as an attorney representing Hogan, talked Bill Goldberg into hiring Henry for the contract negotiations.

That escalated things to a whole new level. Henry and I ended up arguing over the situation to the point where I wouldn't take his phone calls and he wouldn't take mine.

Dealing with Napoleon

Finally I agreed to meet Henry in Beverly Hills. At the time, WCW was represented by CAA, at the time one of the largest agencies in

Hollywood. I didn't want to go to Henry's turf, and he didn't want to go to mine, so we met at CAA.

I booked the largest conference room there. Michael Ovitz had built the place to intimidate anyone the moment they walked in the door, and I was using everything I could to try and get the upper hand. Henry walked into the conference room and found himself at the far end of a table maybe thirty-five feet long, surrounded by agents, assistants, business affairs people, and probably a few mailroom clerks. None of them had any idea why they were in the room, except to sit there and look really fucking important. I was flanked by maybe thirty men and women in dark blue suits with red power ties and highly polished wingtips.

Henry is a very entertaining, charismatic guy. But negotiating sessions with him tend to follow a very similar pattern. Before he came in, I told the CAA people that Henry would start with some small talk. "In the middle of that, Henry will tell you all about the fact that he's the guy who did the George Foreman grill deal. No matter what we are making small talk about, trust me: He will go on and on about the George Foreman grill."

Henry had every reason to be proud of that deal, by the way—Foreman sold fifty-three million grills! But at every meeting I'd ever been in, he rolled out that story. It got to the point I could tell it as well as he could.

So Henry came in, doing his Hollywood attorney thing. "Hey, Eric, good to see you." We were all friends and family. He sits down. "Yeah, Eric, I've been really working on this George Foreman grill thing."

Everybody around me started chuckling. The meeting went downhill at a rapid pace from there.

From my point of view, the session would have been a waste anyway, because Henry had decided not to bring Bill Goldberg along, even though talking to Goldberg face-to-face was the reason I came to L.A.

"Where's Bill?" I asked.

"Well, I wanted to sit down and go through this with you first."

"That wasn't our understanding."

Henry folded up his attaché case and got up. All the CAA guys got up and went back to work.

That was pretty much how things went for weeks.

Feeding Frankenstein

Unfortunately, we had created the monster. We were fairly dependent on Bill Goldberg at that point. He was really driving our programming. Ultimately, we had no choice but to sit across the table from him and give him pretty much everything he wanted.

We could have done what I had done to Ric Flair, locked him up on the sidelines for the rest of his contract period. He wouldn't have been able to go to WWE. We could have paid him under protest, making sure we didn't breach our agreement, then at some point sue him for breech of contract. I suggested as much to Harvey, but by then no one had the appetite for that strategy. By 1999, WCW was in no position to take that hard of a line. Bill and Barry knew it, and he exploited it. He ended up getting well into seven figures for a three-year deal.

Despite all the back-and-forth, Henry Holmes and I remained friends. In fact, Henry represented me in my first contract with WWE. Warriors respect warriors.

Rap Music

Music was one of the few things that I could get past the standards and practices radar without too much of a fight. So when Kevin Nash and Konan came up with the idea of incorporating a rap music angle into *Nitro*, I jumped at the idea. I thought it would give us an opportunity to become relevant again to that younger, cooler demo.

At the time, Master P was the number-one rap star in the country.

The urban music style in general was popular in every walk of life. Someone—I'm not sure whether it was Kevin or Scott or someone else—knew Master P and had a discussion with him about doing something with wrestling. We then arranged for him to appear on several *Nitros* and at the Sturgis Pay-Per-View that August.

Whether it was a good idea with the wrong person, or a wrong idea with the right person, it wasn't effective. We didn't execute it well at all.

I think now it needed to have been a long-term, more fully integrated relationship. For rap to have worked as a co-branding opportunity, Master P—or maybe someone more suited to wrestling—would have to have been involved in more aspects of the show instead of just a single wrestling angle. We treated the whole hip-hop and urban phenomenon as a short-term storyline, rather than embracing it and weaving it into the show. We treated Master P like we treated Dennis Rodman, and it never took hold.

Not that it wasn't fun. We had a rap-versus-country feud. Master P's people, the No Limit Soldiers, took on Curt Hennig and the West Texas Rednecks. I believe it was Curt's idea—though as I've said, it's sometimes hard to say who came up with specific storylines, and even more difficult to remember. Curt and the boys cut a song that got some decent airplay in the South. But we didn't use the rap thing very well, and it just didn't take hold.

And not to bust Curt's cover or anything, but he's the only Texas redneck I know who was born in Minnesota.

Savage Sabbatical

Randy Savage and Hulk Hogan had always had a bizarre relationship. Hogan originally brought Randy to my attention and really sold him. But I noticed early on that there was an undercurrent of hostility between them. They managed it, keeping it out of view and working together. But as time went on, it gradually became more intense.

Randy could be intensely jealous and insecure. He was one of the most paranoid people I have ever met in my life. To this day, I haven't met anyone as intensely paranoid.

And I *liked* Randy. We got along personally. I had no business problems with him either. He was very much a straight shooter. He never played games, and you never had to play games with him. You knew exactly where he was coming from at all times. I really respected that.

But he was always worried about someone being out to get him. He thought someone was always trying to embarrass him. Someone was always setting him up for failure. It was a constant, constant challenge to manage those issues. They weren't real—except in Randy's mind.

Whatever the situation was between Hogan and Randy—there were rumors about personal issues related to Randy's divorce—their issues finally boiled to the surface in the summer of 1999. The two argued pretty fiercely at Sturgis. And when Randy started doing his paranoid thing, I sent him away for a few weeks. I was sick of dealing with the situation. Not Randy, but the situation. Everything was starting to get to me.

The Kiss of Death

Heading for Red Ink

Turner and Time Warner were massaging their books to satisfy Wall Street, and doing that meant hitting projections that called for double-digit growth. Each division had to do its part.

WCW's revenues had grown phenomenally since 1994. But by the summer of 1999, the mandates of "kid friendly" programming, budget cuts, and the brick wall I kept running into each time we were presented an opportunity to turn things around had taken their toll. People quit watching our product and were sold on the

WWE "attitude." While our revenues were still very high, they started to slide. By August, I believe, we were projected to lose money. It wasn't a lot by corporate standards—a million or a million and a half. It was a big number, but not enough to keep me up at night. Because there were a lot of ways to make it up.

And I came up with one: Kiss.

Kiss

I'd met Gene Simmons of the rock band Kiss earlier in the year. We threw around different ways for us to work together. A lot of our ideas involved different licensing deals. Though the band had its heyday in the 1970s and '80s, it still had a large following. To this day, Kiss has a fan base that will buy just about anything that has the Kiss name on it. It's a little like the *Star Trek* thing.

Gene Simmons is a licensing and marketing machine. I have never met anyone who understands promotion to the extent that Gene Simmons does. We said if we're going to work together, we need a line of merchandise and collectables. If we could do that, the licensing end alone would be a good return on our investment. As part of our deal to work together, I brought Kiss onto *Nitro*. I overpaid for their appearance, but in the big picture to launch the Kiss/WCW merchandise, it made good sense.

And by the way—it's been reported that I paid Kiss $500,000. The number was actually $250,000. As always, the numbers that were and still are thrown around, whether in dirtsheets or online or even in other books, are all bullshit. WCW and Turner never released financials on WCW, and no figures are available in the public records. What people have seen are guesses based on bad "inside" information and hearsay at best.

As the Kiss relationship evolved, some people Harvey Schiller knew approached me about doing a WCW event on New Year's Day at the Fiesta Bowl. That gave me an idea.

This was in 1999, and everybody was talking about the "millennium bomb"— the supposed disaster that would strike when the clock struck midnight and the calendar rolled over to the year 2000. If you remember, there was a lot of craziness and paranoia about the computers and other electronic systems being unable to accommodate the new digits. I thought *Wow, what a great way to take advantage of this—a Pay-Per-View that would air from nine to twelve on the West Coast.* People could watch what happened as the clock struck midnight all across the different time zones.

The Pay-Per-View would combine a Kiss concert with a WCW wrestling event. We'd call it *New Year's Evil.* It would be incremental revenue hitting our books, and more than make up for any shortfall we were projecting at that time.

Two or three years earlier, I wouldn't even have had to send a memo informing anyone of my decision. What a difference a merger makes.

We worked through the majority of the logistics. I told Gene we'd cover his expenses and give him a percentage of the net profits, which meant there was no real cost to us to having Kiss. The Fiesta Bowl guys loved the idea. They knew we'd draw a big gate because there were a lot of people in the area for the Fiesta Bowl anyway.

The deal made sense on every level. But logic and common sense no longer had much to do with what was happening to WCW.

The Millennium Bomb

Believe it or not, there were a lot of people at WCW concerned that the world as we knew it would literally come to an end.

I have to admit, it wasn't just the idiots at WCW who thought this. The federal government spent a lot of money on different contingencies, and probably every large corporation in America had some sort of emergency plan just in case. But the people at WCW used it as an excuse to go around me and try and kill the idea. They told Harvey Schiller and the other division heads that they *really* didn't want to do it. Partly because they were scared, I guess, and—mostly in my opinion—because they were lazy and didn't want to work over the holidays.

Once again, I got vetoed.

The Pay-Per-View would have delivered three to five million dollars to the bottom line at a time when WCW really needed the revenue. We'd come up with a solution, everything was in place, and I was told no.

I told the committees that killed the Pay-Per-View that they'd just guaranteed that WCW was going to lose money. "When you come back to me and ask me why it happened, why WCW is in the red, I'll remind you about this Pay-Per-View. If anybody else has a solution, grab a bat and step up to the plate. If not, I'd prefer it if you just stayed the hell out of my way."

Gliding Like a Brick

My finance guy, Bill Busch, told me I had to go over and see Vicki Miller, who headed Turner's financial division. "Work with her," he said, implying that she could help me find a solution.

I flat-out refused. To me, Vicki Miller represented the people who never wanted WCW on the books to begin with. That may not have been reality, but it was certainly my perception. The people at Vicki's level didn't even try to understand wrestling. To me, it was a waste of time even having a conversation.

Bill ended up getting me on the phone with her. I ended up explaining to Vicki why I wanted to do the Pay-Per-View, and why it was a solution to our revenue problems. Her answer was, "Well, we need to find another way."

Well, great. I needed to figure out how to grow wings and fly myself to work every day. But that wasn't going to happen either.

They cut the promotional budget, cut the guts out of my staff, cut the guts out of everything we were doing, and on and on and on. And then said, And oh, by the way, make more money.

"Vicki, this is a unique business. It's not like other business units where growth or losses happen very slowly and you can figure out a way to remanage the business over a six- or twelve-month period and reverse a downward trend. I'm telling you right now. This business has the glide path of a brick. Once these numbers start going down, you're not going to have a chance to correct it."

She didn't have an answer for me.

That was it for me. In my mind, that was the last straw.

Phantom "Losses"

A lot has been written about the losses that WCW was projecting at this point. None of these "facts" were supplied by anyone with first-hand knowledge of the real situation. Here are some facts: even though Time Warner was a public company, WCW's finances were not made public. That's because WCW's revenues and expenses fell into a category referred to as "other income/losses" on the Turner and Time Warner balance sheets.

There were other divisions of Turner and Time Warner that were reported this way. This gave the accountants the ability to shift some of the figures from the others around. GAAP—the Generally Accepted Accounting Principles, a kind of rules of the road for accountants—allowed our accounting division to forecast losses in such a way that they could be estimated (or in some cases overestimated) and included in a forecast that might benefit the division or department in any number of different ways.

This was an internal issue and not necessarily an issue regarding public information. Intercompany allocations and forecasts were used and abused to help various divisions or departments position themselves internally for future budget considerations.

The bottom line here is that in August of 1999, WCW was facing the first quarter in eighteen or twenty where we were projecting a loss. This loss was in the neighborhood of $1.5 million. The numbers that were "reported" by the media later were many times higher.

When I saw those numbers months later, it appeared to me that management had decided to dump as much of a projected loss on the books as possible for fiscal 1999. This way, management could look as good as possible in fiscal 2000. I'd seen it before, and it didn't surprise me.

People Weren't Watching

In retrospect, people have claimed that our guaranteed contracts and my alleged (but nonexistent) romance with Hollywood doomed WCW. Or that I was "ATM Eric" and spent too much money on talent, sealing our fate.

The truth is, people weren't watching our shows. Period. If we could have cut the contracts in half—and miraculously kept the talent—WCW would still have been doomed.

We had lost the audience. Period. If no one is watching your shows, they are not buying your Pay-Per-Views, they are not buying your merchandise, they are not buying tickets to your live events. It wouldn't have mattered if the talent worked for free.

We were dead. We'd lost our audience to WWE and weren't allowed to do anything that had an edge to get them back. Because we had to be "family friendly," we were stuck with a game plan that had nearly driven WWE into bankruptcy a few years before.

If you lose your audience, you lose your revenue.

I want to be objective, but that's the bottom line.

Done

I said to myself, There's no one above me who wants this company to succeed. The limitations they're putting on us make it impossible for us to pull the nose up. They're rejecting every opportunity to turn it around.

I thought back to the meeting a year before, where I'd been told to stop using the Leno jokes. I told myself I should have quit back then. I should have drawn the line in the sand when I had more leverage. Now I had no leverage. I had zero support. I was surrounded by people who were job scared and obsessed with their stock-option packages.

Thursday night, September 9, 1999, I called Harvey from home and told him I was miserable. I'd had it. I wanted out. I was going to do what I should have done a year before.

Harvey talked me out of it. He said I was just under a lot of stress. He was trying to be a friend and a leader, though in my mind I didn't want to hear it. In the end, I agreed with him, reluctantly.

I was driving to work the next morning, and Harvey called me on my cell phone.

"What's up?" I asked.

"Meet me in my office."

"What's up?"

"Just meet me in my office."

I knew right then what was up—I was gone. But the reality of it and Harvey's sudden turn-around still surprised me.

Et tu, Bill?

Here's what I think happened:

Before calling Harvey at home, I had talked with Bill Busch in my office. I confided in him, telling him how frustrated I was. I told him I was pretty sure I was going to throw in the towel.

Bill gave me the impression that he was trying to talk me out of it. He feigned support. In doing so, what I think he was really doing was get me to open up and give him information that he could take back to others above me, including Vicki Miller.

I didn't realize it at the time, but Bill actually wanted my job. He was a slippery little snake, and he blindsided me. He was an accountant, good at adding and subtracting. He wasn't a strategic guy, didn't have a creative strand of DNA in his body, and didn't really understand wrestling, but he was good at navigating the finance side of the business. As a result he'd become a confidant of mine. I had no idea that he and a handful of others saw my unraveling as an opportunity to do what was best for them.

I don't know for sure what Bill did that night. But *someone* called the top people on the financial side of Turner. *Someone* shared information on where my head was at and what I planned on telling Harvey. There was a high-level conference call, either late that night or early the next morning, which was why Harvey had to call me and ask me to come and see him.

It's only my impression, but I think Harvey was told what to do by Vicki Miller.

Harvey told me that I had to go home. Not that I was fired. Just that I had to go home. He was really uncomfortable, and I could tell he didn't want to do what he was doing.

"How can I go home, Harvey? I have a Pay-Per-View this Sunday."

"Not this Sunday, you don't."

Harvey was very careful in what he said. He didn't say I was *not* coming back, just that I had to go home. He didn't fire me. I had two and a half years left on my contract.

As much as I was disappointed with Harvey for not standing up for WCW earlier, I still trusted him, and do to this day. He's an honest person—sometimes painfully so. There may be a lot of political DNA in Harvey, but I don't think there's a dishonest bone in his body. When he said, "Look, Eric, just go home," I took it at face value.

I got in my car. I drove home. It was like ten-thirty or eleven o'clock on a Friday morning by the time I got home. I sat down with my wife and told her what had happened.

She was more relieved than anything.

I was eerily relieved as well.

We talked for maybe an hour or two. I decided to fly to Wyoming and go trout fishing.

By three o'clock that afternoon I had filed my flight plan, had clearance from air traffic control, and was rolling down the runway, headed west.

Loree, Garett, and Montanna.

Return to Hell

Time Off for Bad Behavior

A Sign from God

Somewhere about ten miles outside of the east entrance of Yellowstone, on the Shoshone River, I found a little hole in the river where a monkey with a fly rod could have caught fish. I literally thought it was a sign from God that I should give up wrestling and have my own fishing show on Saturday morning on ESPN.

Not only was the fishing incredible, but the fall weather in the Rockies was great, and the scenery was amazing. I wanted my wife to share it all with me. I called her and said, "Loree, fly your mom from Phoenix to Atlanta to watch the kids, then hop on a plane and come out and go fishing with me."

She did, and we had a ball. And it was the best fishing I've ever had in my life.

A Break

I was relieved that I was out of WCW. I was disappointed that I hadn't done it a year before. But there was also a level of disorientation. For the first time since 1993, I wasn't working fifteen or sixteen hours a day. After having this company occupy my mind even when I wasn't working—or even awake, for that matter, because I used to dream about it—it was all suddenly gone. It was like a chemical imbalance in my brain. I kept wanting to pick up the phone and tackle the next issue.

I wanted to keep working, but there was nothing to work on. I was under contract to WCW, and Time Warner wouldn't let me out of my contract. I think in Harvey's mind, the situation was temporary. I think he felt I was just pushing too hard and needed a clear perspective.

I also think Harvey believed he was going to get the job of president of Turner Broadcasting. He understood that WCW was being hogtied, blindfolded, and put in the closet. He knew what was going on. He couldn't change it, because he would have burned up too much political capital. But I think, looking back, that Harvey believed that when he won the battle to become president of Turner Broadcasting, he'd call me back, and then he'd be able to give us all the support we needed.

Let Me Out of My Deal

My first reaction to being sent home was, "Fuck you; let me out of my deal."

They wouldn't.

I asked them to let me out of the contract mostly because I was angry and pissed off. I didn't have any plans or other offers.

Asking to be released was also a test to see where their heads were at. If they had entertained the idea of letting me out of the contract, I would have known that they had absolutely no intention of bringing me back. It also would have been clear to me that they were going to pull the plug on WCW.

I was so sick of the company and pissed off that I didn't want to go back, ever. I hated the politics, I hated the environment. On the other hand, the fact that they wouldn't let me out of my contract meant that I had no immediate financial concerns. So I spent the time enjoying my wife and my children—and the fishing.

Now Batting for the Yankees . . .

I was in Montana at a fishing lodge when a friend of mine, Jamie Waldron, called. Jamie was an agent at CAA at the time, and he was plugged into what was going on at Time Warner.

"Have you heard the rumors about Harvey?" he asked.

"No. I've been fishing. I don't even have a TV in my room."

"Schiller's out. He's going to the Yankees."

Harvey had lost his battle to become president of Turner Broadcasting, and had moved on, taking a position with George Steinbrenner. Steve Heyer was named Turner president. In retrospect, Harvey was probably hurt by the fact that he had been Ted's guy, though I have no insight into what actually happened. I do know that Harvey was very much caught up in the political machinations of the restructuring of Turner after the AOL Time Warner acquisition. Harvey was probably the only executive in Turner who made more enemies than I did.

When I heard that Harvey was gone, I thought that my situation with WCW was pretty much over and done with. I didn't think that Steve Heyer or anybody else at that executive level would be interested in bringing me back.

Jason Hervey and I were talking about different opportunities, but the WCW contract had me pretty well tied up. So I just kept taking things easy.

Meanwhile, Back at the WCW

While I Was Gone

I had a great fall. I spent a lot of time in Wyoming. Then I took my plane and flew up to Montana for some more fishing. We had a great Thanksgiving, a great Christmas. I quit thinking about wrestling. I'd watch it, and sometimes get a phone call from Hulk Hogan or Diamond Dallas Page or another wrestler, but for the most part I put it out of my mind.

I watched *Nitro* a few times. It was just miserable to watch. My personal view was so tainted that they could have produced the best shows in the history of sports entertainment, and I would have thought they sucked.

Bill Busch was running the company. That was a joke. I can't even begin to describe how ill equipped he was to be in the situation he was in. I sat back and laughed when people told me about what was going on. Busch looked a lot like the character Gomer Pyle. He commanded all the respect of a Cub Scout leader in a room full of gangbangers. I knew it was only a matter of time before he was eaten alive.

Then Bill brought in Vince Russo from WWE to book the shows and run the creative side of the company. I laughed even harder.

The only positive thing that I heard was that a reorganization brought WCW under Brad Siegel, who headed Turner's entertainment division. Not only was Brad a competent executive, but it made a lot of sense to have WCW under the entertainment side of the business.

Brad was a rational guy. I respected him. He would try to make things work and give people the opportunity to succeed. But he was also smart enough, and under enough pressure, that if something wasn't working, he'd try to fix it. I'd had a lot of success with Brad, and we thought alike in a lot of ways. Knowing that, I told my wife in January that it was just a matter of time before WCW called me back.

Did I want the phone call?

I guess so. I had mixed emotions.

By that time, I'd been away from it long enough that my spirit was coming back. After a few months off, the part of my personality that would rather fight than have sex came back to the surface. I was looking at the gloves hanging in the corner and thinking, *Hmmm*. With Brad in place, I thought there was a reasonable chance that I'd have support. We could do some things that we hadn't been able to do before.

But another part of me said, *No way—I don't want to go back to that mess.*

A Train Car Full of Options

While I was away, AOL and Time Warner made public their plans to merge. The dance would continue for roughly twelve months, but the deal was essentially closed by January 2000. Quite honestly, when I heard that there was going to be a merger, I thought Time Warner was going to acquire AOL, not the other way around. It made no sense to me that Time Warner, this American icon of the business community, was going to be absorbed by a dot-com company. I didn't get it.

The merger wasn't on my radar screen at all—until one day in January when my wife and I took my daughter to a dance class. We went to a nearby Applebee's to grab a quick bite to eat. While we were sitting down, I got a phone call from Bill Shaw.

"Congratulations, Eric. Have you heard the news?"

"No, Bill, I haven't. What are you congratulating me for?"

"Remember when I told you one day I'll make you a millionaire?"

"Sure."

"Well, congratulations."

I had no idea what he was talking about until he explained: the stock options I'd gotten while working at WCW were about to make me rich.

Early on, Bill made sure that what he couldn't pay me in salary was made up for in stock options. But I never thought about them, and didn't even know how they worked. As far as I was concerned, it was paper money I couldn't spend.

The price of Time Warner stock shot skyward because of news of the merger. My options entitled me to buy stock at a relatively low price. If I exercised the options, the difference between the option strike price and the market price would be my profit once I sold the stock.

When I got home, I pulled out my file and saw how many I had— a train car's worth.

I went, *Oh, my God. This is great! I get it now.*

The options immediately vested because of the merger, which meant that I could exercise or use them whenever I wanted. The strike price of the majority of my options were in the $14 and $15 range; the stock was now trading for several times that.

Life was great.

I'd get up every morning and watch CNBC. I'd sit there for hours, watching the little ticker at the bottom of the screen. Every time I saw Time Warner, my heart would skip a beat, because it kept going up and up and up. I had a whole different view of the world.

Touching Base

I called Brad not too long after that, probably around mid-January. It was a social call, though I wanted to get some insight into where his head was at as well.

Sure enough, I could tell from the tone in his voice that he was under tremendous pressure and things were not going well. We both danced around the issue of whether I would come back or not without mentioning it.

A few weeks later, I was in Minnesota with my wife, having dinner at a restaurant. There was a TV in the corner turned to *Raw*. I was trying to carry on a conversation with my wife, watching out of the corner of my eye and trying not to let her know I'm watching *Raw*. Suddenly I saw Eddie Guerrero, Chris Benoit, Dean Malenko, and Perry Saturn all come out. Those were my guys, on *their* show.

Now I knew how Vince McMahon felt.

I looked at my wife and said, "They're going to call me."

She said, "I know."

Forty-eight hours later, I got a call at home from Brad.

"What if you were going to come back? What would it take?"

"Let me give it some thought."

As I was saying that, my wife walked by the room. She stopped, turned around, and looked at me.

I could see in her eyes that she didn't want to hear what she was about to hear.

"You're going back, aren't you?" she said when I hung up the phone.

"I don't know. I might. I'm going to give it some thought. But I'm not sure."

"You're going back."

She didn't want it to happen. But it did.

Same as the Old Boss

An Aggressive Deal

Things at WCW were deteriorating at such a fast pace that they really didn't have much choice but to bring me back. The whole Vince Russo experiment was an unmitigated disaster. Vince was a one-trick pony and pretty much full of shit. He was sent home in mid-January because of all the problems he'd caused. And Bill Busch didn't have a clue how to turn the company around.

But politically, Brad couldn't bring me back as the president of WCW. That would have been too controversial for him. He wanted me back, particularly as a guy who understood the wrestling business, the entertainment business, and someone who had a strong creative point of view. But he also knew that putting me in charge of the company would have burned up a lot of his political capital.

At the same time, I didn't want to go back as the president of the company.

I played it pretty aggressively.

"Brad, you're going to pay me one hundred cents on the dollar on my existing contract." The company had been trying to buy people out by offering lump sums up front for less than the entire contract, and I wasn't going for that. "This company is more screwed up than when I left. I will not be an employee of AOL Time Warner. I will be an independent contractor. I'll provide you many of the same services, overseeing the creative direction of the company and all that. . . . In addition to paying me off on the old contract, you'll write me a new one."

I think it was a two-year deal, for a pretty substantial amount of money.

"And in addition to all that, you're going to guarantee three movie contracts."

That's called a "put deal" in the entertainment industry. I was asking for a guarantee that I would have three slots for television movies on TBS. Producers covet those commitments. What I wanted to do was take these commitments and walk into a meeting and say, "I have a put commitment at TBS. Come to me with your ideas." As a producer, it puts me in the driver's seat. It was a great piece of leverage to have.

I kind of threw that out there, being very aggressive.

They took it all. I basically got everything I wanted. My contract called for me to manage and oversee the creative process. I had nothing to do with contracts, finance, or anything else. I was, in effect, the executive producer again.

Vince Russo

After we'd agreed on terms but before I officially came back to WCW, Brad asked me to go meet Vince Russo.

"Tell me if you think you can work with him," Brad said. "If you think you can, I'd like to try and make that work. The two of you might be able to make some magic."

I called Vince. He probably knew when they sent him home that they'd end up calling me back. He wasn't surprised at all.

We met at a restaurant far enough outside of Atlanta where I didn't think either one of us would be recognized. I didn't want anyone putting two and two together.

I liked him. Vince can be a fairly charming guy. He can come off kind of humble when you first meet him. It's anything but the truth, but he comes off as a pretty sincere guy. Prior to our lunch, Vince had said a lot of stupid shit to the dirtsheets about me, trying to put himself over. While I should have been pissed off enough to reach across the table and pull his tongue out of his skull, instead I took it in context.

I called Brad back that afternoon and told him that I had no problem working with Vince. I don't have to like someone to be able to work with him. I just have to be able to trust him, and I thought I could trust Russo.

By the way, we were never coequals, as Vince later claimed. The dirtsheets never seemed able to get that right. Vince reported to me, which was another reason I didn't think there'd be a problem.

Bill Busch resigned right before I came back, probably because he knew I'd chew off my leg before I worked with him again. Not only was he was a miserable failure as head of WCW, but he knew that I knew what he had done to me.

An Unhappy Millionaire

Once I signed the deal and was no longer an employee, I got a letter in the mail telling me that I had thirty days to exercise my stock options. I went, *Wait a minute!* My stock was going through the roof—every day it went up. I thought in a year it could be at $150, which would mean a much bigger profit if I waited to sell.

I called my attorney. "How can we fight this? You've got to find a way."

"Eric, there is no way. Just sell your stock and be happy."

I was the most miserable millionaire on the planet.

Fast-forward twelve months: the stock was worth less than half of what it had been when I sold, and heading south. Even to this day, it's worth less than twenty bucks. A lot of guys who held on to their options watched millions of dollars evaporate into thin air. In retrospect, that I was forced to cash in my stock options was one of the best things that ever happened to me.

He's Back

As bad as things were at WCW when I left in September 1999, now it was worse in ways that are hard to describe.

One of the raps on me was that I focused on the big names, the Hulk Hogans and Ric Flairs and Roddy Pipers and Bill Goldbergs and Stings. In my mind, a handful of big names drive the majority of the business. That's been proven countless times.

The dirtsheet community always criticized me for that. They claimed I didn't let the "young guys" get their opportunities, or said that I held them down. That sort of criticism has always been around, and always will be around, in the entertainment business. The difference is, I admitted it.

Vince Russo, more than anybody, loved to see his name in the dirtsheets. He would do an interview with anybody, anytime, anywhere. He maintained a dialogue with the Internet and dirtsheet community that was almost obsessive-compulsive. To get them to talk about what a great guy he was, he decided to bring a bunch of no-names, journeymen, and rookies to WCW. He wanted to prop them up them in high-profile roles. But the guys he thought should be stars didn't project much charisma. They didn't dress like stars. They didn't look like stars. It was like he went to a biker bar in New York, found some big guys who looked tough, and said, "Hey, follow me; I'm going to make you a star."

The storylines that went along with them had the same feel. They were unsophisticated and dark. There was no apparent arc or purpose.

Vince's particular take on interesting characters, interesting storylines, and interesting *anything* was generally very dark. His storylines had a dark, angry—I don't want to say trailer park feel, but they were dark. It was more the tone than anything else.

Bischoff vs. Russo

I looked around at my first WCW meeting and said to myself, *Wow. We don't have a lot to work with.*

We still had some of the bigger names, guys like Sting, Diamond Dallas Page, Hogan, Goldberg. But I think a lot of the talent had become so disillusioned and tired that they were simply worn out. The whole Vince Russo disaster—or "experiment," as I like to refer to it—had a pretty negative impact on all of their characters. They were shells of their former selves.

Man, this place is miserable. It's not fun. There's just not a lot of light at the end of the tunnel.

But we tried.

I laid out an angle that would have Russo and I feuding, with two camps of wrestlers opposing each other. I think one of the things that helped convince Vince to come back was the fact that the storyline called for him to be on television.

I didn't know how badly Russo wanted to be on TV. He was already a monster in many respects, but the newfound "celebrity" really got to him. He went off the deep end.

Soon, the storyline was reality.

Crash TV

The more I worked with Russo, the less I liked him, and the less I trusted him.

As I've said, it's not important for me that I like someone. It's nice when it happens, but it's not a requisite. But when I start looking at people and start realizing that I can't trust them, it has a serious impact on how I move forward.

When you sit across from someone and you're talking to them, whether about the weather or politics or business, you get a sense of whether they're honest people with integrity or not. At first, I couldn't pinpoint it. It was just a feeling creeping in.

I wanted to make the situation work. One of the things I decided to do early on was give Russo a lot of room. That may have been a mistake. Many of the things that he came up with didn't fit my SARSA formula. There was action because they involved wrestling, but they didn't have story, anticipation, reality, surprise. They were shock for the sake of shock. There's no structure to that.

Okay, Vince, I get it—but where's that going to go?

It was crash TV for the sake of crash TV.

I didn't like it, but I didn't want to stifle him to the point where he just threw up his hands and said it wouldn't work. I gave him a lot of room.

Room, not rope—I didn't want him to hang himself. I wanted him to prove himself right. I was hoping he'd show me something that would make me go, You know what? This guy does have a point of view that makes sense.

So I sat back a lot. By May or June, I decided it wasn't working. The stories remained dark, weren't going anywhere, and weren't connecting with the audience. Siegel told me to put a bridle on Russo and his dark tones. So I began exerting more control.

Fiasco at the Beach

Nothing for Hogan

It seemed to me when there was pressure on him, Russo would tend to go home for any number of reasons. Maybe it was a coincidence, but I think he'd get so frustrated with things that he couldn't function. Then he'd throw up his hands and go home for a week or two at a time. At least it seemed that way to me. He had the emotional constitution of an eggshell in my opinion. Brad, not knowing what else to do, was okay with this.

I didn't really care. It was easier to not have him around.

Russo was on one of his emotional sabbaticals while we were laying things out for the July *Bash at the Beach* Pay-Per-View. Hogan and I bounced some ideas around generally. We didn't have a real good handle on anything that felt great. He was going to be in the main event, but we couldn't come up with a finish.

The Pay-Per-View was July 9. I flew out to Wyoming to be with my family, as I did every Fourth of July, continuing to talk to everyone by phone. When I left, Russo decided he would return and plug himself back in. It was a bit of a nuisance, but okay with me.

We talked through the majority of the matches. I don't recall the details, because they all flow together, but we were pretty much okay with everything except for the Hogan match.

I asked Russo what he saw for the Hogan match, and he said he really didn't know what to do with him.

Not the right answer. Russo didn't like the character or believe in it. That was fine, but we had a responsibility—and a long-term contract with Hogan. We couldn't just bury the guy because Russo didn't like him. Whatever our personal tastes were, he was still one of the biggest draws in the history of the business. It was up to us to figure out the best way to take advantage of him.

I called Hogan and told him I had two or three options.

"If either one of us comes up with anything that we feel really strong about over the next two or three days, you call me or I'll call you. Otherwise we'll flesh this out at the event."

I planned on getting there the night before the show, which would give us enough time to plan the finish.

Father's Death

I got up on the Fourth of July and went to the parade, partied on the steps of the hotel that Buffalo Bill Cody built, and cooked for my family and friends the way we do every year. Later that evening I got the news that my father had passed away. That turned things upside down.

I put the Pay-Per-View off to the side. With the exception of the Hogan finish, everything was under control anyway. I went to Minneapolis for the funeral, which I believe would have been on Friday.

I remember being in the parking lot of the funeral home before the service and being on the phone with Russo. And I could tell by the tone in his voice that he had a shitty attitude. He just didn't want Hogan on the roster.

As it turned out, I had to spend a little more time in Minneapolis than I had planned, and didn't leave until early Sunday morning. That put me into Daytona around noon or so. I called Russo when I landed and told him that I was on my way and to hold on until I was there.

"Yeah, yeah, no problem."

I got into the building, and the production meeting was almost over. Russo had started the meeting without me, trying to get it done before I arrived.

It was a very bizarre situation. It was clear to me that Russo thought my preoccupation with my father's death had given him the chance to slip in and take over everything that was going on.

Rather than making a big scene and disrupting the meeting, I sat back and let it go on. When it was done, I cornered Russo and asked, "What was that about?"

He made some piss-ant excuse about wanting to get ahead of schedule. It was just Vice Russo bullshit. I would deal with Russo later.

I let that go and went to find Hogan. I found him and headed with him to a motor home I used as an office. I laid out an idea I had been thinking of for the past few days.

The Title

Because of the way we had used the WCW Championship belt over the past few years, it had ceased to have any real meaning. I had been working on an angle involving Hogan that would fix that.

"What if we create a situation where you win by disqualification, but you're so disgusted with everything that happened until that moment that you grab the microphone and basically say, 'Screw you. I'm done. I've achieved everything I want to achieve. This belt is my belt. Kiss my ass, I'm out of here!'?"

I would feign confusion and try to calm Hulk down. There'd be plenty of people and press around. We'd work everyone there, trying to make it look as if Hogan was quitting with the title. He was quitting and taking the title with him.

That would force WCW to have a tournament to decide the new champion. The anticipation would build over the months, culminating with a title match at *Halloween Havoc*. The storylines with everyone striving for the title would give it back its credibility and meaning. As I laid it out, the idea was for WCW to acknowledge that Hogan had retired with the title. We'd create a new one.

Hogan liked it. It made sense. There was an arc and a reason for what happened.

"So what happens next, brother?"

"We'll end up having two heels in the finals at *Halloween Havoc*," I told him. "As these two show up to wrestle, you come out of nowhere and say, 'Uh-uh—this is the championship belt. This is the WCW title. It has a history and tradition. You want it, you have to go through me.' "

Bam, we have an impromptu match. We surprise everyone. We've added credibility to the World Heavyweight title. We have Hogan in the ring with a heel. It all made sense.

Hogan agreed. I told him that for it to work, he had to go away for three months. That was no big deal, though. It worked into the framework of his contract anyway, and he was okay with it.

I got on the phone and ran it by Brad. I didn't want him to panic if he heard the news that I'd chased Hogan out of the building. Brad liked it, and he, I, and Hogan decided that was what we were going to do.

I didn't want to tell Russo. By that time, I knew I couldn't trust him. I knew he wouldn't keep his mouth shut. A leak to the dirtsheets, even by accident, would kill the plan. But Brad said, "No, you can't do that; you can't keep the secret from him." Brad was still trying to make it work.

So I pulled Russo in and told him what the deal was in front of Hogan. Russo went, "Okay, great. That's what you want to do? Great."

The plan was set. He fully understood everything we were going to do.

I thought.

Hogan compromised a little with Jeff Jarrett on how the match ended, but to me it was irrelevant. As long as it ended with him saying, "Screw you, WCW," and me running out the door after him like I was trying to put Humpty Dumpty back together again, it didn't matter to me.

We went out and did what we were supposed to do. Jeff Jarrett lay down. Hogan, disgusted, denounced us all. He told me to take the company and stick it, then jumped in his limo. I ran after him, yelling, "No, no, wait." I jumped in the car, and it took off.

In Business for Himself

We were laughing our asses off. We high-fived each other and congratulated each other. We thought we had a really good plan.

The Pay-Per-View was over with, so there was no reason for us to go back to the building. Hogan and I drove to the airport and hopped on his plane to fly back to Tampa.

When the plane landed maybe twenty or thirty minutes later, both of our phones were lit up with calls.

We quickly learned that right after Hogan and I left, Russo got on the microphone and went into business for himself. He said, basically, Hulk Hogan is a piece of shit, he's never going to work for this company again. He vented, burying Hogan in slanderous terms. He then set up an *immediate* championship match, completely at odds with what we had worked out. Booker T pinned Jeff Jarrett in what Russo declared was the championship match. He'd rebooked the show and pulled the rug out from under the entire tournament plan.

It didn't make any sense, but he did it.

We were stunned. We couldn't believe that Russo would be so stupid and arrogant to take it on himself to change the finish.

Hogan was livid. The first thing he did was call his attorney.

I called Brad Siegel and said, "What the fuck? What was that about?"

Brad was in a total state of confusion.

That was it for me as far as Russo went. I told Brad I couldn't work with him.

Showdown

Siegel, who was working in L.A. at the time, told me to meet him out in L.A. and talk about it. I thought, Fine; I was doing what he asked me to do and assumed he was going to explain that to Russo. I was pretty sure where he was going to come down in the discussion. Brad had approved the plan, and the storyline I'd laid out for the company wasn't exactly complicated. I thought he'd pull the trigger on Russo on the spot.

But Brad, instead of taking a stand and coming down on one side or the other—preferably the side he'd laid out earlier—began to vacillate, trying to find a middle ground.

Middle ground?

I don't think Brad understood the magnitude of the problem, or the fact that Hogan intended to sue. Russo was a great whiner—he'd get these puppy-dog eyes and be very emotional. He was a good con artist.

I was shocked that Brad seemed to be trying to find a way to compromise. Maybe he was overwhelmed by Russo's passion for his position. But looking back, I think Brad didn't want to report to the people he reported to that he'd had to fire Russo. Even though he didn't like the dark, no-star approach and the stunts Russo had pulled, he couldn't bring himself to pull the plug.

So I made it easy on him:

"If you think Russo's approach is going to be a great approach," I told Brad, "I'll just step aside. I have some things I have to work on."

I'd just sold a show to UPN. And besides, the fishing was just getting good in Wyoming.

Brad seems to have seen this as the path of least resistance, so he took it. Brad didn't like confrontation or tough decisions.

I was happy. I was tired of working with Russo, knew I didn't trust him, and knew that he had nothing under the hood creatively. *Now* I wanted to give Russo enough rope to hang himself with. That way, he'd be out of my hair for good.

Hogan's Lawsuit

Let me make this point very clear: I think that if Brad Siegel fully understood the magnitude of the legal problem he was about to have with Hulk Hogan because of what Vince Russo did, he would have fired Vince Russo on the spot, if for no other reason than to protect the company legally.

Hogan did go ahead and sue, alleging that he had been defamed by Russo and that WCW had broken its contract to him. The defamation portion of his suit was later dismissed, but Hogan wound up with a significant amount of cash after a protracted legal battle. *Bash at the Beach* was probably the costliest Pay-Per-View ever for WCW, thanks to the self-serving bullshit Russo pulled.

Vince Russo

Vince Russo came to WCW claiming to be *the* guy. Bill Busch, because he was an idiot in my opinion, went, "Here's the guy who turned WWE around. Let's grab him."

The others didn't know any better and went along. They were desperate to find somebody to fill the void that I'd left. They didn't do any real diligence; they took his claims at face value.

The truth is, Vince Russo is not the guy who turned WWE around. Now that I'm part of WWE and talk to some of the people who were there then, I've found out that they all wet their pants laughing when they heard that claim.

Vince Russo was *part* of the turnaround. But Steve Austin, Vince McMahon, and the realistic storylines built around them were the biggest factors in the turnaround, and Russo was not part of much of that. And, from what I've been told, the top people had no respect for him.

Russo was smart enough to look at *Nitro* and apply many of our formulas to his storylines. And he was able to convince a lot of people, including himself, that he was the guy. But anyone who worked with him for a few weeks would have known better—he *wasn't* the guy.

Ready to Rumble

Laugh With Us, Not at Us

The movie, *Ready to Rumble,* came out in 2000. A lot of WCW people including Sting, Bill Goldberg, and Diamond Dallas Page had parts in the movie. I'd played a big role in making the movie happen, though my departure from WCW may have ultimately hurt it.

In the summer of 1998 or thereabouts, I was approached by Jeffrey Silver and Robert Newmyer from Outlaw Productions, which had a deal with Warner Brothers to do a movie. Because of the synergy within Time Warner and the popularity of WCW at the time, Bobby and Jeff suggested we come up with an idea for a wrestling-themed film. We met over a period of a couple of months and discussed some ideas. They had some ideas and I had some ideas, and for a couple of months we just bounced them back and forth. WCW's concern was that the movie was fun and funny, but didn't necessarily make fun of our business.

In Hollywood, poking fun of the audience is a very easy thing to do. While that may be very funny to people *outside* the industry, fans and those inside the industry don't find it that entertaining. My role was not so much to come up with a great idea for a movie; my role was to help them find ways to have fun with the content without making fun of wrestling fans and wrestling in general.

We collaborated for a few months and came up with a really interesting idea. They cast some really good people. David Arquette, who already was a big star, is the name everyone recognizes of course, but the entire cast was very substantial. There was Oliver Platt, who may not have been an A-lister but had had a lot of interesting movie and TV roles and was a legitimate star. There was James Caan's kid Scott, who's gone on to do some pretty good stuff, including *Gone in Sixty Seconds*.

The movie had a great cast and a good budget, and we were all excited. The idea was that WCW would work with the producers and get as much of our talent integrated in the movie. We also hoped to do some of the things we had done previously with TBS and TNT, using our shows as a promotional platform for the movie, putting it over the top.

A "Bischoff Project"

It was all going great until I left WCW in September of 1999. By that time, Outlaw had already started production. All Bill Busch and the rest of the brain trust had to do was follow through on the plans we'd made. But the problem was, the movie was an Eric Bischoff project. So despite the fact that it was a Warner Brothers' feature film, internally it got very little support, other than what was contractually required. Once it came out, it got very little promotional support.

That's just bizarre. When you look at the way Vince McMahon puts together a great infrastructure and management team when WWE is involved with a movie, you see how it should be done. That's because Vince understands the power of the brand and the media platform, and how it can reach out to the audience and help motivate them to see movies. *See No Evil*, released in 2006, was a perfect example.

WCW didn't do that for *Ready to Rumble*, and I think that hurt the movie at the box office. It only did about $5.3 million on its opening weekend. I'm sure it did better in rentals and DVD sales and that sort of thing over the years, but in my opinion it could have done much better out of the gate if WCW had pushed it.

Selling Out

Are You Serious About Buying This Company?

WCW deteriorated, and deteriorated, and deteriorated. Russo wasn't the only problem. The company was still hamstrung by everything that had hamstrung it before I left.

Stepping away a second time, it all crystallized for me. After a short while I called Brad. "It's not going to work, Brad. You can't fix it. I can't fix it. If Steven Spielberg came in and took over WCW, he couldn't fix it. In my opinion, WCW is a square peg that will never fit into the round hole that is AOL Time Warner." The conglomerate does not want WCW to succeed.

"Rather than beat this thing to death, let me buy it. It's going to go away, one way or another. So let me buy it."

He laughed. "No thanks, Eric. That's not going to work. You keep doing what you're doing. We will never sell this company."

A month later, I got a phone call from him.

"Uh, Eric, are you *serious* about buying this company?"

I started pulling the financing together right away.

The Art of the Non-Deal

Dialing for Dollars

False Start

i didn't have the resources to buy WCW myself, but I was sure I could find the money. I picked up the phone and called a couple of people who I thought might be interested.

Peter Gruber at Mandalay Entertainment was one. Peter had been the former chairman and CEO at Sony Pictures. He was a pretty impressive dude. Mandalay was producing some high-budget movies that were doing very well. They also owned a bunch of baseball teams. They were well respected in the entertainment business and had a lot of bread.

I had a pretty good working relationship with Peter. My friend Jason Hervey was also working with him at the time, so it was easy to get a meeting. But Peter likes to do deals that are lopsided and aggressive. He also doesn't like to use his own money to do anything. It became obvious that he wouldn't mind being involved, but he wasn't going to step up in a substantial way to make it happen. So I started looking around for other people.

The Package

Jason told me about a guy named Brian Bedol who headed Fusient Media Ventures. Brian and his partner, Steve Greenberg, had spent years acquiring old footage of sports events. They spent a lot of time aggregating old video that no one thought had much value. Then they used it to launch the Classic Sports Network, then subsequently sold the network to ESPN. You know it today as ESPN Classic.

Jason got me Brian's number. I called him and told him about the opportunity with WCW.

He immediately got his partner on the phone, and I walked them through a potential deal. "Great," they told me. "Come on out to New York and let's talk."

They decided they wanted to take a run at it. Our arrangement called for me to own part of the company. I would run the wrestling and TV side, leaving Brian to handle the business side. He was far more qualified there than I was.

Brian and Steve were part of Allen & Company, a venture capital company, so we brought them in. We made a presentation to Warburg Pinkus, another venture capital firm. In the end, we had a package worth $67 million.

Start by Closing the Doors

While Brian negotiated the deal with Turner Broadcasting, I worked on developing the go-forward strategy. The first thing we would do, I decided, was shut the company down.

The WCW brand had been dragged through the mud for so long that it had to die and be reborn if it was going to be worth anything. It had to go away and then come back looking and feeling completely different. Otherwise the audience wouldn't give it a chance. Gradual change wouldn't have worked, because it would never feel different enough for the audience to give it a chance.

We planned to keep it off the air for a period of time, rebuild it creatively, then launch it with a fair amount of fanfare. It would be kind of like a re–grand opening. That was the only way we'd get the audience to sample us.

No More House Shows

One of the other strategies was to shut down the live event business. Just as in 1994, the live event business was way, way down. I knew that we couldn't tour successfully until we built the brand back up. And since it was bleeding money, it wasn't a very hard decision.

We also agreed that it was critically important that, for a year to eighteen months, we cut down on television production costs. That meant doing the shows at the same location, giving us a base to work at week after week.

I had some relationships at the Hard Rock Café in Vegas. Brian had some relationships there as well. So we started talking to them about building a small arena on top of one of their parking decks. The arena would be WCW's new home.

Hard Rock was a hip, pop-culture place to be, and we'd gain from the cobranding. Vegas being Vegas, we knew we could always get an audience. In the short run, it would be a great situation for us.

Take Two

WWE's Offer

WWE made some inquiries about buying WCW, which gave Turner a second possible buyer. We weren't worried about the competition, until Brian uncovered some pretty "creative" bookkeeping (a couple of years later the SEC found AOL's accounting a little too creative as well, and laid a pretty heavy fine on the conglomerate). That made us revise our initial offer, which gave Brad Siegel an opportunity to pursue WWE's inquiries. We backed out.

I was disappointed. We had spent a fair amount of time and a lot of money, and for them to shop it without trying to renegotiate the deal felt pretty sleazy. But there was nothing I could do about it.

WWE pursued a deal, and in fact got pretty close to buying WCW in the fall of 2000. Vince McMahon got a call from Viacom, with whom he'd recently entered into a comprehensive, long-term deal. Basically, they told him that there was no way they were going to let him buy WCW and air what would then be his show on a rival network. He had to back out of the deal, though I didn't know that until I got a phone call from Brad Siegel.

"Hey, Eric, you think you can put that deal back together again?"

"Hey, Brad—fuck you."

Silence.

"Brad, if I do put this back together, will you guys act in good faith? Because if you do, then I think I can. But I don't want to get these guys back to the plate if you're using us to leverage a better deal."

He gave me his word that wasn't the case.

I called up Brian, and asked whether we should pick the ball back up and run with it.

Fusient wasn't thrilled. They weren't convinced that Brad and the rest of AOL Time Warner were operating in good faith. But Brian gave Brad a call and convinced himself. We began renegotiating the deal.

Clean Sweep

By that time, Vince Russo had left WCW for good. There were some decent human beings left at WCW, though they were struggling under all of the old constraints and dealing with poor morale as well.

Ed Ferrara had come in with Vince Russo to help write the shows. Ed was an okay guy, and a real writer. He'd done some feature films and understood television. He understood wrestling and was a good guy to work with.

There were others at WCW who weren't. It seemed to me that the only qualification anyone needed to get a job there was to stand up and say, "I watch wrestling on TV every week and I love it." In Brad's mind, that qualified you to play a major role in running the company.

Terry Taylor was there, and a guy named Bill Banks who in my opinion was the most underwhelming person I'd ever met, creatively speaking. There was a guy named Aaron Blitzstein who was, for reasons I couldn't understand after meeting him, supposed to oversee branding and marketing. For the most part, I had a collection of underqualified misfits. Miraculously, Sharon Sidello and Gary Juster were still there. I wouldn't make the same mistake twice when it came to them.

Brian suggested we sit down and talk about whom we wanted to keep.

"We can do that on the phone. And you won't run up much of a phone bill."

The people there were part of the problem; they were never going to be part of the solution. It was better to just start all over. Brian was very hesitant to take that position until he went to Atlanta and met some of them. Then he called me and said, "Okay, you're right. We're going to wipe the slate clean and start from scratch."

A Done Deal

The deal was announced in January. We had a signed letter of intent. We met with the employees. We held a press conference. We had a call with Wall Street. It was a done deal.

We spent the next month or two working out the mountain of legal and business details involved in the sale. The closing was set for sometime in April or May. In the meantime, Brad arranged for me to work behind the scenes so that we could position the creative for the eventual takeover.

I told my wife that when the deal finalized, my life would change dramatically. It would be back to the way things were in 1995 and 1996; there wouldn't be a lot of family time, or even the opportunity to take a vacation for quite a while. We decided to take advantage of the kids' spring break for one last splurge. We booked flights to Hawaii. I told each of my kids they could bring one friend. My wife and I even planned to renew our wedding vows there, and invited some friends from Japan to meet us. I took everybody out there, and we had a great, great time. Life was really, really good.

I was excited again. I believed our strategy would work. WCW was going to be a successful franchise once more. I had the support of the important wrestlers. Brian Bedol and his partner had the horsepower and business acumen to help us achieve great things. Everybody was locking arms and stepping up to the plate to go forward.

It's Over

Three or four days after we got to Hawaii, I went down to the beach with my wife. While I was there, I got a phone call from Brian Bedol.

"Eric, it's over."

"Great, deal's closed. Finally."

"No, you don't understand. The deal's not going to happen. It's off the table. Over."

Shock doesn't begin to cover what I felt.

Kellner Kills It

Jamie Kellner killed the deal.

Kellner, who had formerly run the WB Network, had just taken over TBS and TNT. I assume—I've never spoken to Kellner about it—that when he got there he said, "Show me all the deals that are pending." Our deal would have been at the top of the list.

The deal called for us to acquire copyrights, trademarks, assets, all the things that would normally go along with an acquisition. But the most important part of the deal was a ten-year broadcast window at TBS. The window gave us four hours a week, for both *Thunder* and *Nitro*. We controlled the inventory—meaning that we got the revenues from the commercials during that time.

Kellner said he didn't mind selling WCW, but he didn't want wrestling on his networks. He took the distribution element out of the agreement, eliminating the broadcast window.

That took the deal from something worth roughly $67 million to something worth $67.

Maybe.

It made absolutely no sense for us to do the deal under those circumstances.

WWE Swoops In

I had been talking to Peter Ligouri at Fox during the months leading up to the closing of the acquisition about airing one of our shows on FX. They wanted *Nitro;* I wanted to give them *Thunder.* In any event, we intended on flipping one of them over. Even though *Nitro* and *Thunder* had fallen from the ratings heights they'd been at a few years before, their numbers were still pretty good for cable shows. But Fox wasn't interested in giving us the kind of commitment we would have needed to resuscitate the deal. Our deal was dead.

That left Vince McMahon and WWE. Now that there was no broadcasting involved, Viacom no longer had any objections. So Vince bought what was left—basically, the copyrights and video library. I'm sure whatever he paid, it was worth it in the end.

For me, it was a long flight home from Hawaii.

Meet the Devil

Getting On with Life

Out of Wrestling

hen the deal fell apart, and because of the way it fell apart, I was disheartened and disappointed. My life in pro wrestling was over, not with a sparkle but a splat.

There was no way in the world I was ever going to work for Vince McMahon. Joining WWE was out of the question—I didn't see that happening in my lifetime. So I geared my mind toward developing other projects.

Out of sheer boredom, I took a couple of consulting jobs. A group out of Canada wanted to develop an MTV-like wrestling format called *Mat Rats*. They were relatively well funded. I worked with them for a short time, trying to help them develop the concept. Ultimately, their project didn't get off the ground.

I was also approached by a group out of Los Angeles called Battle Management. They represented probably a dozen or so mixed martial arts fighters who were fighting in Kl, UFC, and Pride. They wanted to develop a business plan similar to a wrestling model. I worked with them for a little while, though their project was too advanced for its time. The television networks were a little too leery of the whole mixed martial arts genre, and it was still pretty raw. They've gotten more used to it now, but back then it would have taken way too much money to fund a wrestling-like business structure.

Most of what I did was develop projects on my own. Among other things, I worked with Mark Burnett, best known as the creator of *Survivor* and *The Apprentice*. With Battle Management, we created a show that was loosely a martial arts version of *Survivor*.

A Call from WWE

In my family, the Fourth of July is the biggest holiday of the year. For one thing, it's my wife's birthday. For another, July 4 in Cody, Wyoming, is very special, unlike any other Fourth of July celebration I've ever been to. I don't want to say that the people of Cody are more patriotic than the rest of America, but they have a real sense of small-town patriotism that you don't get in a lot of places.

Celebrating the Fourth of July in Wyoming has been a tradition for my family for probably fifteen years, even before I owned a home there. But in 2001, it was a little more special and a little different, because it was the first Fourth of July after my dad passed away.

We'd been there for a week or so. On a Thursday night, I got home, and my answering machine was blinking. John Taylor had left a message.

John was an attorney in Atlanta who represented WWE. He wanted me to give him a call. So I did.

He told me WWE wanted to talk to me. Would that be okay?

"Sure. Have them give me a call."

Jim Ross called back a short time later. Jim and I have since mended our fences. I won't say that we're great friends, but I think we've dealt with our issues. But up to that point, Ross hated my guts. He blamed me for every bad thing that had ever happened to him. He'd told people I fired him, when that wasn't true. In fact, he'd made such a public enemy of me—I think to endear himself to the crowd and get himself over—that in real life it carried over.

I could tell he wasn't excited about talking to me. Vince or someone must have put him up to it. WWE had decided that it would be a good idea to shoot an angle with Vince McMahon and me the following Monday.

I asked what they were thinking. Ross was pretty vague.

"We don't really know if it'll work," said Jim. "It's a short-term deal. Come in, we'll try it. If it works, great. If not, hey, part friends."

A couple of things occurred to me. One was, if they were calling me on a Thursday night for an angle they wanted to do on Monday, they probably hadn't given it a lot of thought. It seemed like an idea that came up at the last minute. If that was the case, it probably hadn't been planned to go very long or very far—it would be a hot-shot moment, as we say in the business.

The other thing was that I wasn't in any kind of shape. I'd been eating and drinking for a week straight.

I was also stuck in Wyoming. There are only two or three planes that go into Cody on any given day, and over the July 4 holiday you have to make your reservation months in advance or you won't be able to get a flight out. I honestly didn't think I'd be able to get out of there.

On top of everything else, I didn't feel like leaving my entire family, which had just flown and driven in from different parts of the country. *Hi everybody! Thanks for showing up! I'm gone!*

I called Ross back and thanked him. "Maybe we can do something down the road. The timing just isn't right."

When I hung up the phone, I said to myself, *That's it*. Not too many people tell Vince McMahon no and hear from him again.

A Year Goes By . . .

I continued working on different projects. I had pretty much made up my mind that I didn't really want to work for anyone else again. After everything that I had been through with Turner and AOL Time Warner, I didn't see myself working for another big company again. I had enough money in the bank and wasn't under any financial pressure. I've never really been the type of person who overspends. The only money that I'd ever really spent foolishly was on my airplane. Aside from that, I've lived under my means.

A year went by. I started developing a lot of relationships in Hollywood. I pitched various ideas for shows. We had some false starts and near misses, but didn't really develop anything substantial.

I was in Los Angeles in May 2002 when I got a phone call from Kevin Nash. He was working for WWE—it was right around this time that World Wrestling Entertainment changed its name from World Wrestling Federation. Kevin and I were still pretty good friends, though we hadn't talked in a while.

"Hey, Eric. There's a rumor going around that you're going to be getting a call from Vince. Would you be interested if he calls you?"

I told him I didn't believe that would happen. But I said I'd be interested. By this time, I'd put all of my bitterness and ill feeling behind me. I'd moved on, emotionally and psychologically.

"Sure, if Vince calls, it'd be great. But if it doesn't happen, let's go catch a beer next time you're in L.A."

A day later, I got a call from Vince.

A Fellow Warrior

Whatever anxiety or doubt I had, Vince eliminated immediately by saying something to the effect of: "I would like to think that if the shoe was on the other foot, and you had acquired WWE, we would have been able to work together."

It was odd. I was on the phone with him for, maybe, two minutes, and I felt like I'd known Vince for my whole life. It was as if I was talking to an old friend.

Vince was very gracious. The feeling I got was that he understood what I had gone through. While he came out on top, he understood what the Monday Night Wars and everything else had meant and had some empathy for me. He didn't say it, but I felt it.

I hung up the phone and I said to my wife, "I can work for this guy. If the offer's right, I'd like to go back."

I wanted to go back because my career in the wrestling industry had ended in a bitter and ugly way. I had spent nearly twenty years of my professional career in the wrestling business. To have achieved everything I achieved and have it end on such a down note bothered me. I didn't want to be remembered like that.

If nothing else, I thought, WWE would be an opportunity for me to go out and have some fun. It would give me a chance to end my career on a high note.

And in the meantime, make people realize that much of what they'd heard or read about me wasn't true.

Or, if it *was* true, give me a chance to learn something about myself.

Tell Me What to Do

Vince and I talked two or three more times. It was a very easy negotiation. We're all motivated by money to various degrees, but the money wasn't really that important to me. After some back-and-forth between our attorneys, we did the deal.

Vince told me what he had in mind for me in a very general sense, but we didn't talk about storylines in a detailed way. I guess that had to do with the way I was brought up in the industry. I didn't get hung up on how they were going to use me and didn't worry about it. The agreement didn't have any language that said they owed me any explanation creatively. I pretty much signed over my character when I went to work for them. They were going to tell me what I was supposed to do, and I would do it to the best of my ability. That's how I work.

There were a lot of people in the WWE who claimed to have insight into what kind of person I was and what made me tick. All that kind of crap. Somehow, I believe Vince was under the impression that I would be difficult to work with, and that I might not be willing to do certain things creatively. But nothing's further from the truth. If you look at what's happened since I got there, there's nothing they've asked me to do that I haven't done. I've enjoyed almost

all of it. I don't get hung up on the difference between my character and the person I really am. The two are not really connected.

Vince did ask me early on if there was anything I wouldn't be willing to do.

"Yeah. I wouldn't be willing to move to Connecticut. But other than that, I'm wide open."

Just Acting, Thanks

I was never interested in being a real general manager or taking *any* management role at WWE. And no one ever offered it.

Running WWE is Vince McMahon's job, and I don't think he'd ever offer it to anyone. He's got a wife that is very competent. He's got a daughter who is quite competent, a son who is very competent, a son-in-law who is very competent—I don't think he's looking for anyone, especially me, to come in and run things.

In fact, that was one of the things that made the WWE offer attractive to me. My schedule would be limited, allowing me to do all the things I wanted to do to build my business outside of wrestling.

I had the best of both worlds. I could step back into the limelight, so to speak, with WWE as a performer. Yet I'd still have enough time to pursue the projects I'd been developing in the entertainment industry.

Right about the same time, Jerry Jarrett and his son Jeff were starting TNA, and they asked me about coming in and being part of that organization. I didn't believe that they had the vision to pull something off that would be successful, and I didn't want to be part of a failed wrestling company again. I also didn't completely trust Jerry. But the biggest reason I didn't get involved was that I didn't want to give up everything I was doing in Los Angeles. I told them, *Thank you but no thank you.*

Heat with the Boys

The Power of Surprise

After the second or third discussion I had with Vince, I started getting phone calls from people, asking what was going on. "Hey, I heard you did a deal," said Kevin Nash. "I heard you did a deal."

As much as I hated to, I had to deny it. Technically it wasn't true. I hadn't signed anything yet. And I wanted my appearance with WWE, assuming I went through with it, to be a surprise.

The wrestling audience is a funky audience, particularly because of the power of the Internet. The Internet really does have an impact on the business. If the wrong person found out I was coming back, the news would be online in seconds.

I knew that that if the word got out, the initial reaction would be, "Oh, cool." But then you would have people tearing it down. That's kind of the nature of that community. There are very few positive things said on the Internet. It's more about everyone's negative view of what everyone else is trying to do. So I knew it would turn quickly to "Oh, Bischoff's going to ruin WWE. He's going to do to them what he did to WCW. The morale's going to go down, the guys are going to hate it."

It'd be one big negative thing before it even started.

I called Vince and said, "Vince, there are leaks in your organization. I'm getting phone calls I shouldn't be getting, from people who shouldn't know that you and I are talking. If we're going to do this, can we do everything in our power to keep it quiet? Don't tell anyone you don't have to tell."

He agreed.

"And you know what? I want to go so far as to fly myself in. Because the minute you book an airline ticket through your office, everyone's going to know. I'll book my own hotel. You tell me where to be and when, and I'll be there."

And we did.

Back to Black

In the year-plus that I'd been away from television, I'd let my hair grow pretty long. I'd also stopped dying it, which meant it was completely silver. I decided that, to make the best impact, I'd show up looking as close to the guy people remembered from *Nitro* as possible. So I got out the dye and had my hair cut Ken doll style.

A week or so before the show, I got a call from Stephanie McMahon, Vince's daughter and one of the company vice presidents. Like the rest of the family, she was very cordial on the phone. That's one thing I have to say about the McMahons: they're very classy people. Despite what the perception may be, I've found them all, Vince, Linda, Shane, and Stephanie, to be genuinely nice people.

"Eric, I want you to know you've got a lot of heat here with a lot of the boys. I'm not sure if you know what you're getting into."

"Stephanie, you don't know me, but here's the deal. I've had heat from the day I started in this business. I pretty much believe that if I show up and work hard, all of that stuff will take care of itself. If I don't do that, the fact that I may have heat is going to be a problem. Don't worry about it. It'll all be fine."

Committed to Memory

The *Raw* I was going to appear on was at Continental Airlines Arena in East Rutherford, New Jersey. I came into New York City and stayed across the river near LaGuardia Airport. Monday morning, a town car came over and picked me up, bringing me to another hotel not far from the arena, but not the one where the wrestlers were staying.

Around two or three in the afternoon, a script was slipped under my door. There were two or three pages of material they wanted me to memorize. Up until then, I'd never had to memorize that much material. Usually I'd work with bullet points and improve it. That's the way a lot of guys who've been in the business for a while work.

I wasn't sure whether they wanted it word for word or not. But I figured if they'd spent this much time preparing this much script, I better do it word for word.

For the next few hours, I walked back and forth in my room, talking to myself, reciting my lines.

Ready to Rock

About seven o'clock, a stretch limo arrived at my hotel to take me to the arena.

We stayed out in the parking lot, outside the arena area, until nine. Then the limo pulled inside the arena. I remained inside so no one could see me.

I was smiling so hard my face hurt. I knew it was going to be big. I knew I was going to get a huge reaction from the crowd. I was excited to get out in that ring again and let it rip, just hear that audience react.

There is nothing like that.

There is nothing like standing in the middle of a ring, surrounded by fifteen or twenty thousand people, and having the ability to make them do exactly what you want them to do, exactly when you want them to do it.

I wasn't nervous. There wasn't any anxiety. I didn't second-guess myself. Nothing. It was about as perfect as it could have been.

As the time came closer to my debut, I saw guys passing and trying to get a look in the limo, hoping to figure out who the surprise general manager was going to be. Steve Lombardi—he's a great guy who works behind the scenes at WWE after a career as the Brooklyn Brawler—squinted at the blacked-out windows. He couldn't figure out who was inside. It was still a secret.

About twenty minutes before I was supposed to go out, Vince McMahon came by. It was the first time we had met face to face since that interview in 1990. He sat in the car and gave me a little pep talk.

"When you come out, Eric, I want you to give me a big hug. Let's embrace."

Which was kind of odd, because I'd hardly even shaken his hand until this point.

"Sure, Vince."

He went back to the show. A few minutes later Stephanie came by, and we were ready to go.

A Train Wreck

"Okay, Eric, now none of the boys know. It's going to shock a lot of people. Don't let that bother you. Just go out and do your thing."

I think she probably thought I was a mental train wreck. She was sure that half the guys in her locker room were going to want to kill me, and the other half would cheer them on.

But I was just as calm and relaxed as I've ever been. We got out, and I followed as Stephanie walked me up to the gorilla position, which is a kind of holding area right behind the stage. It's the last thing you see right before you walk out.

Either by design or accident, she made a wrong turn. Instead of walking me into the gorilla position, she swung me through an area backstage where twenty or twenty-five wrestlers were watching the show around a monitor.

The looks on their faces was priceless.

There was shock. There was fear. There was disbelief. There was anger. There was laughter.

Big Show stood up. "Oh ho, ho, I can't believe this!"

We reversed course and went up to the gorilla position. I stood there and waited.

Out on the stage, Vince was telling the crowd that WWE needed to be shaken up. He wanted a general manager who was going to be ruthless, someone who lived and breathed "ruthless aggression."

And he had found the perfect SOB.

My music started, and I walked out.

Milking It

The Hug

The crowd was in utter shock. I walked to the center of the stage and gave Vince a big hug.

A very, very big hug. We milked it to the point where it was almost homoerotic.

"That rumbling beneath your feet," I said as we embraced, "is a whole lot of people turning over in their graves."

The audience was so surprised they didn't know how to react. They were quiet—until I started running off at the mouth. Within a few seconds, I started noticing the scowls, then the howls and the boos.

It was the reaction I wanted. Once again, I'd found my inner heel.

Paying Respects

We did some backstage shots right after the show. The first was with Booker T, who'd been a WCW Champion. It was just fun. Everybody was so professional that if I'd had any anxiety, it would have all gone away.

I went around and said hello, seeking out people I thought I ought to approach first to let them know I had no hard feelings. A lot of WWE people were still carrying the wounds of the Monday Night Wars. I'm sure a few would have gladly volunteered to drive a stake through my heart because of everything they'd gone through. But many, especially the production people, were also anxious to see what I was like, and what I was like to work with on camera. Not to sound too arrogant, but I think that even though they may have hated me and thought I was the devil incarnate, everyone realized that as a performer I was pretty damn good.

I walked up to Undertaker. He's been around a long time, with a very successful career, and it's protocol for a newcomer to pay respects to someone of his stature. He was, I won't say indifferent, I won't say unfriendly, but he didn't go out of his way to acknowledge me. I thought to myself, *Okay, I've got to work hard and contribute, and then he and I will get along. And that's pretty much what's happened in the years since.*

As ironic as this sounds, I probably have better relationships with the people at WWE today than I had with the guys at WCW when I was there. Guys like Bruce Prichard, Gerry Brisco, Pat Patterson, and Ann Russo, who does my travel. Vince. The production people. I get along with all of them far better than most people who worked for me at WCW.

Part of it is that I'm a different person in a different situation. But the staff at WWE are all hardworking, competent professionals. I'm amazed by most of them. I've never met more hardworking or committed people than the ones who work at WWE, at every level.

Vince himself is a freak of nature when it comes to work ethic. I have a great work ethic. He makes me look like I'm going backward. If he sleeps three hours at night, I'd be amazed. He's one of the most intense, focused people I've ever met in my life. Much as Ted Turner set the tone for his company, the same is true in WWE. Some people may think that if they don't try to keep up with Vince, they'll be on shaky ground. But more than the intimidation, they respect what he does and know how hard he works.

Wrestler Feuds

The heat that was supposedly following me around either dissipated right away or wasn't there to begin with.

So much of what the public read about and heard about was bullshit. Chris Benoit and Eric Bischoff never had problems at WCW. I always got along with Chris. Dean Malenko and I had never had a problem.

Chris Jericho was one of the guys who used me and whatever tension existed between us as part of his character. From the public's point of view, there was a problem. But personally, there really wasn't much there.

Eddie Guerrero and I had problems when we didn't see eye to eye creatively. Eddie could get emotional and I could get emotional, and when you get two guys who both have tempers in a room, shit's going to happen. Once or twice it did. But those incidents were blown way out of proportion. I took care of Eddie, and he knew it. He got into a bad car wreck in Florida one time when his contract was up. I called him up and told him not to worry about it. Not to say that he wasn't disappointed in things I was doing, but it wasn't a personal thing.

Of all the guys at WWE when I came over, Arn Anderson and Ric Flair were probably the only ones who were clearly not comfortable with me being there. But even they put it in their back pockets. Within a month, Ric and I were going out together and having a beer.

Stone Cold Steve Austin

A couple of things have really stood out during my time at WWE. My showdown with Steve Austin—who'd stepped away from wrestling after I left WCW—was one of them.

I can't remember who came to me and said he was coming back to WWE. It may have been Vince, asking me if I wanted to do an angle with him that would end up with me in the ring with him.

"Hey, now, I know there's some history between you and Austin," said Vince, pulling me aside. "Don't worry about it. He's not the kind of guy who's going to get into the ring and take advantage of you."

Quite honestly, that was the furthest thing from my mind. I knew Steve was a pro—as are 99 percent of the guys in WWE.

There's a code. When it comes to what they do in the ring, wrestlers take things very, very seriously. Two guys who absolutely hate each other and would normally come to blows anywhere else would never settle their personal issues in the ring. It's just not done.

Once they laid out what they wanted to happen and where they wanted it to end up, I suggested the "hunt for Steve Austin" skits. Since the urban legend was that Steve Austin hated Eric Bischoff because Eric Bischoff fired him by FedEx, I suggested we play off that. "Obviously if he's coming back, my character is going to want to make amends. He's not going to want this guy pissed off at him."

So I went down to Texas and began looking all over for him. Steve showed up while we were filming one of the skits. It was the first time I'd seen him since 1994 or 1995. He looked great. It was clear that he'd been working out and getting into shape for his comeback.

Steve pulled me off to the side. "Hey, I just want you to know, the past is the past, I got no heat with you."

Within three minutes, we were in a conversation about how my firing him had actually been the best thing that ever happened to him. It was a very good conversation.

"Hey, Eric, when we get in that ring, I'm a little stiff anyway," he told me. "But don't worry, I'm not going to take advantage of you."

"Stiff" in wrestling terms means that what's supposed to be fake is sometimes real by accident. A punch might connect a little harder if a stiff guy throws it.

"Steve, don't worry about it. As long as I can walk out to the car when it's over, we're in good shape."

The match turned out exactly the way it needed to turn out. He pretty much beat me up.

Much better to get potatoed, and walk out with a broken nose or black eye, than to have someone so careful with you that the match ends up looking phony. I'd rather have my ass kicked than come out without a scratch and have the audience shit on the match.

Steve got a great reaction. I had a tremendous amount of heat

and he was a big babyface, and the match worked perfectly.

We became pretty good friends after that. Although we don't socialize and hang out now, I've spent a fair amount of time reliving some memories with him after the shows.

Out with the Trash

In early December 2005 I got a call from Stephanie McMahon.

"Look, Eric, we want to do an angle with you. You're going to overreact to this thing and think it's really bad, but it's not. We really like working with you. You're a great performer. We have every intention of keeping you on. This is not the end of your contract, and we're not going to close your deal."

I was about to be fired.

She laid it out and I said, *Hmmm, that could be fun.*

The writers in WWE are some of the hardest-working people I've ever met. Brian Gewirtz, Ed Koskey Michael Hayes—they have the most thankless jobs you can have in the entertainment industry. The number of hours of content they write and the travel that they have to do for the job make network sitcoms look like a vacation. Because of negativity on the Internet, these guys take a tremendous amount of criticism. The fact that they're able to do it day in and day out, year round, amazes me.

Brian Gewirtz is a great guy, but he's kind of a nervous little character. He tiptoes around a lot. Brian called me about it, and he was kind of tentative. "Take a look at it. If you have any concerns, we'll talk about it."

I got the script and I thought it was funny as hell.

They had to get my character off the air to give it a rest. I'd been doing the general manager for three and a half years. For all that time I'd been the evil dictator who was angry at the babyface performer, because he wasn't giving me my respect. It was the underlying premise for every angle I was in.

Honestly, in the last angle, when we were doing everything we could to get the belt off of John Cena and onto Kurt Angle, there was nowhere else to go with the character. It was time to give the character a rest and an overhaul.

The angle built over a couple of weeks, until finally I was put on trial and my fate "decided" by Vince in a kangaroo court sequence revisiting my sins as WWE's weasely general manager. The way things were originally laid out, I would go back to the ring for judgment. There, John Cena was going to hit me with his finishing move, propelling me into a garbage truck so that I would be taken out with the trash.

I went to Vince and told him that it would make more sense if he did it.

"You're the chairman of the board. The storyline has been that I haven't met your expectations. It makes more sense to have you throw me in the garbage truck."

And that's the way we did it.

In Character

They had steam-cleaned the truck, and you probably could have performed surgery inside it. They'd welded two giant stops to keep the scoop from crushing me in the back. The idea was that after I got bodyslammed into the back, I would keep my eyes closed until I heard the scoop closing. We'd talked through it, but we didn't actually rehearse it.

I waited until the thing closed and tried crawling up into the

back. Vince jumped into the driver's seat and drove out of the building. Within seconds the truck was moving too fast for me to get anywhere. It was so dark I couldn't see, and on the way out of the building, Vince hit some cable covers that bounced my face against the compactor. When I finally got out of the truck, I had a three-inch gash under my eye.

Vince hopped out of the truck and was looking at me like, *Oh, my God, are you all right?*

We were out in the parking lot. There were fans all over the place. I didn't want to come out of character. So I started yelling at him. "You don't give a shit if I'm all right. You brought me into this company to embarrass me, to humiliate me. What the hell do you care?"

I screamed at him the whole way back into the building.

Professionalism

My character has a lot of heat. It's a natural character. I don't have to force it. It's not at all who I really am, but there's enough of who I really am to make up for my lack of acting ability. I can reach into my personality and find those elements that the audience reacts to. Then I turn up the volume and act them out in a way that works.

One of the reasons why me coming to WWE has worked has been the professionalism of WWE's staff and talent. I've tried to be just as professional. I show up on time. I do my job to the best of my ability. And I mind my own business.

I made up my mind early on that I was never going to get myself involved in politics. There are politics in WWE. I will tell you, though, they're not *anything* like the politics that existed in WCW.

Despite the fact that WWE is a public company, in a lot of ways it's still a family-run business. Vince McMahon is the only head of WWE, and everybody recognizes it. There's not a lot of jockeying for position in WWE. My sense is, that it's frowned upon. There is a corporate culture of professionalism. But there are politics. Any human enterprise has them.

I'm as apolitical as possible. I don't hang out with too many people. I'm a loner. For the most part, when I show up, I read a book or work on my computer, and stay out of everybody else's way.

The Bigger Picture

Good Guys, Bad Guys

Professional wrestling has prospered greatly in the last fifty years, despite the many changes the world of entertainment has gone through. If you look at WWE today, it's the most-watched program on ad-supported cable television. I think that really says a lot for the basic psychological and emotional attraction of sports entertainment and what it has to offer.

It's simple. It's good guys, it's bad guys. It's storylines that keep you coming back for more. It's characters viewers aspire to be.

Scott Hall once told me, if you look at all of the really successful characters, they have this one thing in common: they're characters that guys wish they could be, and that women wish they were married to.

He used different terminology, but you get the idea.

Stone Cold Steve Austin is a great example of why wrestling works. So many people sitting at home, men and women, wish deep down inside they could be someone who stands up to the boss, gives him the finger, and basically says, "Screw you." I don't think there's anyone who works in a factory or office, in a brokerage firm, anywhere, who doesn't wish they had the opportunity to walk up to their boss and tell them that.

Steve Austin became that cultural icon that we all wished to be. At other times, different characters and storylines catch the mood of the country and reflect it back at the viewer. That's a time-tested formula for success, and I think it will continue in the future.

If I Were in Charge

Sometimes I watch Monday night *Raw* or *SmackDown!* and I think about how I would do it if I were running things now. I go back to that formula we used with *Nitro*—SARSA. Story, anticipation, reality, surprise, action.

Action is pretty easy to create in wrestling. But it's not the only thing in wrestling—it's just one of those five elements. The others are just as important and usually even harder to create.

One of the things that I've noticed these days is that the bookers and writers often think they can force-feed conflicts to the audience without bothering to make them believable. The story suffers as a result.

Is it plausible that wrestler A is going to have an issue with wrestler B? If not, you have to make it believable before it happens. You have to ask yourself what kind of backstory to create to get the audience to believe it, and spend the time creating it. We don't take the time, and the story suffers.

The story is suffering because the reality is suffering. And if you have a weak story and no reality, then you don't have anticipation—because no one really cares enough to anticipate it.

The sheer amount of product that we have to produce each year means that we don't have the time to make every story real or believable. But I think it can be done more often than it is.

Entertainment Buffet

One thing that makes wrestling so unique right now is its appeal to different demographics. It's a little bit like an entertainment buffet. There's something there that everyone's going to like. If you're a ten-year-old kid, you have characters and personalities that you're attracted to. If you're sixteen or eighteen, there are different characters you're attracted to for different reasons. If you're twenty-five to forty-nine, you relate to different people for different reasons. And if you're someone who's sixty-five who used to watch wrestling when you were young, there are things that remind you what wrestling was back in the day.

When you look at the television landscape today, and the proliferation of cable channels, the networks have largely become niche programmers. Nearly all have narrowly defined audiences, and therefore narrowly defined content. Wrestling reaches across all of those demos. That's one reason it's so powerful on cable. It's literally attractive to a whole range of audiences.

Breaking New Ground

For me, surprise has always been an important element in wrestling. It's tough to achieve that now, I think. There's so much television programming out there, and there has been so much over the past ten years or so, that there is very little possibility of doing something that hasn't been done before in one way, shape, or form. The good news is, we've pushed the envelope and come up with many different ideas. The bad news is, we've just about scorched the earth, leaving no creative possibility untried.

The audience knows that. They're so smart, so sophisticated—not too many people use the words *sophisticated, wrestling,* and *audience* in the same sentence, but it's true—and it's hard to surprise them.

People outside the industry don't realize how sophisticated the wrestling audience is, how dedicated and diverse the viewers are, how demanding they can be. Those things are great, because they tend to create brand loyalty. But they're also a challenge, because it's very hard to sneak something past that kind of audience. They know when you're tilting an old idea five degrees one way or another and trying to palm it off as something new and fresh.

Better-Defined Characters

In my opinion, over the next three to five years, rather than trying to pretend that we're coming up with new ideas, we re going to go back to the future in some respects. I don't think that wrestling will ever return to the dark, dingy, and small wrestling arenas with very basic wrestling formulas and stripped-down presentation. But I do think we're going to go back to some of the fundamental things that worked. And one of those things is going to be more clearly defined characters.

For the last couple of years, we've embraced a philosophy that lets the audience decide whether they like a character or not. We've had a lot of characters who are ambiguous, not completely good and not completely bad. You can see some of that with Triple H and John Cena. Triple H is a character who is theoretically a heel. But he's not really a heel. Guys kind of like him. John Cena is a character who's supposed to be a babyface—but he's not really a babyface. It's up to the audience to decide whether they like the characters or not.

Flattening Out

That works when the industry and your brand is firing on all eight cylinders and you reach the WCW 1997 fever pitch, or the WWE 1999–2000–2001 pitch. But as you start to soften up a little bit, as things get more competitive or the numbers level out, you don't have that luxury of letting the audience decide. You have to take control of your product more. I see that starting to happen. We're maintaining the audience very well, but it's harder to grow the audience. And one of the responses, I think, is going to be a trend toward more clearly defined good guys and bad.

If you make things too ambiguous, you end up with that gray area. You tend to fall into a problem Verne Gagne warned me about years ago: People won't care. It's not important whether the audience loves you or hates you, Verne used to say. But they have to feel strongly one way or another.

Corporations and Creativity

The Turner–Time Warner–AOL serial mergers were a recipe for disaster, in particular for WCW, for two reasons. First, WCW was a square peg in the round hole that Time Warner wanted their networks to fit. They wanted golf, HBO-quality movies, and high-end programming. To 95 percent of the executives at Time Warner, WCW was an embarrassment. Once the people who really wanted it off the books took control, it was a foregone conclusion that WCW was never going to be successful, regardless of what Eric Bischoff did or didn't do.

But WCW was also strangled by a corporate mentality that was strongly anti-creative. We were an example of what's still happening across the board in entertainment today.

With the exception of HBO, risk is not rewarded in the entertainment properties that are part of the vertical integration of corporate America.

Creativity—real creativity—depends on risk and chances. In entertainment, if you don't take chances, if you don't reach out for the most creative people in the marketplace and give them an opportunity to be unencumbered and as creative as they can be, you end up having a bunch of bankers and accountants and people who are anything but creative making the creative decisions. Nothing can be more devastating for entertainment.

Look at the television networks and the programming on those networks. Most of the programming decisions are made by the most noncreative, unimaginative, nonvisionary people I've ever met in my life. When it comes to instinct and vision, they're woefully inept. But they're great in a meeting. They're great corporate suits.

The Warrior at Peace

Sometimes I look at the people around me in the WWE, and I realize how ironic it is that I'm there. The fact is, I'm the guy who almost put them out of business. There were a lot of people—some of whom I'm now friends with—who were worried that they were going to lose their jobs, their houses.

Much like any war, we were both fighting for a just cause. They were fighting to survive. To them, I was the devil incarnate.

We felt it was important for us to be number one and to be successful, and we were willing to do just about anything we needed to do to achieve that. We were not worrying about how employees at WWE were going to feed their families.

I oftentimes wonder if Vince, Kevin Dunn, and the others really understand and appreciate that many of the things that have led to WWE's success—in some ways more obviously than others—are really tied to the things that I either created or did first.

I don't want to suggest that I'm responsible for their success, because no one is responsible for their success other than them. But I forced them to embrace a course different than the one they were on before *Nitro*. If you look at the live television component, the fact that they're a two-hour show, that they went from cartoon-type characters aimed at children to a formula I created for *Nitro*, that they feature a cruiserweight division—why did they do all that? Who were they reacting to?

Look at WWE log pre-nWo, and look at it now. Where did it come from?

You tell me where *attitude* came from.

So many of those things were born on *Nitro*.

I often wonder if they realize it.

EPILOGUE

Never Say Never

riting this book and chronicling the events that led up to the sale of WCW to WWE required me to write about some of the negative things that happened to me over the last few chapters. But make no mistake about it. Eric Bischoff is not a bitter man.

From a purely financial point of view, my family has benefited tremendously from pro wrestling. Every parent hopes to provide opportunities for their children, and this business has helped me achieve that goal. This business and my role in it have given my family an opportunity to see the world and experience things that most families can only dream about. I am very grateful for that.

Often when people recognize me, or realize who I am, they start asking questions about the business. The first one or two start off: "Hey, whatever happened to . . . [insert famous wrestler here]?" After they get through the who's-who of past and current wrestlers, the questions are along the lines of: "Do you think anyone is ever going to challenge WWE the way *Nitro* did?"

Inevitably, they get more specific and ask if I ever want to compete with Vince McMahon again. More often than not I have fun with those questions. I tease them by saying something like, "Absolutely. As we speak, I'm scheduled for a meeting next week with network executives, planning a new program." I'll get them all excited, and then I'll let them in on the joke.

More seriously, a number of times every year I'm approached by individuals or companies who want to launch a program competing with WWE. Some are not legitimate at all, some are very legitimate. Invariably I tell them the truth, because I don't want to waste anyone's time, especially my own: the conditions have changed so much over the last five or six years that in my opinion, there will never be another situation like the one that existed in the mid-1990s when WCW and WWE went head-to-head.

The most profound change is the vertical integration of the media industry. Cable television is no longer competitive in the same way it was ten years ago. When you look at the television landscape and the cable networks now, while there may be hundreds of channels available to the viewer, and dozens and dozens of cable companies or networks, the truth is that most are owned by one of the big four media companies. Viacom has a large piece of the cable industry. NBC-Universal has a big piece of the cable industry. ABC has a big piece. And so does Fox.

Very few, if any, of these companies have the kind of entrepreneurial spirit and vision that Ted Turner and Turner Broadcasting had back in the mid-1990s. Most are managed by committees and focus groups. The majority of media executives make decisions now based on fear, not vision. The television business today is extremely risk-averse. And once you eliminate the cable companies that are controlled directly or indirectly by one of the big four, what's left are niche networks that don't have the resources to compete on the level necessary to launch a competitive product. Those conditions more than anything prevent anyone from taking on WWE.

That's not to say that it wouldn't be better for WWE and the business overall to have true competition, because it most certainly would—I proved that—but the conditions as they exist today don't provide that opportunity.

And just as the business conditions have changed, I've changed as well. While I am still an extremely competitive person, I tend not to be as hyperaggressive as I was ten years ago.

Part of that may be because I'm just getting older. But another part is simply the fact that I've already been there and done it. No one else in the history of the business has been able to compete with Vince McMahon and beat him at his own game. That was a very powerful motivation for me. To this day, there's only one person in the history of this business who's done it, and it's me. Because I've already been to the top of that mountain and achieved that goal, it's now less important. I have other goals, other things I'd like to achieve.

Don't get me wrong: I would have liked to camp out on that mountaintop a lot longer than I did. But I'm proud of what I achieved, nonetheless.

Another thing that has changed for me is the fact that I can now attach faces, and in some cases families, to the names at WWE. Even if all of the conditions I've described changed, and there was a huge competitive opportunity, I'm not sure that deep down inside I could do some of the crazy things I did at WCW that made us so successful. Back then I didn't worry about whether or not the employees at WWE would be able to feed their families. I didn't know them. They were names I didn't recognize, faces I couldn't pick out of a crowd. Now, it would be hard to do anything that might hurt them. I wouldn't want to jeopardize people for whom I have a tremendous amount of respect, and in many cases feel real affection for.

These days, when I think about sports entertainment and professional wrestling, I'm grateful for the opportunity I have right now. In many ways, I have the best of all worlds. Thanks to wrestling, I have some great friends, people like Hulk Hogan, who's probably one of my best friends to this day, and others both from the WCW days and now WWE. Jason Hervey, the actor who spent six or eight years as a star on ABC's *Wonder Years* and whom I met fifteen years ago through wrestling, is now my business partner. Together we have created and produced both network and cable reality projects, launched a licensing business, and are partners in a gaming company and an energy drink company with international distribution.

And I'm still involved in the wrestling business, which is something that's been a large part of my life for the last twenty years. And I can still perform. I am grateful for that.

I love performing in front of a large audience. I love manipulating them. I love the challenge of getting the reaction necessary to advance a storyline, however big or small my role may be. I love the challenge of trying to get better every time I go out in front of an audience. It's all part of my DNA.

Did I make mistakes building WCW? Of course I did. I don't think there is an executive in America that can look back and say they did everything right while building their company. But does the criticism by so-called experts, or by wrestlers who didn't have a clue about what was really happening behind the scenes, bother me? Not a bit. The very fact that Ted Turner himself, as recently as about a year ago, helped me secure a deal with one of the biggest names in NASCAR by providing a personal reference (something he rarely if ever does), confirms to me that the people who were actually in the trenches, who really understood what was going on, know what I accomplished and know why WCW ended up where it did.

More importantly, I know what I achieved. When you make a list of the people who have had the most positive impact on the sports entertainment business as we know it today, it's a very short list. The list of people who have actually *changed* the business is even shorter. Clearly at the top of that list is Vince McMahon. Inarguably, he is the individual who took professional wrestling from the regional territory business and rolled it out nationally on cable and network television and subsequently changed the business forever. Below Vince McMahon, there's probably only one person who has had anywhere near the impact on the *way* the *business* is conducted today—and that's Eric Bischoff.

I take a lot of pride in that. The things I did to make WCW competitive changed the business fundamentally, from a creative and strategic point of view. Today I watch *Raw* and *SmackDown!* and see things that originated at WCW. I know where WWE and the wrestling business were prior to the launch of *Nitro*. I'm convinced that the competition I created grew the audience to such an extent that networks were willing to compete for the business, which gave Vince the opportunity to move WWE from USA Network to Viacom and ultimately back to USA Network. I believe that if it weren't for that competition, WWE would have continued along the path it had been on. The wrestling business would have gotten flat—so flat that the WWE might not have had the opportunities it's had over the past several years, including becoming a public company.

I don't know that for sure. No one can say what would or would not have happened for certain. But when you look at wrestling ten or fifteen years ago, it was a limited niche product. It's still hard to sell advertising inside wrestling today, but it was much harder back then. The launch of *Nitro* and the change I forced upon WWE created competition that grew the audience—and more importantly, changed the demographics of that audience to a point that the advertising revenue had to follow. No one could deny the size and purchasing power of the pro wrestling audience. WCW *Nitro* and, yes, Eric Bischoff helped create a pop culture phenomenon on cable television.

Would WWE exist today if it weren't for the pop culture phenomenon born from competition with the WCW?

As I said, no one can go back and definitively say what would have happened if things were different. But I think it's safe to say that WWE would not exist at the level it is at now.

So at the very end of the day, when people ask, "Do you think there'll be another competitor to the WWE?" my answer is, "I don't think so." When people ask, "Will you ever go head-to-head with Vince McMahon again?" my answer is, "Probably not."

But never say never.